the

Byzantines

Averil Cameron

Blackwell
Publishing

BLACKWELL PUBLISHING
350 Main Street, Malden, MA 02148–5020, USA
9600 Garsington Road, Oxford OX4 2DQ, UK
550 Swanston Street, Carlton, Victoria 3053, Australia

The right of Averil Cameron to be identified as the Author of this Work has been
asserted in accordance with the UK Copyright, Designs, and Patents Act 1988.

First published 2006 by Blackwell Publishing Ltd

1   2006

Library of Congress Cataloging-in-Publication Data

Cameron, Averil.
  The Byzantines / Averil Cameron.
    p. cm. – (The peoples of Europe)
  Includes bibliographical references and index.
  ISBN-13: 978-0-631-20262-2 (hardback : alk. paper)
  ISBN-10: 0-631-20262-5 (hardback : alk. paper)
    1.   Byzantine Empire—History.   I. Title.   II. Series.

DF552.C36 2006
949.5′02—dc22

                              2006004744

A catalogue record for this title is available from the British Library.

Set in 10/12pt Sabon
by Graphicraft Limited, Hong Kong
Printed and bound in Singapore
by Markono Print Media Pte Ltd

The publisher's policy is to use permanent paper from mills that operate a
sustainable forestry policy, and which has been manufactured from pulp processed
using acid-free and elementary chlorine-free practices. Furthermore, the publisher
ensures that the text paper and cover board used have met acceptable
environmental accreditation standards.

For further information on
Blackwell Publishing, visit our website:
www.blackwellpublishing.com

Contents

Figures

Maps

Preface

Byzantium – an Absence

For most historians, Byzantium is an absence.

A few examples will suffice. To take intellectual history first: in the volume entitled *Medieval Philosophy*, the second volume of *A New History of Western Philosophy* published by Oxford University Press in 2005, we read that from about AD 600 'philosophy went into hibernation for two centuries'.[1] Hibernation might imply an awakening, but whatever awakening there may have been is simply ignored in the rest of the book. Another example can found in the debate about nations and nationalism. Some, like Anthony D. Smith, have argued against the prevailing view that nations and nationalism are the children of modernity, and have debated the question of whether there were nations in antiquity.[2] But while the discussion of possible earlier examples includes ancient Egypt, classical Greece, Edom, Arpad, Aram and Armenia,[3] Byzantium is nowhere to be found. Two recent books on the end of the Roman empire do no more than briefly allude to the fact that the Roman empire in the east did not 'fall' but continued until the capture of Constantinople by the Ottomans in 1453.[4] A study of Eurasia in the eleventh century CE from a 'world-historical' perspective does no more than remark that even some specialists on Byzantium have been asking themselves why its reform and renaissance in the eleventh century were 'so much less thorough-going than their Latin counterparts'.[5] Finally – and by now it is no surprise – Byzantium is also absent from discussions of the rise of the (Western) individual,[6] while in an interesting collection of responses to a recent work on Mediterranean history, with a long time-span extending to AD 1000, the only entry for Byzantium in the index is to a passage in which the Byzantine empire appears only in passing, albeit in a paper in which Byzantium does at least have a role. In the same book, in a general map labelled 'The Mediterranean in

Greek, Roman and medieval times', 'Byzantium' seems to be used as the name for the city of Constantinople, which is not itself labelled.[7]

Byzantium therefore occupies an uncertain place in historiography, which is to say no-one knows what to do with it. Was it part of Europe? Or does it belong rather to the East? How does the history of Orthodoxy sit with the conception of Western Christendom?[8] (The contemporary relevance of this question is amply demonstrated by its recent and explicit evocation by some member states of the European Union.) Another point of uncertainty is the role of Byzantium in the Crusades, somehow poised between the Latin West and the Saracen East. This is despite the fact that, like its successor empire, that of the Ottomans, the territory of Byzantium included large swathes of Europe, where its influence after 1453 has continued until today. Moreover, as an integral factor in the political and cultural histories of the emerging post-Communist states of central and eastern Europe, Byzantium has acquired a newly sensitive role, both as the predecessor of the Ottoman empire and the bringer and guarantee of Orthodox Christianity, and as conveying an uneasily 'Eastern' inheritance.

These ambivalences make the inclusion of Byzantium in this series, and its re-insertion into the history of Europe and of the wider Mediterranean world especially necessary, at a time when the extent and nature of Europe are again urgent questions, and when the relation of the 'West' with the Islamic world is a matter of tension and anxiety. Unlike the barbarian groups who settled in the territories of the late Roman empire, and whose identity and ethnogenesis are currently the subject of much debate,[9] the Byzantines were not a people who arrived from the north or the steppes and found their identity through interaction with the Romans. It is a moot point when one can first call them Byzantines, rather than Romans (as they continued to refer to themselves), and indeed the term 'Byzantine', used in this sense, is an innovation of the sixteenth century. Edward Gibbon referred to seven centuries of a 'Greek empire' after the age of Justinian, and was unsure whether Justinian himself should properly be assigned to the Roman empire or to this Greek successor. But the Byzantines themselves were deeply involved in the ethnogenesis of other peoples, including the Bulgarians, the Serbs, the Hungarians and the Russians. Byzantium, no less than Rome or the papacy, shaped the development of Europe.

In the often partial and, from the western European point of view, rather insular, historiography of Byzantium, certain powerful narratives have held the field. These include the idea of Byzantium as an overwhelmingly Orthodox society, dominated by an alliance between Church and emperor sometimes described as Caesaropapism, in which the emperor was able to, and often did, intervene by *diktat* in the affairs of the church. Closely connected with the narrative of Byzantium as an overwhelmingly religious society is the idea that it was static and even fossilised, dominated by a stifling court ritual. In land-holding and economic relations the theme of 'Byzantine feudalism' dominated older scholarship and features in books that are still very widely read. Finally, the Gibbonian image of Byzantium as the weak successor of the Roman empire is in danger of being reinforced from two new directions. First, the reinvention and relabelling of the period from roughly the fourth to the seventh or even the eighth centuries AD as 'late antiquity', and the very positive evaluation placed on it in much recent scholarship, invite us to question the evaluation of Byzantium as either late antiquity's extension or its contrast. Secondly, while on the one hand crusader historiography is at last permitting some degree of recognition of the Byzantine involvement, the evaluation of Byzantium in the Comnenian period from the late eleventh century, one of the greatest periods in its history, now has to contend with a competing narrative of an energetic, developing and expanding western Europe, characterised by the rise of towns and universities and the development of self-consciousness.[10] In this context, the awareness among historians of the approaching catastrophe of the sack of Constantinople by the Fourth Crusade in 1204, and still more of the difficulties of the succeeding period up to 1453, make adverse comparison between Byzantium and western Europe all too tempting. We need here to ask how far any of these narratives of Byzantium will still stand, and if not, how they should be replaced.

Writing accessibly about Byzantium presents many challenges. One must in the first place attempt to overcome the prejudice that still exists against the eastern empire and the stereotypes with which it is surrounded. In addition, not only is the subject matter unfamiliar, but the written material that the historian needs to use is often difficult to find and exists only in editions in obscure publications and difficult languages. This situation has improved greatly in recent years with the appearance of an increasing number of English translations, and these are used wherever possible in this book. But some important Byzantine source material is still not edited and exists only in manuscript form, and a great deal more has to be read in old and uncritical editions. Writing about a society from which so few archives or official documents have survived also requires techniques of imagination and analysis very different from those familiar to modern historians. Byzantinists employ quantitative methods when they can, but given the nature of the sources this can only be done with great care, and much more often they must draw on comparative material or use other theoretical tools in order to interpret their evidence.[11] Finally, the Byzantines are unlike most of the other 'peoples' in the present series, not only because they were not a 'people' in the ethnic sense, but also in that their state lasted for many centuries, during which it underwent many changes even while retaining some of its most salient characteristics. The transition from the ancient to the medieval world is again a major topic of historical attention with Peter Brown and others on the side of a 'long' late antiquity, stretching to c.AD 800, or even, in some formulations, to AD 1000. Where Byzantium fits in such a model is not easy to decide, but I have chosen to begin with the key moment of the inauguration of the city of Constantinople by Constantine the Great in AD 330, and to attempt to convey something of the changing characteristics of Byzantium throughout its long history until the capture of the city by the Ottomans in 1453. It is impossible in this compass to deal in detail with all the aspects that might be included, or to provide a detailed narrative history, which in any case is available in other publications. But it was, after all, the city of Constantinople, seat of the imperial power for eleven centuries, with only a short break from 1204 to 1261, that constituted the very centre of Byzantine identity.

In writing for non-specialists as well as for Byzantinists, my aim has been to ask questions rather than to overwhelm the reader with detail; however, Chapters 2 and 3 provide an outline chronological narrative – in which less attention is paid to the late antique or early Byzantine period than to the later centuries – that I hope will give a context for the thematic discussion in the rest of the book. There are real problems of scale and coverage: Byzantine history is complicated, with many unfamiliar peoples and places so that even the thematic chapters must contain some narrative, while, equally, much has necessarily to be omitted. A central theme, however, is reception. The Byzantines still suffer from being thought of as obscure, or indeed obscurantist (hence the ubiquitous appearance of the term 'byzantine' to denote unnecessary complexity). I believe that the Byzantines need to be brought into the mainstream and Byzantium needs to be normalised as a subject for historians. There are, however, distinct problems for the historian of Byzantium. For example, while the amount of written source material is very large most of it is literary or theological and emanates from the educated elite, and historians need to work hard if they want to uncover the everyday, or the average Byzantine to whom Norman Baynes referred as 'the man in the East Roman street'. Documentary evidence is much smaller in volume than literary material, since no state archives survived the sack of Constantinople, and the historian has to resort to ecclesiastical or local records where they exist, or the archives of other states such as Venice or to the documents preserved in literary sources or occasionally in manuscripts. Many thousands of lead seals survive that were once attached to official documents and that carry information about the officials who issued them, from which deductions can be made about wider economic or administrative practice, but while these are now being seriously studied and published their interpretation is a highly specialised matter. As for archaeological evidence, while there has been an explosion of archaeological work dealing with the late antique or early Byzantine period, and this has dramatically changed the way historians view that period, the same level of archaeological interest has not yet been felt in relation to later periods of Byzantine history.[12] In contrast, the current trend for a contextualised or historicist approach among Byzantine art historians, in clear reaction to the earlier concentration on style, is making a major contribution to knowledge; this is particularly welcome, in view of the fact that a disproportionate amount of work has been done in the past on ecclesiastical buildings, especially from an architectural and stylistic viewpoint.

A book of this kind cannot be, and does not try to be, a history of Byzantium. In any case, several historical introductions to Byzantium have recently been published in English, and because of these and other easily available reference tools the subject is now becoming much more accessible. My treatment has had to be highly selective, and readers will find that many important aspects of the subject, or series of events, are either omitted or referred to only briefly. Nor can the references do more than indicate some of the key sources and modern literature, mostly in English; this will not satisfy specialist readers, but I hope that the references will be helpful to others and act as pointers to further reading.

Acknowledgements

This is a book in a well-established series, and I am grateful for the chance to include Byzantium. Blackwell is also the publisher of the series The Making of Europe, which contains several distinguished studies that either have direct relevance for Byzantium, such as Peter Brown's *The Rise of Western Christendom*, or that, like R. I. Moore's *The First European Revolution* or Jacques Le Goff's *The Birth of Europe*, provoke a Byzantinist to respond. I must also thank those persons and institutions that have given me the opportunity and the challenge to broaden my interests to embrace the Byzantine empire. They include my students both at King's College London when I taught Byzantine history there after the foundation of the Centre for Hellenic Studies in 1989 and at Oxford after I became Warden of Keble College in 1994. Keble has given me two periods of research leave, in Athens and at Princeton, during which I have worked on this book, and I am very grateful to the College and to colleagues in both places, especially Evangelos Chrysos and Niki Tsironis, and to the British School of Archaeology in Athens, as well as to Peter Brown and Dimitri Gondicas of the Program in Hellenic Studies at Princeton. It was an especial pleasure to spend time in the company of Peter Brown, who has been a support and an inspiration for many years. John Haldon was a generous friend during my stay at Princeton, and I owe a great deal also, in Princeton and elsewhere, to Emmanuel Papoutsakis, Petre Guran, Glen Bowersock, Philip Rousseau, Alice-Mary Talbot, Natalia Teteriatnikov and the group of Princeton graduate students, including Daniel Schwartz and David Michelson, with whom I enjoyed regular encounters over coffee or in Firestone Library. I should also like to thank a number of other colleagues and friends for their help in different ways including Jean-Claude Cheynet, Michael Jeffreys, Tim Jenkinson, Tassos Papacostas, James Pettifer, Trish Long, Anne Dude and Joseph Wang. I am also grateful to the editors of the series, James Campbell and Barrie Cunliffe, and to the production and editorial staff at Blackwell, especially Tessa Harvey, Angela Cohen and Gillian Kane. Felicity Marsh was an exceptionally helpful and intelligent copy-editor. Finally, I am very conscious indeed of the debt I owe to the many other colleagues, friends and family, who have encouraged me to persist.

Averil Cameron
Oxford, January 2006

Abbreviations

ACO   *Acta Conciliorum Oecumenicorum*, ed. E. Schwartz (Berlin, 1914–40), J. Straub (1971), R. Riedinger, series secunda (Berlin, 1984–92)

CFHB   Corpus Fontium Historiae Byzantinae

CCSG   Corpus Christianorum, Series Graeca (Turnhout)

CSCO   Corpus Scriptorum Christianorum Orientalium (Louvain)

CFHB   Corpus Fontium Historicorum Byzantinorum

CSHB   Corpus Scriptorum Historicorum Byzantinorum

Mansi   J. D. Mansi, *Sacrorum Conciliorum Nova et Amplissima Collectio*, 31 vols. (Florence and Venice, 1759–98) (still the standard edition for council acts and proceedings, though gradually being superseded by new critical editions)

MGH   Monumenta Germaniae Historica

PBE   *Prosopography of the Byzantine Empire, Vol. I* AD *641–867*, ed. J. Martindale (Aldershot, 2001, CD-rom)

PG   J.-P. Migne, ed., *Patrologiae Cursus Completus*, Series Graeca (Paris, 1857–66) (the fundamental publication of Byzantine writings, with Latin translation, but often based on much older editions)

PLP   *Prosopographisches Lexikon der Palaiologenzeit*, ed. E. Trapp et al. (Vienna, 1976–96)

PLRE   J. R. Martindale, ed., *The Prosopography of the Later Roman Empire, Vol. III* AD *527–640* (Cambridge, 1992)

PmbZ   *Prosopographie der mittelbyzantinischen Zeit*, ed. R.-J. Lilie and F. Winkelmann, 7 vols. (Berlin, 1998–2002)

TIB   *Tabula Imperii Byzantini*, vols. 1–9, various authors, Denkschr. d Österr. Akad. d. Wiss., phil-hist. Kl., Vienna, 1976–

1

What was Byzantium?

> 'Hellene' is the glory of ancient Greece; 'Romaic' the splendours and the
> sorrows of Byzantium, above all the sorrows. 'Hellenism' is symbolized
> by the columns of the Parthenon; Byzantium, the imperial golden age of
> Christian Greece, by the great dome of St Sophia.
>
> Patrick Leigh Fermor, *Roumeli: Travels in Northern Greece*

Byzantium is the modern name given to the state and society ruled
almost continuously from Constantinople (modern Istanbul) from the
dedication of the city by the Emperor Constantine in AD 330 until its
sack by the Ottomans under the young Mehmed II ('the Conqueror') in
1453. But Byzantium is hard to grasp, and 'the Byzantines' even more
so. Even the seemingly innocuous statement in the first sentence raises
several questions. For example, how significant was the supposed separation of the eastern and western parts of the Roman Empire in AD 395?
Did Byzantium begin with the reign of Constantine the Great (proclaimed emperor at York, 25 July AD 306), or with the dedication of
Constantinople (AD 330) or later, perhaps in the sixth century or the
seventh? Was Byzantium a society, a state or an empire? What were its
geographical limits at any one period? And, above all, who were its
inhabitants, how were they defined and how did they think of themselves?
Byzantine high culture used Greek as its medium, and the language
of the state was always Greek. But while the title of this book implies
that the Byzantines were a distinct people, the inhabitants of the empire
were defined neither by language or ethnicity, but by their belonging to
the Byzantine state, and during much of the period by their Orthodox
Christianity. They called themselves 'Romans', or at times, simply
'Christians'. The nature of their state, and the role played in it by
Orthodoxy, are both fundamental questions addressed in this book. But
before approaching either of them we need to address some problems
of definition, and these are the subject of this first chapter.

Fig. 1   Head found at York, probably of Constantine, York Museums Trust
(Yorkshire Museum)

It is essential to grasp the changing size and shape of the Byzantine
state through the eleven centuries of its existence (for I shall here take
the dedication of Constantinople in 330 as a conventional beginning).
No state could possibly stay the same for so long, and the history
of Byzantium is a history, in part, of sheer staying power in the midst of
substantial historical change. There is a real problem about defining
and assessing this Janus-like society which looked in different directions
during its history – across the Mediterranean; to the east, towards
what we now call Turkey and the Middle East; to the west towards
Sicily and Italy, towards central and eastern Europe and the Balkans
and to the north towards Russia. Different 'units of analysis' will be
needed at different times, and mapping the Byzantine Empire calls for

a series of different maps for different stages in its history. Furthermore, the world around Byzantium was dramatically transformed during this long period: territory was conquered and lost again, empires and dynasties rose and fell, the ancient world gave way to the medieval, Islam became a great power and the later centuries saw the vigorous expansion of western Europe. No single definition or characterization of Byzantium or the Byzantines could do justice to all of this, and part of the aim of this book is to draw attention to the sheer pace of historical change.

Attitudes to Byzantium

Why study Byzantium? Even now, to most Europeans, apart from Greeks and others of the Eastern Orthodox tradition, the very word, Byzantium, suggests something exotic and (probably) bureaucratic and even corrupt. According to the *Oxford English Reference Dictionary*, the term 'Byzantine' denotes something that is 'a) extremely complicated, b) inflexible, or c) carried on by underhand means'. An anthropological work about the Nupe of Nigeria based on field work done in the 1930s used the title *A Black Byzantium*, apparently to denote hierarchy, social stratification and complexity.[1] To describe oneself in ordinary conversation as a Byzantine historian provokes incomprehension or disbelief. In the western European popular consciousness mention of Byzantium attracts two main responses: either it is still thought of as irrelevant and backward, the precursor of the Ottoman Empire and somehow implicated in the religious and political problems of the contemporary Balkans, or else it seems in some mysterious way powerfully attractive,[2] associated as it is with icons and spirituality or with the revival of religion in post-Communist Europe. Each of these responses reveals the persistence of deep-rooted stereotypes and neither does justice to Byzantium or the Byzantines as they actually existed. There is also a great difference between the perceptions of the Byzantines held by the Orthodox and the non-Orthodox worlds, corresponding to the degree to which Byzantium does or does not belong to national histories. This presents an even greater challenge to historians than before, in view of the political changes that have taken place since the late twentieth century.

Why then is it that historians seem unable to avoid looking back on the long centuries of the Byzantine state except with the consciousness of eventual fall? This is not how most people think of the classical Greek city states or even of imperial Rome. Yet the idea of Byzantium still goes hand in hand with an acute awareness of the Ottoman sack of

Constantinople in 1453.[3] Mindful of Edward Gibbon and many other writers since, the one thing we think we know is that the Byzantines were doomed. In this familiar scenario the tiny population of Palaiologan Constantinople heroically and tragically held out to the last; the fragment that remained of the once great empire was surrounded and could never have prevailed. Many books still talk of the decline that is assumed to have set in during the Palaiologan period from 1261 to 1453, forgetting that this final phase in the empire's history had opened, in the return of the exiled emperor to Constantinople, with a success, and had gone on to produce some of the most brilliant cultural artefacts in Byzantium's history. The difficulties that Byzantium experienced in the fourteenth and fifteenth centuries were to a great degree the result of dramatic historical developments in the world around it. Yet Byzantium's Western critics are still wont to claim that its future did not lie in a Western-style renaissance leading to a European Enlightenment. Its destiny, they maintain, was to be engulfed by the Turks, the ancestors of the proverbial sick man of Europe and the representatives of the East. It was Byzantine scholars and churchmen who carried Greek manuscripts and Greek learning to Italy and made possible the development of Greek humanism in the West. Yet the poignancy of the last days of Constantinople and the singing of the last liturgy in Hagia Sophia on the eve of the final assault on 29 May 1453 have, in much of the most influential scholarship on Byzantium, forever branded the last Byzantines with the stigma of romantic failure.[4]

An important aim of this book is to demonstrate the inadequacy of these assumptions. As I have suggested, part of the difficulty in the past has been connected with the way in which Byzantium has been studied and by whom. Not only is the inaccessibility of many of the voluminous literary and theological writings of the Byzantines themselves a serious problem for contemporary students, but the scholarly study of Byzantium also requires linguistic and other skills nowadays in short supply. There is a notable tradition of philological research and publication in patristics (the study of the Fathers of the Church), and of the broader study of Byzantium in such European centres as Paris and Vienna, and the study of Byzantium has flourished in modern Greece and the Orthodox world. The subject had a distinguished history in pre-revolutionary Russia, and a predictably ambivalent one in the Soviet period, from which it is now emerging.[5] But in Britain, while a few major scholars such as Steven Runciman have made Byzantium their special field,[6] its history has never been part of the general curriculum either in schools or universities, nor has it generally been seen as playing more than a peripheral role in European history. It was not, for example, held to be central in the planning of a five-year research programme on the transformation of the Roman world between AD 400 and AD 900, sponsored during the 1990s by the European Science Foundation.

The situation has changed in the past few decades, particularly under the influence of the re-emergence in eastern Europe since 1989 of national states with a stake in rediscovering their own history and the concomitant questioning of the concept of 'Europe'. Under these influences we are seeing a contemporary effort to present Byzantium as a 'world civilisation' on a par with any other.[7] There has also been a distinct rise in the number of scholars working on Byzantium both in Britain and in North America, many of whom have not themselves had the classical training shared by most Byzantinists in the past. This marks an important change, for while in the past writers in the English-speaking world such as J. B. Bury and many other historians, and Robert Byron and Patrick Leigh Fermor among travel writers, saw Byzantium through a classicist's eyes,[8] their successors today are far more likely to approach it as a medieval society in its own right.

How and When Did 'Byzantium' Begin?

A complicating factor during the last generation has been the explosion of interest in the period now often referred to as 'late antiquity', which reaches from roughly the third to at least the seventh century AD.[9] A whole discipline has grown up around the idea of late antiquity as an identifiable field of study in its own right, vested in the concept of a united, or at least shared, Mediterranean culture, and a continuity up to the eighth century or even later, as suggested by the use by some archaeologists of the term 'the long classical millenium' to refer to the period from the fourth century BC to the eighth century AD. The very success of this changed perspective blurs the question of a transition from classical to Byzantine, and calls into question the date from which Byzantium can be said to have come into being. However the issues of periodisation, as well as the 'transition' from the ancient world to the medieval, or Byzantine one, have been endlessly debated both before and after this recent development, and are not susceptible of any final answer. Some would place the real beginning of Byzantium as late as the seventh century when much of the territory stretching from Anatolia to Egypt and North Africa was lost as a result of the Arab invasions, and when the urban landscape of Asia Minor underwent sharp contraction.

Others, more conventionally, date the beginnings of Byzantium from the foundation of Constantinople on the site of the classical city of Byzantion by the Emperor Constantine. Logical though this seems, it has the twin disadvantages of suggesting that there was somehow a distinct Byzantine or eastern empire at a time when the Roman empire was not yet formally divided, and of assuming that in the first phase of its existence the city of Constantinople marked much more of a departure than most scholars are now willing to admit.[10] A third option might be to start from the reign of Justinian (AD 527–65), which indeed seemed pivotal to Edward Gibbon, while recent archaeological work might suggest a break in the late sixth.

All these options have their merits, but choosing to begin from the reign of Constantine has the advantage of recognising the symbolic importance that his foundation of Constantinople came to play in Byzantine consciousness. This does not imply separation between the eastern and western empires in this early period, or any drastic change of attitude on the part of the citizens of the east. Unlike most empires, the Byzantine Empire did not grow out of conquest. Rather, it evolved from an existing political system that had itself developed from the 'high empire' of Augustus and his successors.[11] New settlers in fourth-century Constantinople were not immigrants from outside: they came from within the existing territories of the Roman Empire. This makes the change from Roman Empire to Byzantium both difficult and challenging for historians to trace.

'Greeks' and 'Romans'

Constantine's city (Constantinople, 'the city of Constantine') occupied the site of the classical Greek city of Byzantion, whence the term 'Byzantine' and our use of 'Byzantium', but the citizens of the eastern Empire referred to themselves as 'Romans'. From this came the term *Rum*, used for the Byzantine empire in Arabic and Turkish sources, and *Rumis* for the Greek Christian population under the Ottomans. Similarly, *Romios* was used to denote a Greek until, with the development of the modern Greek state, it came to be replaced by 'Hellene'. Though Greek was, and continued to be, the language of Byzantine government and culture a large part of the population at many periods of the empire's history spoke other languages. This was certainly true in the early period when the empire included Egypt, Palestine, Syria and Mesopotamia, whose languages included Coptic, Aramaic and Syriac, as well as

Latin-speaking North Africa, Italy and Illyricum. The Byzantine success in driving the Vandals from Carthage and North Africa in AD 533–4 led to the introduction of some Greek for official purposes until Carthage eventually fell to the Arabs in 696. At times in later periods large areas of the Balkans came under Byzantine authority, and places formerly under Arab rule were recovered, with the result that the empire included Slavs and Bulgarians on its European side and Muslim populations in the east. 'By the eighth century, versions of Slavonic appear to have been spoken throughout much of central Europe east of the Elbe',[12] and some of these regions, with their existing populations, later came for periods under Byzantine rule. Latin, Italian and Hebrew also coexisted with Greek. There were also other changes: in the Comnenian period (1081–1204) 'Hellene' begins to be used as a self-description, and a character in one of the twelfth-century romances is identified as 'a Greek [Hellene] from Cyprus',[13] while in the last phase of the Byzantine state the term 'Hellene' came back into use in conscious evocation of Byzantium's classical heritage. In earlier periods, in contrast, the term 'Hellene' denoted pagan ideas or persons, and for the Christian Byzantines it carried very negative connotations. Plato, for example, was considered a 'Hellene', and his philosophy was condemned by the Church, and saints' lives, especially from the early period, are full of improving tales of the discomfiture of pagans ('Hellenes') by Christian holy men and women; similarly, collections of miracle stories contain anecdotes demonstrating the triumph of Christian healing over 'Hellenic' medicine. When the Emperor Justinian collected and codified the law in the sixth century it was Roman law in Latin that his team of lawyers made available to the Latin west and which became the basis of several European law codes.[14] Justinian's Code also remained the basis of law in Byzantium, although after this mammoth task of codification, completed in a very few years at the start of his reign, Justinian began to issue some of his new laws (*Novels*) in Greek. There were Latin-speakers in Constantinople in the sixth century, among them the emperor himself, as well as North African bishops and exiles from the war in Italy who included Cassiodorus, quaestor and praetorian prefect under the Ostrogothic kings of Italy and the author of the *Variae*, a collection of official correspondence, a *Chronicle*, a *Gothic History* and later the *Institutiones*, written for his monastery at Vivarium in Italy. But Greek had already been in use for centuries as the standard official language in the eastern Empire outside the specialised fields of law and the army; the future pope Gregory the Great was a Latin-speaker in Constantinople in the 580s, but from the end of the sixth century the use of Latin declined to the point where few were familiar with it, and there was little desire to master Latin or to read Latin texts until much later. The works of Augustine, so fundamental for the medieval West, went unread in Byzantium.

However the question of Greek in Byzantium is not straightforward. Already in the early period a gulf had opened up between the written, high-style language and the spoken one. Those with literary aspirations adopted a formal, rhetorical style using classical vocabulary far removed both from the spoken language and that used in literary works of a more practical and less ambitious nature.[15] As late as the fourteenth century writers aimed at a linguistic register and a literary style that was as close as possible to classical models. Thus imitation or *mimesis*, an explicit aim in Byzantine rhetoric, has commonly taken to be a hallmark, or even the sum, of Byzantine cultural expression.[16] The use of this 'high' linguistic and stylistic register is one of the most characteristic features of Byzantine literature and has done more than anything else to convey an impression of artificiality and sameness. In fact it is not so very different from the divide in recent times in modern Greek between *katharevousa* ('pure') and demotic ('popular'). Linguistically, at least, Byzantium was a multicultural state and its emphasis on language rather than ethnicity as the badge of culture followed a Roman precedent of toleration. The modern nation-state lay in the future, and racial prejudice as such was not a feature of Byzantine culture;[17] Byzantine prejudice existed in plenty, but it was directed in other ways.[18]

Who Were the 'Byzantines'?

The Byzantines were not a 'people' in any ethnic sense. If we consider only Anatolia, the population had been thoroughly mixed for many centuries.[19] Nor did an education in classicising Greek, such as was normal for Christians and pagans alike when Constantinople was founded, and which continued to be the badge of culture in Byzantium, carry any ethnic implications.[20] In this sense advancement in Byzantium was open to anyone with the means to acquire the education in the first place and the necessary connections. This was an inheritance from the Roman Empire, which included Asia Minor and the other territory which came to be ruled from Constantinople. By the early third century AD there was no longer any formal distinction in the empire between citizens and the non-citizens who formed the population of conquered or assimilated provinces; what mattered was not ethnicity or local background but shared culture, connections and status. In the eastern part of the empire there was also an inheritance from even earlier conquests and earlier regimes, those of Alexander the Great and the successor states that were set up after his death, whose enduring legacy was to spread urban culture and the Greek language to the east. Byzantium did not therefore emerge out of an ethnic grouping or in a region occupied by a population with a particular ethnic background but developed its own characteristics out of and in response to centuries of earlier history and settlement. One of the features that it took over from this background was a willingness to incorporate those who were willing to adapt to its norms, including using Greek as the language of culture.

With these beginnings, the Byzantine Empire also underwent a striking degree of expansion and contraction during its history. The tenth-century treatise of Constantine VII Porphyrogenitus on the administration of the empire vividly underlines the extent of Slav settlement and population change in the Balkans in the early medieval period, and the Byzantine state contributed to this mixing from an early stage by moving populations, sometimes for strategic reasons though more often in order to resolve demographic or security problems. Thus, the Emperor Justinian II (685–95, 705–11) settled Slavs in Asia Minor and moved easterners to the Balkans. When Constantinople became severely depopulated in the eighth century, Constantine V (741–75) repopulated it from outside, and also moved people from the east to Thrace. Nikephoros I (802–11) moved soldiers and their families from Asia Minor to Thrace and repopulated Lakedaimon with settlers from the Armeniakon, Thrakesion and Cibyrrheotikon themes, and Basil I (867–86) moved defeated Paulicians from Anatolia to the Balkans. Population change and the spontaneous or enforced movements of peoples accelerated with the military campaigns in the east in the tenth and eleventh centuries with their corresponding changes in political and religious control. Both Muslim and Christian populations fled from approaching armies while yet others were deported, among them Muslims from cities such as Adana, Mopsuestia in Cilicia, Antioch and Emesa (Homs in Syria) to Byzantine territory and non-Muslims into empty lands. The capture of large numbers of prisoners might lead to enslavement and sale or ransom, or to deportation, and conversion was a further possible result of changes brought by military conquest. Later still, it was convenient for the despots of the Morea in the fourteenth and fifteenth centuries to take advantage of Albanian emigration into Greece to use them as settlers in the Peloponnese.[21] The population shifts of the nineteenth-century Balkans and the 'ethnic cleansing' of more recent times therefore had precedents in the Byzantine Empire over many centuries, even if with different motivation and scale, and these shifts in population were important in continuing the assimilationist characteristics that Byzantium had inherited from its Roman roots.

We refer to Byzantium as an empire, because it had an emperor (*basileus*), and quite often more than one, and because at most periods of its history it governed other peoples and territories by reason of conquest. Yet the extent to which Byzantium was a territorial state, or was perceived as such by the Byzantines themselves, is far less clear. There are no surviving Byzantine maps; the image of the world envisaged by the sixth-century writer known as Cosmas Indicopleustes is based on biblical cosmology and was designed to show the superiority of Scripture over Ptolemy's *Geography*. The latter continued to be studied, at least in later periods, but most of the Byzantine wars of conquest, or indeed defence, must, like Roman ones, have been undertaken without detailed mapping and on the basis of local guides. Modern maps of the Byzantine Empire in its various stages run the risk of imposing a clarity that was not felt or even envisaged by contemporaries, and this is especially true in relation to the lines on modern maps which represent 'frontiers'.[22] The art of war itself was highly developed in Byzantium, and numerous military treatises survive.[23] In the period from Constantine to Justinian frontiers in some parts of the empires were marked by fortresses, and both Anastasius (491–518) and Justinian (527–65) devoted a great deal of resources and much energy to repairing and rebuilding them. Procopius's *Buildings*, probably written in 554, is a panegyrical account of Justinian's building activity with a strong focus on military installations and churches, and while, as a panegyric, it is tendentious of its very nature, it can sometimes be used with care as a guide to actual sites. However, Justinian's work on fortification at the isthmus of Corinth in Greece did not keep out the Huns in 559, and Slavs penetrated Greece and the islands in the late sixth century and attacked Thessalonike in the early seventh; their presence throughout the Balkans in this period is undoubted, though it is often hard to trace.

The eastern frontier, and in particular the military aims of late Roman emperors, have been the subject of much recent debate. It seems clear that the number of soldiers in the frontier forts had been reduced in the sixth century, and that a retreat had taken place from some parts of the frontier area.[24] For the defence of this region Justinian relied heavily on 'Saracen' (that is, Arab) allied troops. It was not a matter of linear fortifications even in areas where there were legionary forts, and the *strata Diocletiana* from north-east Arabia and Damascus to Palmyra

Fig. 2   Part of the walls at Dyrrachium (Durres, Albania), birthplace of the Emperor Anastasius (AD 491–518)

and the Euphrates was a military road, not a fortified line. The 'frontiers' of the early Byzantine period were very different from the closed and policed borders of modern states, and in later periods of Byzantine history the notion of a frontier was even more fluid; there was also a high degree of regional variation. We should think rather in terms of broad frontier zones that were zones of contact rather than of exclusion: there was no standing army stationed along fixed boundaries. This permeability was at its most pronounced in Anatolia and the east where for several centuries Christian and Muslim populations were fought over and intermingled; these borderlands form the background, however distant, to the romance of Digenes Akrites, whose father was an Arab emir and whose mother was the daughter of a Byzantine *strategos* in Cappadocia.[25]

Nor should the lines drawn on even the best modern maps of the Byzantine Empire in its various stages be taken to imply that when conquests or reconquests happened there was an immediate imposition of state apparatus over a whole area; the Byzantine state was mainly interested in the exaction of revenues, and law enforcement was extremely variable; security consisted largely of using military force to repel or diplomacy to make deals with predatory neighbours or potential invaders. Diplomacy was very important in Byzantine foreign relations, and the Byzantines liked to think of themselves as heading a family of nations, an idea which led Dimitri Obolensky to use the term 'commonwealth' for the Byzantine system.[26] It may now be necessary to revise that rather benign picture, for Byzantium was certainly capable of aggressive wars. Yet trade and religion carried Byzantine influence as far as China, and at certain phases in its history Byzantium's sphere of influence did indeed stretch far enough in all directions to make the Byzantines' own term, the *oikoumene*, or 'inhabited world', appear convincing.

This empire was held together by a strong ideology based on its court and capital at Constantinople. This ideology revolved round two axes: the imperial power and the Orthodox religion. Each was in practice flexible, and their interrelationship was far from fixed. The empire was also defined by the state's capacity to tax and to operate military and legal systems. To this extent Byzantium was, and remained, a centralised state, at least until 1204, even though the physical limits of its control varied very greatly from one period to another.

Change and Byzantine Identity

Officially, and in the minds of its elite, the Byzantine Empire remained the centre of the civilised world, protected by God. So strong was this idea that during the seventh century when it was under threat, and even after its eastern provinces had been brought within Umayyad rule, the powerful idea of a universal God-protected empire was restated by provincials who had themselves become the subjects of the Caliph.[27] Constantine VII's tenth-century handbook for his son, *On the Administration of the Empire*, set out for the latter's benefit a description of all the peoples (*ethne*) with which Byzantium, which he calls 'The Empire of the Romans', might have dealings. During the Palaiologan period the ecumenical posture expressed here was no longer credible (though it was still stated), and Byzantine foreign policy relied at all periods on an elaborately developed diplomacy that was very likely to involve concessions and had as its object the procurement of benefits. Even now, however, it drew on long traditions, and, in the circumstances, as Nicholas Oikonomides observed, it was remarkably successful.[28] In the Comnenian period, from the eleventh century and later, the Byzantines were also renowned for other kinds of alliance, such as dynastic marriages, even though Constantine VII had claimed that the practice had been forbidden by Constantine I.[29] Again, they demonstrated flexibility in the face of changing circumstances.

Minorities and Social Cohesion

Whatever the immediate conditions, for much of the history of the Byzantine Empire political coherence was less a matter of policing fixed frontiers than of finding ways by which to hold the allegiance of populations that were often highly varied. How this was achieved in military and economic terms will be considered later. There were, however, other mechanisms of assimilation and integration. As we have noted, Byzantium was from the start polyglot and cosmopolitan. It was also centralised, in that the legal system was based on imperially issued legislation, and provincial governors and officials were centrally appointed. This was reinforced by the ecclesiastical structures, and by the sixth century, if not before, bishops had become key players in their local communities;[30] we can see this in action from numerous saints' lives, such as the early-seventh century *Life* of Theodore of Sykeon. However, the imperial system of Byzantium was also able to allow considerable local freedom and variety. In late antique Syria and Mesopotamia, for example, a lively local culture existed, using Syriac as its written language and developing through the fifth and sixth centuries an identity based on the rejection of the Council of Chalcedon (451). This rejection was not indeed universal, yet it was enough to give Eastern Christians a coherence which stood them in good stead in the seventh century and later under Islamic rule. To the north-west of Constantinople, Slavs and Avars invaded the Balkans in the sixth and seventh centuries, and this occupation was followed in the late seventh century by that of the Bulgars. Here, however complex and varied Byzantium's relations with both groups in subsequent years proved to be, they were accompanied by processes of acculturation in both directions, and Byzantine cultural influence was also felt further afield in the later states of Croatia, Serbia, Russia and Wallachia and Moldavia.[31] Another group were the Jews, who are known to us partly through unsympathetic Christian sources, but also from the documents from the Cairo Genizah, dating from the tenth to the thirteenth centuries, which reveal active and well-established links between Jewish families and communities across the Mediterranean whose language was Hebrew. In later periods many westerners came to live within the empire, both in Constantinople and elsewhere, some from the

Italian trading city-states such as Venice and Genoa, and they brought their social mores with them as well as their language. Conversely, there had been a substantial Greek-speaking presence in Sicily and south Italy since the seventh century, when many had fled there from the eastern provinces under pressure from the Persian and Arab invasions. Parts of Italy were ruled directly from Byzantium, for example the Exarchate of Ravenna, which lasted with some disruption until the mid-eighth century; there was a line of Greek popes in the seventh and eighth centuries,[32] Venice became fully independent from Constantinople only in the ninth century and Bari fell to the Normans as late as 1071. Many areas of Asia Minor passed at different times from Byzantine to Arab rule and back, and then fell to the Seljuk or Ottoman Turks.

Byzantium was remarkable both for its capacity to absorb and integrate and for the diffusion of its culture. Examples of the latter are the continuity of existing, Byzantine patterns of life during the Umayyad caliphate and, much later, the continuance of Byzantine culture in the Balkans and central Europe after 1453.[33] It has also been common to regard Byzantine culture as based on two elements: the Greek, classical influence, exemplified for instance in the educational system and the teaching of rhetoric, and the Judaic and Christian tradition. Cyril Mango sees Byzantine culture as an amalgam of the two, with the latter predominating; in this view the superstitious and 'medieval' elements of Byzantine culture are most strongly emphasised.[34] In contrast, Speros Vryonis refers to this combination as a 'hybrid', and Byzantine culture as having a 'hybrid character'.[35]

These terms are typical of much of the scholarship about Byzantium. However, the traditional notions of 'influence', or of the Byzantine debt to the classical past now seem too simplistic; equally, the notions of ethnicity and identity have come under scrutiny in recent years. We can no longer accept Arnold Toynbee's notorious appeal to ideas of race and ethnicity in relation to Byzantium, yet the rise of nationalism and of appeals to ethnic consciousness in the contemporary Balkans shows that such ideas are far from obsolete.[36] In addition to the political implications inherent in language of ethnicity and race, a large body of theoretical writing has concluded that these concepts are themselves constructs and cannot be regarded as objective terms. The introduction to a recent collection dealing with the subject of ethnicity in late antiquity states firmly that 'the ethnicity of any community is subjectively defined', and makes the point that the term itself is a modern coinage.[37]

Byzantine Identity

'Identity' is hardly less difficult to define. The sense in which the Byzantines felt themselves to have a shared identity and the factors that bound them together at the different stages of Byzantium's history are questions addressed by Cyril Mango in the first chapter of his *Byzantium: The Empire of New Rome*. Mango emphasises cultural and ethnic diversity, claiming that if we look at the situation towards the end of the eighth century 'we find a population that had been so thoroughly churned up that it is difficult to tell what ethnic groups were living where and in what numbers'.[38] Even if overstated, this acts as a valuable reminder that our available sources permit only somewhat impressionistic estimates of the mix of the Byzantine population at any given time. As for 'Greekness', this can be reasonably applied to the language of education, court and high literature in Byzantium but is far from doing justice to Byzantine society as a whole.[39] In the search for a unifying or identifying factor religion seems at first sight to be a better candidate, and this is certainly how many Byzantines saw it. In the words of Steven Runciman, '[the Byzantine] had an overriding sense of religion . . . He had a deep devotion towards his Church and its ceremonies. The Divine Liturgy was to him the great experience of his regular life and his loyalty to it was unbounded.'[40] In contrast, Mango emphasises the divisions that the search for orthodoxy caused, and indeed Byzantium was bitterly divided to the very end on religious matters. It may well be that even here, loyalties were just as, or more, likely to be regional and local than directed to Constantinople or to the empire as a whole.

A theme that Byzantinists are currently addressing is the issue of how people actually lived, what was the condition of their material and social lives, and what difference it makes that while the literature and surviving sources for Byzantium are overwhelmingly urban the vast majority of the Byzantines actually lived in villages.[41] Vryonis's notion of hybridity is innocent of theoretical connotations and the two elements that he identifies as its constituents, Hellenism and Orthodoxy, are themselves matters open to debate. Nevertheless the notion of hybridity may still be a useful tool in relation to Byzantium. In recent years it has come to be used for a major strand within the discussion of colonial and post-colonial identities.[42] In this context, hybridity denotes 'border lives', typically of migrants or those living as part of a diaspora. Consideration of hybridity is appropriate for any study of identity that has to do with 'the great history of the languages and landscapes of migration and diaspora'.[43] These mixed cultural identities seem particularly evident in the Byzantine Empire, and, in their recent collection, Hélène Ahrweiler and Angeliki Laiou, both of them senior and well-known Byzantinists of Greek origin, address the multi-ethnic quality of Byzantine civilisation, even while maintaining that 'in order to be a full-blown and unquestioned "Roman" . . . it was best to be an Orthodox Christian and a Greek-speaker, at least in one's public *persona*'.[44] The book's focus on personal identity and methods of integration has resulted in some important contributions, not least Laiou's own chapter on institutional mechanisms of integration,[45] though it does not address the issues from the 'post-colonial' perspective. Identity as interpreted in that context will be subjective, even though the culture in question is liable, as in the case of the Byzantines, to present it within a series of binary oppositions. The reality, as post-colonial theorists argue, is that such identities are 'hybrid' in that they come about as the result of complex negotiation through a process of 'hybridisation'.

In the past Byzantium has been seen in a very different way, especially in the Western literary and artistic imagination. Even historians have tended to see the Byzantine Empire as a more or less fixed entity.[46] Such an idea of Byzantium as unchanging, exotic and 'different', that is, different from post-Enlightenment western European culture, has come into being for several reasons. To cite Runciman in the same essay,

> Gibbon, whose flashes of historical insight often pierced through his eighteenth-century prejudices, declared roundly that the historian's eye must always be fixed on the city of Constantinople. He made it clear that he himself did not much like fixing his gaze there; but his judgement was sound. The great fortress-city stood for centuries as the bulwark of Christian civilisation against the forces of the East. Its citizens by their respectful devotion to past standards of civilisation preserved traditions that would otherwise have been lost to us.[47]

In the late seventeenth and early eighteenth century some Anglicans had looked to the Orthodox for a common alliance in the face of both Roman Catholicism and Protestantism, and some Orthodox had looked to the West, but these initiatives were soon to founder.[48] For Gibbon, who was preceded in this by Montesquieu, it was difficult to separate the history of Byzantium from the political and cultural issues that surrounded the Ottoman Empire and its relationships with the rest of Europe. Byzantium was also identified with the Greeks, and the present and past condition of the Greeks was also a topic much discussed both before and after the creation of the modern Greek state; some Greeks also lamented their 'backwardness', and thought in terms of introducing European culture to the Greek world. The idea of Byzantium remained contested: for J. B. Bury, quite simply, 'no "Byzantine empire" ever began to exist; the Roman empire did not come to an end until 1453'.[49] Byzantium was not classical Greece; it could not easily be accommodated either by romantic Hellenists in the eighteenth and nineteenth centuries or by classicists since. For Arnold Toynbee, for example, Byzantium represented servility in comparison with the Hellenic love of freedom.[50] Finally, the tendency towards negativity in relation to Byzantium has to do with a tradition of orientalising approaches to the East. These issues will recur through the rest of this book and point to the need for an evaluation of Byzantium more appropriate to modern conditions and current questions.

All Byzantinists, especially the compilers of biographical dictionaries and other such tools, are familiar with the broader question 'who is a Byzantine?' Should the category also include the many individuals and groups of Byzantine culture, upbringing and education who were not actually living within the empire's borders at any given time? An obvious example is provided by the theologian John of Damascus (d. c.750). Though he is generally regarded as one of the most important of all Byzantine theologians he was born and brought up in Damascus under the Umayyads and spent his life as a monk of the Mar Saba monastery near Jerusalem, never setting foot in Byzantine territory. His many works of theology, all written in Greek, do not seem to have been available in Constantinople during his lifetime even though he was well-known by reputation. John's connections within the culture of the Umayyad Caliphate thus pose sharp questions of hybridity, but it would be perverse to deny him a place within a study of Byzantium. One could cite many other such examples from every period of the history of Byzantium, and most historians, as well as the compilers of prosopographies of Byzantium, have realistically concluded that the term 'the Byzantines' has to be understood so as to include them.[51]

Byzantium presents yet another problem in terms of its written source material in that it is much easier for us to hear the voices of the elite than of the governed. However, this difficulty can be exaggerated. The literature of Byzantium, like that of the classical world, is on the whole an elite and high-style literature, but it is not only that. Scholars are increasingly interested in stories, apocrypha, 'low-level' saints' lives and non-literary texts, and if properly used, these can help us a great deal. A substantial amount is also available in languages other than Greek, though this is not necessarily less formal or elite in origin. It is more a matter of refusing to listen only to the 'official' Byzantine voices, and of really listening to what the sources can tell us. Nor can we understand the Byzantines from their written sources alone, let alone only the literary ones.

Much of Byzantium's territory at various stages in its history fell outside any conventional definition of Europe, and Byzantium has suffered from a body of Western scholarship imbued with orientalising assumptions. The Byzantine capital of Constantinople sat on the European side of the Bosphorus, apparently consciously bridging Europe and Asia, and with an eye to trade with the coastal areas of the Black Sea. It has seemed obvious that this realisation, together with its strategic potential, must have been in Constantine's mind when, as sole ruler of the empire after his defeat of Licinius in 324, he chose to make it the basis for his 'New Rome'. In fact the advantages of the site are not nearly so clear as this suggests: the site was dangerously exposed to the landward side, both to attack and to lack of water; it does not have a favourable climate and is liable to earthquakes; it is not particularly well-situated for provisioning by sea, and the Black Sea is notoriously inhospitable (which is why the Greeks took care to call it the Euxine, or 'hospitable' sea).[52]

Fig. 3 Justinian's church of Hagia Sophia, Constantinople

Despite what one reads in many modern books, we do not know exactly why Constantine chose it in preference, say, to Nicomedia, Diocletian's capital, or whether he intended it to replace Rome; still less can we assume that he foresaw that it would become the capital of a long-lived 'Byzantine' empire. Nevertheless, by the sixth century and the reign of Justinian (527–65), Rome had severely contracted, while Constantinople's population had risen. It was now the single imperial city, recognised as such both in the West and the East. Yet in Runciman's words, 'There has always been a tendency amongst western historians to neglect Byzantium because it seems to them to stand a little apart from the main course of the history of our Christian civilisation.' This question of the European versus the Eastern identity of Byzantium, discussed further in Chapter 9 below, is still one of its most intriguing features, and central to the theme of its hybridity.

2

The Changing Shape of Byzantium: From Late Antiquity to 1025

'Procopius of Caesarea has written the history of the wars which Justinian, the Roman Emperor, waged against the barbarians in the East and West, just as each happened, that great deeds might not go unrecorded and that the vast progression of time might not overwhelm them, consign them to oblivion, and wipe them wholly from sight – deeds whose record he thought would be something great and highly beneficial to both the present generation and to those to come, if ever time should place men in the same kind of crisis again.'

Procopius, *History of the Wars* I.1

For the average English-speaking reader Byzantium needs to be reinserted into general history. This means not only the history of Europe but also that of the wider Mediterranean world, the Middle East and the immense geographical spread of Slavic territories as far as Russia, through which Byzantine influence touched Lithuania, Poland and the whole of central and south-eastern Europe. Its history is not merely integral to that of Europe, but also to the world of Islam. Once we begin to grasp the spread of territory either ruled directly by Byzantium or influenced by it through strong political, religious and cultural ties, its importance is obvious. Yet for most of us, and especially from the perspective of Britain or North America, which are outside Byzantium's direct sphere of influence, this needs something of a leap of the imagination, and it comes as something of a shock to learn that one Byzantine emperor actually visited England.

When the city of Constantinople was officially dedicated in AD 330 the Roman Empire was still undivided. Between AD 395 and 476 there were emperors in both east and west, but this was not new; indeed the imperial system from which Constantine emerged had allowed for a plurality of emperors. However, during the fifth century the impact and level of barbarian incursion and settlement grew, especially in the west, until in AD 476 the last Western Roman emperor was deposed. In the early sixth century Italy came under the rule of the Ostrogoths, while other barbarian kingdoms were established in France, Spain and North Africa by the Franks, the Burgundians, the Visigoths and the Vandals. Meanwhile Constantinople had grown as a city and the cities of the Eastern empire prospered, especially in the eastern Mediterranean provinces.[1] Even after 476 it was still possible to think of a united Mediterranean world. But the Eastern empire, with its capital at Constantinople and Greek as its language of administration and bureaucracy, had begun to take on a new role. It is a moot point whether the Eastern empire in this period should be seen as Byzantine. But it is important to realise that Byzantium was no monolith. Whenever its 'beginning' is postulated, whether in the reign of Constantine (sole rule 324–37), or that of Justinian (527–65) or in the seventh century, it came into being as a separate entity slowly, developing out of the existing structures, and it changed shape many times during its long history.

The religious life of late antiquity has caught the imagination of many. This was the period during which, with the benefit of imperial support, Christianity gradually came to dominate the empire. Constantine was in no position to declare Christianity the 'official' religion, but the later fourth century was the age of such great Christian figures as Jerome, Basil of Caesarea, Gregory of Nazianzus, John Chrysostom, Ambrose and Augustine, and at the end of the fourth century Theodosius I (378–95) legislated to make paganism illegal and to bring heretics within the orbit of the secular law. At the same time Christianity quickly spread as the Church became more visible. The new class of Christian bishops were builders of churches and church complexes and were a source of social welfare to the poor; thus the message they spread by their writings and in their preaching rested on solid grounds of advantage.[2] But this was still a world of religious variety in which older beliefs and practices had a powerful appeal and might themselves be influenced by Christianity. The birth of Dionysus, for example, is a theme of late antique mosaics in Syria and Cyprus in scenes reminiscent of the Nativity, and Neoplatonic philosophy received a new upsurge of vitality in a more mystical and quasi-religious form. The vivid spirituality expressed in contemporary visual art was shared across the entire spectrum of Christianity, Judaism and polytheism;[3] moreover ideas and practices spread easily both across the east–west axis of the empire itself and across its borders.

However, religion was not the whole story, and indeed some contemporary research has sought to pull back from the emphasis placed in

Fig. 4 Colonnaded street, Apamea, Syria, one of the centres of Neoplatonism in late antiquity

Fig. 5 Sasanian period silver-gilt vase depicting Dionysus, Ariadne and Herakles arriving in India, fifth to seventh century, Arthur M. Sackler Gallery, Smithsonian Institution, Washington, DC, gift of Arthur M. Sackler, S1987.117

recent historiography of late antiquity on religion and culture and return to older models of barbarian invasion and the 'decline and fall of the Roman empire'.[4] Such a reaction has come from historians of the west, and neither they themselves nor their emphasis on the traditional 'end of the Roman empire' in AD 476 tell us much about the Eastern empire of the time, where this event made little impact. At the beginning of the fifth century the east had surmounted a Germanic crisis in its government and successfully deflected its own barbarian threat westwards; this freed the young Emperor Theodosius II (408–50) to embark on a codification of Roman law since Constantine (the Theodosian Code) and to summon the Council of Ephesus in AD 431, which was followed by the Council of Chalcedon in 451, held under his successor Marcian (450–57), who had been chosen on Theodosius's death as the husband of the latter's forceful and religious sister Pulcheria.[5] The Council of Ephesus was extremely important for religious and political divisions in the east thereafter; it recognised the title of Theotokos ('she who gave birth to God') for the Virgin, and in so doing endorsed the intense lobbying carried out by Cyril of Alexandria, and condemned Nestorius, the bishop of Constantinople, who refused to accept this formula, and prepared the way for a later separation in the Eastern Church between the 'orthodox' Church and those who made a strong division between the human and divine natures. In this tradition Nestorius was claimed as the founding father of Christian communities in Mesopotamia, Persia and further east, including China, where Nestorians are recorded on inscriptions as early as the seventh century.[6] The Christological issues were addressed again in a second Council of Ephesus in 449, (known as the 'Robber Council'), which condemned a monk called Eutyches for arguing that Christ had only one, divine, nature. The matter was felt to be unresolved, and the Council of Chalcedon in 451, which declared that Christ had two natures, human and divine, but that they were indivisible, is crucial for understanding the later relations between the Eastern and Western Churches. Western Church historians tend to believe that Chalcedon settled the issue once and for all, and many Western-based histories of the early Church end with it. In contrast, large numbers of Eastern Christians believed that it leaned too far towards the Nestorian position and never accepted it; these miaphysites ('one-nature people'), after many more struggles eventually started to ordain their own clergy during the sixth century and formed the basis of a further separated Church, which has lasted to this day in Syria and Egypt.[7]

The fifth-century century Church historian Sozomen depicts the court of the young Theodosius and his three older sisters as almost a house of prayer, and Pulcheria, fourteen years old when the infant Theodosius became emperor, as dedicating herself to virginity and to bringing up and guiding her young brother;[8] she was given a heroic importance in later Byzantine consciousness for influencing the Council of Ephesus and bringing the relics of the Virgin's robe and girdle to Constantinople. Whether or not she did all that she is credited with, the fifth century in the East was a time of preoccupation with religious politics and legislation; it was also a time of consolidation for the government, after Zeno (474–91) had successfully fought off internal challenges. Both Marcian and Anastasius (491–518) became emperor as the safe choice of a female regent, in Anastasius's case Ariadne, the widow of Zeno, and both had useful even if not recent military connections. Anastasius was known for his prudent fiscal policy and his strengthening of fortifications. The Eastern empire continued during the fifth century to intervene in Western affairs and used its barbarian allies in the attempt, but by the early sixth century the political geography of the Mediterranean had very significantly changed.

The 'fall of the Roman Empire' is a venerable historical question. As we have seen, Gibbon concluded that the Roman Empire continued for many centuries after AD 476, and the Byzantines themselves continued to think of themselves and their empire as Roman. Thus the revisionist emphasis on the importance of AD 476 noted above makes it difficult to explain the survival of the Eastern empire. Equally, whatever traditional structural weaknesses have been adduced in the past to explain the end of antiquity and the transition to the medieval world – over-taxation, a top-heavy military and bureaucratic structure, slavery, or class-struggle – they usually fail to account sufficiently for the very different circumstances and outcomes in East and West. A. H. M. Jones was followed by Geoffrey de Ste Croix in taking the end of the sixth century as the effective end of the ancient world, and J. H. W. G. Liebeschuetz's recent study focusing on urbanism as an indicator of change sees 'decline' as having set in well before this,[9] but these conceptualisations too leave in the air (perhaps deliberately) questions about the development of Byzantium and its ability to ride out and deal with the severe challenges of the seventh century.

Faced with the fragmentation of the Western empire into the new 'barbarian' kingdoms, the East struck back during the reign of Justinian (527–65). This was officially a 'reconquest', to use the terminology of restoration also found in the propagandistic preamble to Justinian's codification of Roman law. Vandal North Africa was quickly recovered by Justinian's general Belisarius in AD 534, and a Byzantine administration imposed. The recovery of Italy took longer, and the effects of a prolonged war that ended only in AD 554 were felt both in Italy and in Byzantium; yet here too Justinian was able to impose a settlement outlining the basis of future rule. A contemporary official and Latin writer known as John the Lydian sums it up succinctly: 'For Rome he preserved what was Rome's'.[10] We have detailed accounts of Justinian's military campaigns in the *History of the Wars* by the historian Procopius, originally from Caesarea in Palestine, and a scathing critique in the same author's subversive *Secret History*, where he accuses Justinian and his wife Theodora of 'blood-lust', making them responsible for the deaths of five million people in North Africa alone.[11] This is the language of opposition, and it is a feature of Byzantium that the rulers of this ostensibly autocratic state never lacked their critics. The reign of Justinian was a period of considerable strain in relation to the imperial regime. This was most evident in the serious 'Nika' riot in Constantinople in AD 532, which was put down with great severity and bloodshed, and is vividly demonstrated in Procopius's sharply contrasting works, not only his 'truth-telling' *Secret History*, or 'Unpublished Work', but also his panegyrical account of Justinian's building programme in the *Buildings*. Justinian's reign also saw an outbreak of bubonic plague in 541, the impact of which was still felt even a century later.[12] Justinian's great achievement in codifying Roman law and the swift victories of Belisarius's early campaigns were followed by manpower problems and financial difficulties; the emperor struggled unsuccessfully to deal with the continuing religious division in the empire and became fearful of plots and conspiracies. The administration and organisation of the empire of Justinian in the sixth century were still based on the system put in place in the late third and early fourth century by Diocletian and Constantine, but contemporaries were aware of the strains, and modern historians have found it hard to assess.[13] Justinian was as ready to use diplomacy and mission as other Byzantine emperors if the opportunity arose, and a benign interpretation has recently been put forward of Byzantine relations with the various states of the eastern Mediterranean rim in terms of a 'Christian commonwealth'.[14] However the same emperor was capable of browbeating Eastern Christians, offending North African bishops and driving through his own policies against opposition.

According to Procopius in the passage already quoted, probably written in AD 550–1, and thus before the end of the Gothic War, 'Italy, which is at least three times as large as Libya, has been far more completely depopulated than the latter'. Procopius also blamed Justinian for allowing Huns, Slavs and Antae to overrun Illyricum, Thrace, Greece and the Chersonnese. But Justinian's policy paid off for a time. While the incursion of the Lombards into Italy in AD 568 could not have been foreseen, Byzantine rule was maintained at Ravenna and Venice in the north and also in south Italy (Apulia, Calabria, Lucania and Campania) and Sicily. Parts of southern Spain were also recovered, and North Africa remained technically under Byzantine control until the late seventh century.

Nevertheless it is clear that Justinian's ambitious policy of reconquest was not sustainable overall. According to Michael Hendy, 'as a source of surplus revenue, Justinian's reconquest was a dead loss'. Its prospects of success were also badly affected by the need to deal at the same time with the powerful military power of the Sasanians in the east, and to defend Greece and the hinterland of Constantinople from incursions from Huns and others from the north. As Procopius's *Buildings* demonstrates, Justinian put great efforts into strengthening the existing system of frontier fortifications, but this did not in the long run keep the empire secure. While taxation was imposed after the reconquest of North Africa, Byzantine rule there required a heavy investment in buildings and in military and civilian personnel and infrastructure; the Byzantines quickly found themselves having both to maintain an army of uncertain loyalty and to confront Berber attacks. The Byzantine administration was Greek in character, and it was not easy for Constantinople to deal with the aftermath of Vandal Arianism, or with the Latin-speaking North African Catholic Church, the church of St Augustine, several of whose bishops led the opposition to Justinian's religious policy in the 540s. Against this, recent scholarship has established that North Africa under the Vandals still engaged in long-distance Mediterranean exchange, if on a reduced level, and grain and olive production continued into the Byzantine period; Eastern saints also found a following in North Africa, and Greek-speaking Eastern monks and clergy from Palestine including St Maximus Confessor arrived in Carthage in the seventh century in the wake of the Persian conquest of Syria, Palestine and Egypt. But the Arab conquest of Egypt in AD 641 left North Africa exposed, and the Arab foundation of Kairouan in Tunisia in AD 662 predated the fall of Carthage by more than thirty years.[15]

Throughout their history the Byzantines were faced with profoundly important developments outside the empire to which they found themselves reacting. The Arab invasions in the eastern provinces, the Slav inroads into the Balkans, the rise of the Italian maritime cities, the advent of the crusaders and the threats presented by the Turks and the Mongols are all examples of this. The Byzantine Empire existed during

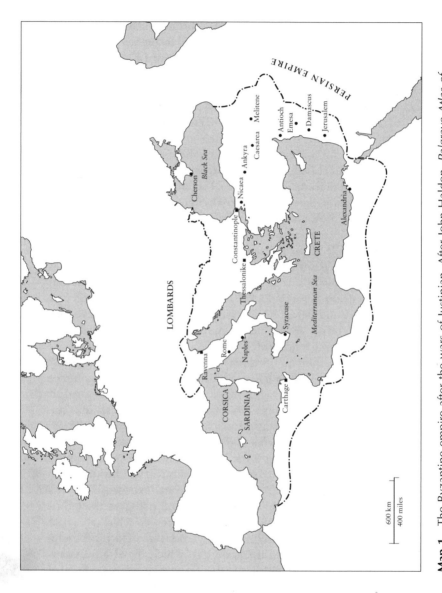

Map 1 The Byzantine empire after the wars of Justinian. After John Haldon, *Palgrave Atlas of Byzantine History* (Basingstoke, 2005), p. 23

many centuries, indeed throughout the Western Middle Ages, and towards the end of this long period, and irrespective of the internal history of Byzantium, both western and central Europe were acquiring a recognisably different shape. For much of their history, too, the world of the Byzantines coexisted with the world of Islam, whether in the shape of the Umayyad caliphate ruled from Damascus, or the Arab empire of the Abbasids and their new capital at Baghdad, with their various successors, or finally the Seljuks and Ottomans from the eleventh century onwards. Byzantium was also deeply affected by the developing papacy and the medieval Catholic Church. There were times when the Byzantines engaged in an aggressive or imperialistic foreign policy, for example under Justinian, or in the tenth and early eleventh centuries with renewed success against the Arabs and the annexation of Bulgaria as a Byzantine province. It remains striking, however, that their military initiatives were so often a matter of attempting to recover or reconquer a position which they had previously held.[16]

Sasanian Persia presented the most dangerous and best equipped military threat to the early Byzantine state, and Rome and Iran had been in a state of alternating war and expensive truce since the rise of the Sasanian dynasty in the third century AD. To campaign against the Persians was a matter of honour; when Constantine died in AD 337 he had been preparing an expedition against Persia, and the Emperor Julian died in mysterious circumstances in AD 363 while on a Persian campaign. Religious factors were also involved in relation to the treatment of Christians in Persia and the Christian populations of Syria and Mesopotamia in the areas over which the armies of both sides had to pass. Justinian's renewed war against Persia under his rival Chosroes I (531–578/9) ended with a peace treaty in 561, achieved with much elaborate diplomacy but at great cost. However, after the Emperor Maurice (582–602) had helped to restore Chosroes II (590–628) to the throne in 591 the latter invaded Byzantine territory in 604. From 611 onwards the Sasanians sacked important cities in Asia Minor and invaded Syria and Palestine, capturing Jerusalem in 614 and deporting many Christians together with the relic of the True Cross to Ctesiphon; from Palestine they then advanced into Egypt. In 622 Heraclius launched an almighty effort of recruitment and military drive, and successfully pushed the Persian army back to its capital at Ctesiphon before entering Jerusalem and restoring the relic of the True Cross. Chosroes II was dethroned, and the Sasanian Empire fell shortly afterwards.

Heraclius's exploit was one of the most brilliant in the whole history of Byzantium, but it was also the most risky and the most short-lived.

The emperor had left Constantinople to lead his army, and was absent when the city came perilously near to falling to a combined siege by the Avars and the Persians in 626. His success was spectacular. The Sasanian Empire fell after three hundred years of existence, and the emperor returned to Constantinople in triumph in 630, bringing the relic of the True Cross with him. His victory was celebrated with maximum pomp and ceremonial, and his wars were praised in grandiose epic poetry drawing on Old Testament kingly analogies by the panegyrical writer George of Pisidia. Constantine's wars against Maxentius in 312 and Licinius in 324 had been invested with Old Testament overtones by Eusebius, and the Byzantine wars against Persia in this period also took on a religious character. The events of the early seventh century evoked deep psychological reactions from contemporary Byzantines. Not only had the True Cross, the very symbol of Christianity, been taken into Persian captivity, but Constantinople itself had been in great danger. For the Jews living in Byzantine Palestine, on the other hand, Persian rule was an unimagined liberation from the Christians, and Byzantine writers in Palestine blamed the Jewish population there for assisting the invaders and aiding in massacres of Christians. In Constantinople the deliverance of the city from the Avar and Persian siege was attributed to the active intervention of the Virgin, who was invested from then on with the role of protectress of the city. Amid such heightened religious consciousness Heraclius's restoration of the True Cross to Jerusalem in 630 seemed like divine justification for the Byzantine state.[17]

Almost at once Arab armies invaded Syria and Palestine. The Byzantines were used to dealing with 'Saracens' in this area, both as federate allies in the wars with Persia, and at times as raiders. Their Arab allies in the sixth century, the Ghassanids, were also Christianised, and were the patrons of pilgrimage shrines. However the followers of Muhammad came from Arabia and were a different story, although they too were familiar with both Judaism and Christianity. They turned their sights towards Syria just as Muhammad died in 632, and only a short time after Heraclius's great success in 630. The numbers of Arab invaders were probably quite small, but the Byzantines had worn out their strength, and after a Byzantine defeat at the River Yarmuk in 636 Heraclius led a Byzantine retreat from the territory which had so recently been recovered. This left Syria open to the Arabs, and Egypt also fell in 642; by the 660s the Arabs had established themselves in North Africa. Heraclius remained on the throne until 641, but his military glory was brief, and the rest of his reign was dominated less by the Arab threat than by his attempt to settle the religious divisions in the east that had been a problem for every emperor since the Council of Chalcedon. There too lasting success escaped him. The new imperial solution, known as Monotheletism (asserting the 'one will' of Christ) remained officially in force until the Sixth Ecumenical Council in 681 but it was highly divisive, and its proclamation alienated many of the Christians in the eastern provinces just as they were coming under Arab rule.

Having reached the Mediterranean the Arab invaders set about acquiring a fleet, and in the space of little over fifty years they had gained control of about a third of the entire Byzantine territory, from Syria and Palestine to North Africa and southern Spain, coming very near to capturing Constantinople in 674–78 and 717–18. Contrary to the common view, it has been argued that the Byzantines should have been able to win against the invading Arabs,[18] but the emperor's mobilisation against the Persians in 622, followed by Byzantine military success, had exhausted the potential of the empire. If the army really was still the fighting machine it had once been in the late Roman period it is hard to explain either Heraclius's recruiting difficulties or his willingness to leave Syria to its fate.[19] Heraclius was a realist, and while the fateful importance of this Arab victory is obvious with hindsight, and Heraclius's withdrawal was represented as a historic turning point in Arabic historiography, contemporary Byzantines had no reason to view it in that way. However, the Persian invasions two decades or so earlier had severely damaged the urban infrastructure of Asia Minor, and therefore the empire's essential tax-base from which the cost of the army had to be found, at a time when late Roman urbanism was already showing distinct signs of weakness.[20] Even in the 540s the second campaign of Belisarius against the Persians clearly demonstrated the shortage of manpower on the Byzantine side, and the historian Agathias who continued Procopius's history in the 580s complained that Justinian had run down the army to a dangerous level.[21] Heraclius was spectacularly successful against the Persians, but his monumental efforts at recruitment tell a story of crisis rather than of confidence.

A further major change was the ending of free bread distribution in AD 618 to the citizens of Constantinople, a practice adopted by Constantine on the model of Rome when Constantinople was founded.[22] Constantine had allowed for 80,000 free rations, in itself an impressive indicator of the projected size of the new city, and the organisation of the *annona*, or tax in foodstuffs (principally grain and oil from Egypt and North Africa), and its eventual distribution to the citizens was a massive undertaking while at the same time sending a powerful message of imperial care for the city. After 618 the capital had to obtain its grain from other sources, from its hinterland and from Asia Minor, and new means had to be found to supply it. The effect was dramatic: supplies were no longer secure, given the conditions of the seventh century, and the population dropped accordingly; on one estimate it fell as low as 40,000. Recent scholarship has emphasised the degree to which the city depended for its food supply on outside sources, and ensuring supply was a political necessity for emperors, who still intervened if the price of bread rose to a dangerous level; according to the tenth-century *Book of the Prefect* it was carefully regulated and calculated on a regular basis.[23] By 1200, based on the one figure that we have, the population of Constantinople was around 400,000, which is to say, not far short of what it had been in 500;[24] Paul Magdalino comments that while the number is no doubt merely a guess, it is 'better than nothing',[25] and it seems to be not far off the mark. Maintaining such a population without state distributions of bread was a very considerable achievement indeed.

A wealth of evidence from pottery has shown that 'bulk exchange', the transportation of large amounts of goods, across the Mediterranean, whether for trade or for the *annona*, had already diminished by the late sixth century, and the loss of the rich provinces of Syria, Palestine, Egypt and eventually North Africa, as well as much of Anatolia, to the Arabs brought with it the collapse of the imperial tax-base and of traditional urban culture in large tracts of the Eastern empire. The large number of building projects, synagogues, churches and public works, and also the results of a huge number of excavated shipwrecks, which seem to have been largely trading vessels carrying wine amphorae, reveal the prosperity of the eastern provinces of Syria and Palestine in the sixth century.[26] Now this enormous volume of shipping was drastically reduced, and vessels became smaller and privately owned.[27] From the mid-seventh century onwards a steep decline set in in Byzantine fortunes.[28] The shrunken fiscal base also reduced the capacity of the state to field a significant army, and Heraclius may have initiated structural changes involving partial decentralisation of army pay and recruitment in an attempt to deal with this problem; if so, however, the process took time and the Byzantine 'theme' system (territorial units with local commanders or *strategoi* with military responsibility) came into being only gradually.

The Emperor Constans II (641–68) continued these military changes and campaigned with mixed success against the Arabs, Slavs and Lombards, visiting Rome in 663 and making his base in Sicily; he was even thought to be considering moving the capital from Constantinople.[29] His attempts to enforce Monotheletism by a further *Typos* or imperial edict resulted in the trials, exile and subsequent deaths of Pope Martin I and Maximus Confessor. In spite of Constans's difficulties, the Byzantine emperor was able to order his exarch in Italy to arrest the pope after the Lateran Synod of 649, which opposed the imperial doctrine. However, Byzantine military effort in the difficult conditions after Heraclius amounted to local fire-fighting, for instance the campaigns of Justinian II (685–95, 705–11) against the Slavs and later around Cherson on the north coast of the Black Sea, where he was trying to check the Khazars. The next military emperors were father and son, Leo III (717–41) and Constantine V (741–75). They were energetic rulers in both internal and external matters, attempting to introduce a religious reform movement by banning religious images and rebuilding the walls of Constantinople. Constantine V also repopulated the city, whose numbers were greatly reduced, with settlers from Greece and the islands and restored the aqueduct of Valens, which had been in a ruined state since the siege of 626. Leo III's reign began with a dangerous Arab siege of Constantinople that lasted for more than a year. Leo was not only able to wear down the Arabs but also to halt their advance in Anatolia, and Constantine V campaigned successfully against the Slavs and Bulgarians, and in the east against the Arabs. He also put down a rebellion at the start of his reign by the *strategos* Artavasdos (who had been rewarded for his support of Leo III by marriage with the latter's daughter, Constantine's sister), and managed to regain Constantinople in 742. Constantine dealt with Artavasdos by blinding him and his sons in the Hippodrome. He was the victim of a vitriolic press in the writings of his religious opponents; nevertheless, it is clear that with the new military organisation of the themes now more firmly in place and supplemented by his creation of infantry and cavalry units known as the *tagmata*, he was a very successful commander. Constantine celebrated a spectacular triumph in Constantinople over the Bulgarians, parading Bulgarian prisoners in wooden fetters, just as he had done with the defeated Artavasdos.[30] Even the hostile iconophile chronicler Theophanes admits that he was regarded as a great general.

After the retreat of Heraclius from Syria in the 630s and the Arab conquests of the seventh century, profound changes took place in the military situation in eastern Anatolia. There was no linear frontier between Byzantine and Arab territory: rather, a variety of fortified sites acted as shelters and centres of military activity. The Byzantine aim was to establish a wide frontier zone, and rarely if ever to engage in direct conflict. The Arabs for their part conducted regular raids into Byzantine territory, and frequent exchanges of prisoners took place, but neither side

Fig. 6 Part of an assemblage of pottery from a destruction layer in the Lower City at Amorium, associated by the excavators with the capture of Amorium by the Arabs in AD 838, courtesy of the Amorium Excavations Project

made major gains until the tenth century – the siege and capture by the Arabs of the city of Amorium in 838 was an exception commemorated in Byzantine hagiography (see p. 185). The Byzantine army was not large enough to do more; much was left to local *strategoi* based in the fortified settlements which had largely replaced the open civic urban centres of late antiquity. A military treatise on guerilla warfare reflecting the situation in the tenth century under Nikephoros II Phokas vividly evokes the tactics and nature of this border warfare.

Recovery takes confidence, and needs renewed strength. When Constantine V's father Leo III had come to the throne in 717 Constantinople was weak, the city dramatically depopulated and the empire greatly reduced. The capital had only just managed to survive a great siege, and the onset of plague added to its difficulties. Once-famous buildings fell into disrepair and were half-forgotten; living in it was like living in a deserted landscape littered with half-forgotten monuments of the late antique past. Access to education had also fallen to a low level and contemporaries filled the gaps by resorting to fancy and imagination and developing a literature of nostalgia, speculation and religious anxiety, as is vividly demonstrated by the pretentious but frequently inaccurate and sometimes superstitious set of 'notes' on the historical monuments of Constantinople known as the *Parastaseis*.[31] In some ways the low state of Byzantium at this time was shared by much of western Europe. However the city gradually began to revive in Constantine V's reign and Irene (regent 780, empress 797–802), herself from Athens, had some success against the Slavs in Greece in 782 through the eunuch general Staurakios. Urban renewal slowly began to be felt. Warren Treadgold points to the dramatic increase in the number of provinces between 780 and 842 and the tax census of 809 along with the successful settlement of a large number of displaced Byzantines as signs that the administration was rising to the challenge.[32] In 800 Charlemagne, who had only recently sought to unite his daughter in marriage with the young Byzantine emperor Constantine VI, son of Irene, and who followed this with the prospect of an alliance with Irene herself, was crowned Emperor of the Romans.[33] This was a psychological affront to the Byzantines, but cultural revival had begun in Byzantium by about 800,[34] and the ending of the divisive dispute over iconoclasm in 843 and the weakening of the Abbasid caliphate in the east released a new confidence.

The Bulgars were originally a Turkic people who had appeared in the Byzantine sphere in the seventh century; they merged with the existing Slav population from the late seventh century, and established the 'First Bulgarian Empire' with its capital at Pliska, west of Varna in modern Bulgaria, using Greek for its early inscriptions. The Bulgars were a major threat to Byzantium in this period, especially under Krum and Symeon, although by the 860s Bulgaria had been Christianised, and by the later ninth century disciples of the Byzantine missionaries, the brothers Cyril and Methodius, introduced the Slavonic alphabet for the translation of the Bible and for liturgical use; Byzantine influence in Bulgaria was now strong, and by the early tenth century the capital had moved to Preslav. The Byzantines also had to deal with the Rus', Vikings who came south from Scandinavia and besieged Constantinople in 860, an event memorably described by the Patriarch Photius.[35] The Rus' established their capital at Kiev and in settling mingled with the existing Slav population.[36] By the tenth century formal trade agreements between Byzantium and Rus' allowed Russian merchants to visit Constantinople every year selling furs, wax and honey. This was a world transformed from that of late antiquity.

We owe to the tenth-century emperor Constantine VII Porphyrogenitus an extraordinary insight into the developed ideology of contemporary Byzantium in which foreign relations occupy a central place;[37] in particular, his treatise *On the Administration of the Empire* set out the procedures for dealing with foreign nations.[38] Constantine was a scholar and a thinker. He commissioned a whole series of working papers and compilations that would be useful for an emperor, and particularly for his son and prospective successor Romanos. These included military treatises, a genre in which the Byzantines excelled, as well as the treatise on imperial administration, which deals in fact with foreign relations and what we would call diplomacy, and the compilation known as the *Book of Ceremonies*, a kind of instruction manual or book of protocols for imperial ceremonial.[39] In these texts Byzantium occupies the centre of a diplomatic and military nexus which stretches from Germany to Russia and the Caucasus. The *Book of Ceremonies* conveys a powerful conviction on the part of the Byzantines themselves of the status of Byzantium in the world order. Documentary accounts of the type that found their way into the *Book of Ceremonies* laid down, for example, minute instructions for all the necessary arrangements when an emperor went on campaign: all was prescribed, from the formulae for commissioning a deputy in Constantinople, the place of disembarkation on the Asian side of the Bosphorus and the military and other escorts, to the gold plate needed for entertaining foreign guests and the imperial bath and chamber pots. The judicious dissemination of false rumours was recommended to the imperial deputy as a useful way of handling difficult situations. While on campaign the emperor also carried a supply of books varying in content from military manuals and liturgical books to books of dream interpretation and handbooks about weather for soldiers and sailors.[40] From these sources we gain an idea of the massive amount of equipment and the number of animals that were needed in order to mount an imperial expedition, and, indeed, the drain on those from whom the food and animals were requisitioned. The descriptions of imperial triumphal entries into the capital after successful campaigns are equally striking. On one such occasion, perhaps in AD 837, when the Emperor Theophilus returned to Constantinople after a successful campaign against the Arabs in Asia Minor, he gave orders that he was to be met by all the children of the city.[41] So intimately was the imperial role connected with the idea of victory that in the protocols for the chariot races held in the Hippodrome of Constantinople, which are also preserved in the *Book of Ceremonies,* all victory, even in the races, is ascribed to him, under God.[42] From a Western perspective Byzantium seemed like a centre of power, prestige and riches to which other peoples could hardly begin to aspire, and Liudprand of Cremona, with his famous description of the mechanical lions, self-elevating throne and golden organ in the Great Palace, was just one of the foreign visitors who was impressed, not to say overwhelmed, by the display and ceremony of the Byzantine court.[43]

Diplomacy and military policy were inseparable for the Byzantines. Information about the history, characteristics and strategic capacity of foreign peoples was essential, as Constantine explains to his son: 'I maintain that while learning is a good thing for all the rest as well, who are subjects, yet it is so especially for you, who are bound to take thought for the safety of all, and to steer and guide the laden ship of the world'. Besides informing the reader about potential allies and enemies, the treatise also includes accounts of military actions taken by Constantine's predecessors, from Diocletian and other late Roman emperors to his father, the 'Christ-loving and glorious emperor' Leo VI, his father-in-law and rival Romanos I Lekapenos and himself.

In many ways this period marked the apogee of Byzantine diplomacy, but in practice Byzantine policy was opportunistic, sometimes requiring military action, sometimes diplomacy, sometimes a show of imperial grandeur, and sometimes the gifts and subsidies that had been a traditional part of Roman dealings with barbarians. Constantine VII himself had his critics for resorting too often to the latter. The tension between show and reality is a familiar one in all periods, and the Byzantines were nothing if not pragmatic. Nor were they alone in their desire to impress foreign envoys: when a Byzantine embassy went to Baghdad in AD 917 it received an equally imposing reception, and Charlemagne is said to have received Easterners in a similar fashion. Both the imperial rhetoric and the elaborate self-justifying theory co-existed with a situation in which emperors had continually to think of their own survival. This was true of Constantine VII himself, who despite having been 'born in the purple' in 905 was kept from power by rival emperors for almost forty years and achieved independent rule only in 945. Constantine criticised Romanos Lekapenos for allowing a Byzantine princess to marry Tsar Peter of Bulgaria, though such practices became common enough later. The presence of foreigners at the court, which carried both advantages and disadvantages, needed to be managed. Some even received imperial salaries during their stay and attended major state occasions such as the Christmas banquet in the room in the palace known as the Hall of the Nineteen Beds. We must not be misled by the smooth surface of Constantine's treatises into imagining that the *taxis*, or 'order', which Constantine recommends implies an absence of struggle.

Constantine VII's reign coincided with a time when the Byzantines were able to recover significant ground from the Arabs in Asia Minor. It was also a period that saw demographic growth, and signs of reviving urbanism and economic activity in Greece, where Byzantine influence had been gradually restored since the reign of Constantine V after an obscure period of Slav settlement and retreat from towns.[44] The acquisition for Constantinople in AD 944, during the eastern campaigns of the general John Kourkouas, of the image of Christ's face miraculously imprinted on a cloth, the famous Mandylion from Edessa in Mesopotamia, was made the occasion for a solemn imperial reception and an appropriate retelling of its legendary history. For a relic of such status to be transferred from Arab rule to the Byzantine capital was the epitome of symbolic victory; two and half centuries later it was in turn taken by the crusaders to the West and housed by Louis IX in his newly built Sainte Chapelle in an eerily similar transfer of symbolic capital. Constantine VII's successors Nikephoros II Phokas (963–69) and John I Tzimiskes (969–76) (who staged a coup and murdered Nikephoros, after helping him to seize the throne) energetically pursued the recovery against the Arabs, regaining Crete, Cyprus, Tarsos, Mopsuestia, Antioch and Aleppo; the advance was continued by Basil II (979–1025), who invaded Syria in 999.

Basil II also adopted a successful offensive strategy against Bulgaria, and has been known traditionally as 'the Bulgar-slayer', although the legend that this title conveys was a creation only of the later twelfth century.[45] Basil's campaign against the Bulgarians under Tsar Samuel began with defeat in 986, but in 1014 he won a great victory, after which he is said to have blinded 14,000 captives. The territory ruled by Samuel was reorganised into two Byzantine themes, Paristrion and Bulgaria, and direct Byzantine rule imposed. Basil died in 1025, and had never married. He had carried forward a great expansion of Byzantine influence that had begun in the second half of the ninth century and gathered pace in the tenth. As well as reclaiming Bulgaria for Byzantium, Basil also successfully campaigned in the north and the east, and by the time of his death the empire stretched from Italy to Mesopotamia, and included the whole of Anatolia; in the north its border was the Danube, recalling the territorial extent of the high Roman Empire.[46]

The borders of Byzantine territory had changed again. By now the Russians were also a well-established presence in Byzantine experience. Vladimir, Prince of Kiev, was baptised in 988 and given the hand of Basil II's sister Anna – a great concession bestowed in return for hoped-for aid.[47] But the Russians had already featured in Constantine VII's treatise on administration, and Vladimir's grandmother Olga had already received baptism from Constantine VII. Byzantium could not ignore Russian trade and growing Russian power, and though Russian Orthodoxy developed a distinctively different flavour over the centuries, its roots were and are Byzantine. In staging the baptism of Vladimir, however, Basil was simply pursuing the same strategy as his predecessors of linking Orthodox mission with political interest.

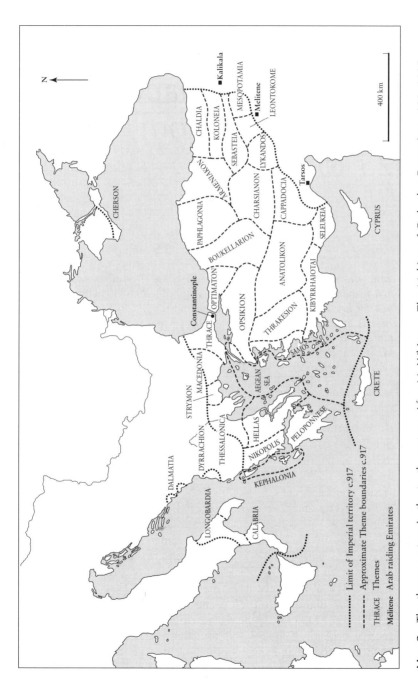

Map 2 The theme system in the tenth century. After M. Whittow, *The Making of Orthodox Byzantium, 600–1025* (Berkeley and Los Angeles, 1996), p. 166

CHERSON

KALIKALA
CHALDIA
KOLONEIA
MESOPOTAMIA
SEBASTEIA
ARMENIAKON
LEONTOKOME
Melitene
LYKANDOS
PAPHLAGONIA
CHARSIANON
CAPPADOCIA
BOUKELLARION
Tarsos
ANATOLIKON
OPTIMATON
Constantinople
SELEUKEIA
THRACE
OPSIKON
KIBYRRHAIOTAI
THRAKESION
CYPRUS
MACEDONIA
STRYMON
SAMOS
AEGEAN SEA
THESSALONICA
DYRRACHION
HELLAS
CRETE
DALMATIA
NIKOPOLIS
PELOPONNESE
LONGOBARDIA
KEPHALONIA
CALABRIA

N

400 km

.... Limit of Imperial territory c.917
- - - - - - Approximate Theme boundaries c.917
THRACE   Themes
Melitene Arab raiding Emirates

3

The Changing Shape of Byzantium: From 1025 to 1453

The emperor, accompanied by the Latins of Count Bryennius who had deserted to him, returned to the capital with the laurels of victory. The date was the first of December in the seventh indiction [AD 1083]. He found the empress in the throes of childbirth, in the room set apart long ago for an empress's confinement. Our ancestors called it the porphyra – hence the world-famous name porphyrogenitus. At dawn (it was a Saturday) a baby girl was born to them, who resembled her father, so they said, in all respects. I was that baby.

Anna Comnena, *Alexiad* VI.7

The fifty years after AD 1025 saw eastern and central Asia Minor lost to the Seljuk Turks after the Battle of Manzikert in 1071 and Bari in southern Italy lost to the Normans in the same year. Alexius I Comnenus, who came to the throne in 1081, had to deal in the north with military threats from the Pechenegs, a troublesome nomadic people originally from Central Asia, and later with the challenges posed by the First Crusade. By 1099 there was a Latin patriarch in Jerusalem, and by 1100 another in Antioch. The impact of the crusaders on Byzantium, and Alexius's dealings with them, were vividly described by the emperor's daughter Anna Comnena, and mark the beginning of a new and significant phase in Byzantium's history. Thus the century that had seen the incorporation of Bulgaria into the Byzantine sphere also saw the arrival in the Mediterranean world where Byzantium had regained its early dominance of both the Seljuk Turks and the western Crusaders. Once again the future survival and shape of the Byzantine state was profoundly affected by what was happening among its neighbours.

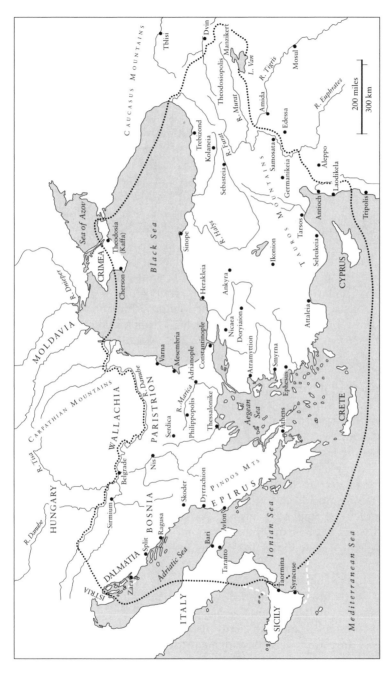

Map 3 The Byzantine Empire c.1025. After A. Kazhdan et al., eds, *The Oxford Dictionary of Byzantium* (New York, 1991), p. 354

At the same time internal changes were taking place. On the older view this was a period of decline and difficulty, accompanied by fiscal crisis; above all, the rise to prominence of landed families represented a triumph of feudalism that spelled decline for the Byzantine state. This scenario, identified most closely with George Ostrogorsky, was challenged by the French historian Paul Lemerle, and the eleventh-century devaluation of the coinage reinterpreted in an influential article by Cécile Morrisson as a sign of economic growth, a position taken much further by Alan Harvey and also developed by Alexander Kazhdan.[1] Alexius I Comnenus came to power only ten years after a Byzantine defeat in Anatolia that has been claimed to have spelled the inevitable decline of Hellenism in Asia Minor,[2] and the battle of Manzikert in 1071 certainly marked a change of focus for Byzantium from Asia Minor to the Balkans, but it did not mean the end of Byzantine interest or influence in the East. Similarly, Alexius's grant of trading privileges to the Venetians in 1082 has been held with hindsight to have been the beginning of a process which sacrificed Byzantine to Western interests. But the Comnenian period, which lasted until 1204, was certainly one of the peaks in Byzantine history in terms of prosperity, cultural life and imperial display, and the Comnenian emperors benefited from social and economic changes that were already happening. There was already a growth of towns and demographic increase in the eleventh century and this continued; the rise of the landed families can be seen as having assisted rather than hindered this process.[3] Trade relations are also part of the story, and so is the impact of the expansion which took place in western Europe in the same period.[4]

The Comnenian period was characterised by the rise to prominence of aristocratic families, a trend which Basil II had already tried to limit, and the power of Alexius Comnenus himself, who became emperor as the result of a coup in 1081, rested on an alliance between his own family, the Comneni, and others, the Doukai, the Palaiologoi and the Melissenoi.[5] The emperor's mother, Anna Dalassena, helped to ensure these alliances by the careful exploitation of marriage ties, and once in power Alexius reshaped the upper echelons of the imperial bureaucracy by creating new ranks and titles held only by those related by blood or marriage to the emperor. Whatever fissures may have existed previously between this landed elite and the civilian bureaucracy (a topic that has been a matter of debate among historians),[6] Alexius's reforms were designed to establish and safeguard his rule for the future on the basis of kinship, an entirely new development for the Byzantine ruling class. His reign has been debated, including the extent to which he showed vision in realising that the economic forces that had led to the rise of the landed families needed to be recognised within the structure of the state.[7] It is indisputable, however, that Byzantine culture in the Comnenian period now came nearer to being based on aristocratic principles, and in this it resembled western European society more than had been the case in earlier periods. In the case of Byzantium, however, this aristocratic society existed in conjunction with a complex and long-established state structure. The Comnenian reforms went a long way towards squaring this circle and in so doing brought about, if only temporarily, more political stability than Byzantium had usually enjoyed.

In 1043 Constantinople was attacked by the Russians under Vladimir of Novgorod. Though the invaders were routed in the Bosphorus with the aid of Greek fire this episode acted as a warning that Christian Rus' was developing into an independent state with pretensions to rival Byzantium. Nor was the result entirely one-sided, as the Byzantines hastened to seal the peace with an imperial marriage alliance, and even paid reparations to the Rus'. The fact that the security of the Russian monastery on Mount Athos was a factor in these arrangements underlines the development of Rus' as a Christian state very much on the Byzantine model. In the following year the schism with the papacy, which was nothing new in itself, came to a head. This had much to do with the intransigence and ambitions of the patriarch Michael Cerularius who found himself at odds not only with the papal legates but also with the Emperor Constantine IX Monomachos (1042–55) who, like later emperors, was anxious to preserve good relations with the papacy for his own political reasons. The Byzantine hold over south Italy was threatened by the activities of the Normans, and the pope was an important ally in dealing with them. However, the vexed question of ecclesiastical jurisdiction over south Italy, and the widespread divergence of practice there between Latin and Orthodox were also concerns. Legates led by Cardinal Humbert were sent by Leo IX to Constantinople, and bad feeling escalated to the point where they laid a papal bull anathematising the patriarch on the altar of St Sophia. Such was Cerularius's indignation that he was able to force the emperor to climb down, and the legates left without having achieved his humiliation or removal. This was not, then, the formal schism it is often said to have been. Most of the differences between the Eastern and Western Churches had been raised before and were not in themselves held to be critical. But now Humbert and Cerularius each learned things they had not known about the other side, and the papal complaints against Byzantine practice were accompanied by claims for papal primacy that the

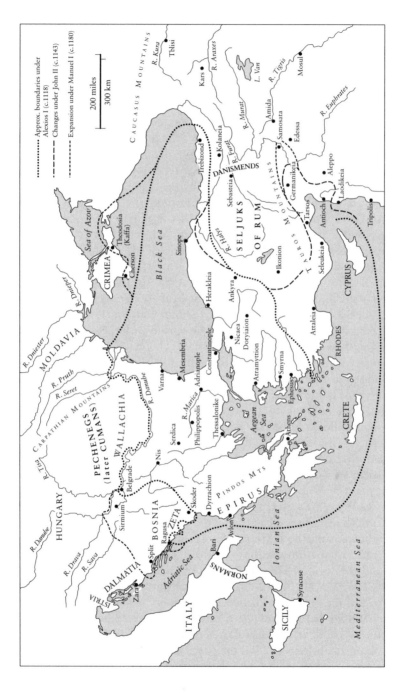

Map 4 The Byzantine Empire under the Comneni. After A. Kazhdan et al., eds, *The Oxford Dictionary of Byzantium* (New York, 1991), p. 355

Byzantines could not accept.[8] The 'schism' of 1054 did not affect the whole Church and it did not prevent individuals from remaining in communion; nor did other Byzantine churchmen necessarily agree with Cerularius. Two years later he was himself deposed by the Emperor Isaac I Comnenus (1057–59). But the political effects of the quarrel were serious in that it destroyed Byzantine hopes that alliance with the papacy would stave off the Norman threat in south Italy. The Normans were, in any case, a growing force in Europe, and would soon embark on the conquest of England. In Italy a formal alliance between the papacy and the Normans was sealed in 1059 and soon Byzantine Italy was lost.

Such was the background to what was to prove the most momentous event of the late eleventh century, the launching of the First Crusade, and its impact on Byzantium. It was the Norman Robert Guiscard who took Bari in 1071, and who had led assaults on the strategically important town of Dyrrachium (modern Durres) in the early years of Alexius's reign, and these Norman incursions across the Adriatic were continued by Robert's son Bohemond in 1107–8.[9] Neither Alexius nor his daughter, Anna Comnena, Byzantium's only female historian, were impressed by the Latins, who as a people seemed to them greedy for wealth and quite unrestrained in any military endeavour.[10] The same Bohemond was one of the leaders of the First Crusade, and Alexius was faced with the difficult and dangerous task of receiving the crusader armies while averting the threat to Constantinople that Anna Comnena, writing from her later perspective, was sure they posed: 'to all appearances they were on pilgrimage to Jerusalem; in reality they planned to dethrone Alexius and seize the capital'.[11] Anna paints Bohemond as the villain, and is both fascinated and appalled by him, but the crusaders themselves were divided and the issue was not so black and white. Their route from Constantinople or Thessalonike lay via Nicaea, just across the Bosphorus in Asia Minor, and now the Seljuk capital, which they attacked with a combined Byzantine and crusader force. The city surrendered to the Byzantines in 1097 in circumstances that presaged the hostilities of the future between Latins and Byzantines.[12] The passage of the Crusade eastwards through Anatolia presented the same dilemmas to the Byzantines as their arrival in Constantinople had done. It is difficult to see what the latter could do except try to manage the delicate balance between providing supplies while attempting to prevent the crusader armies from attacking Byzantine possessions. The situation was all the more ironic in that in 1095 Alexius had asked Pope Urban II for help against the Seljuks and thus provided Urban with a perfect justification for entering Byzantine lands. The pope did not fail to claim that the emperor had asked for a crusade against the Muslims.

The First Crusade reached Jerusalem in 1099 and Baldwin I was crowned there on Christmas Day, 1100. The events of these three years had all the ingredients that were to be found over the next century, as the Byzantines attempted to control these western groups by a mixture of diplomatic and military means. Anna's fears were justified long before 1204. Lombards attacked Constantinople in 1101 and Bohemond joined with the pope against Byzantium in 1108. The Second Crusade in 1147 posed problems for Manuel I Comnenus not unlike those faced by Alexius, and Constantinople was threatened again by Frederick Barbarossa's Third Crusade of 1189–92, which also resulted in the loss of Cyprus. Hostility mounted on both sides well before the Fourth Crusade turned on Constantinople in 1204. It was a considerable achievement that when faced with the obvious dangers to the empire presented by the crusaders, the Comnenian emperors managed on the whole to deal with the very changed situation. In the twelfth century Latin states were established in Jerusalem (until the victory of Saladin in 1187), Tripoli, Antioch and Edessa.[13] The Byzantines no longer had to contend only with the Turks in Anatolia and the east, but with the Latins as well.

Nevertheless the twelfth century was a time of vigour and innovation in Byzantine culture. Western ideas and customs inevitably impacted on Byzantium. One import was jousting, a sport at which the Emperor Manuel I Comnenus (1143–80) vied with the rulers of the Latin kingdoms. Contemporaries remarked on his skill with the lance and his horsemanship and the fact that he introduced jousting to the Byzantine military elite; it is probably Manuel who is the subject of an anonymous panegyrical description of an emperor and his jousts. On Easter Sunday 1159, after a successful campaign in Cilicia, Manuel made a triumphal entry into Antioch, with much display of Byzantine superiority to Baldwin, the king of Jerusalem, and Reynald of Châtillon, prince of Antioch; this imperial pageant was followed by jousts between the Byzantines and the Latins, each side personally led by its lord.[14] In Constantinople much of the area on the Golden Horn was given over by chrysobull (an imperial document with the emperor's signature and gold seal) by the twelfth-century emperors in the form of trading concessions to the Italian city-states of Venice, Pisa and Genoa;[15] there were perhaps sixty thousand Latins living in the city out of a population of three hundred thousand to four hundred thousand. With Western contacts came Western ideas, and with flourishing trade the growth of urban life. The twelfth century saw both revival and innovation in literary output, including the first use of vernacular (i.e. not classicising and high-style) Greek for literary composition. Satire and a revival of the romance were just two among the wide range of literary forms that now flourished, and which raise the question of whether this vigorous activity – clearly linked to social change – amounted to a renaissance, or to an early form of humanism.[16]

In this period no city in the West could compare with Constantinople for its size, its history, its culture and the wealth of its civilisation. To Western visitors it represented the acme of civilisation and luxury. Yet Paul Magdalino, in a careful discussion of the Byzantine twelfth-century 'renaissance',[17] concludes that despite the impressive intellectual and cultural life of Byzantium in this period theirs was not a type of human-ism or a renaissance that led to originality or to a fundamental ques-tioning of the old order. Niketas Choniates complained bitterly of the favour shown by Manuel I to the Latins,[18] and the typical Byzantine hostility to outsiders revealed itself again in a bloody uprising against the Latins in Constantinople in 1182 and a refusal to allow passage to Frederick Barbarossa's crusade in 1189. In fact, the question often asked by historians of whether Byzantium in the twelfth century enjoyed a renaissance of the type that was to follow in Italy, or whether it gave birth to a 'pre-renaissance', rests on several false assumptions, above all the expectation (arrived at with the advantage of hindsight) that Byzantium *should* have gone through a renaissance as the West did, and that if it did not, it must therefore be found wanting. This is effectively an Orientalist assumption born of the standard negative comparison of Byzantium with the West. It reappears in an even stronger form in rela-tion to the Palaiologan period in the thirteenth and fourteenth centuries, and is equally questionable there.

Around Byzantium the world had changed again. The Pechenegs were successfully dealt with by Alexius and by John Comnenus, but the Byzantines now had to live with the Turkish presence in Asia Minor and the considerable threat presented by the Latins. The German empire often impinged on Byzantine interests, and to the north of the Balkans Hungary needed to be kept within the Byzantine orbit. In 1147 the Normans in Sicily took Corfu and plundered Thebes and Corinth on the Greek mainland. Byzantine policy involved a mixture of military action, diplomacy and playing one group off against another. For this the Byzantines acquired a bad name, but it is hard to see what else they could do. In fact they had some success, even if this was limited: Hungary was brought under their protection, if not their control, the Serbs acknowledged Byzantine authority, Bari was recovered and Ancona

Fig. 7 Ivory statuette of the Theotokos Hodegetria (Virgin and Child), late eleventh or twelfth century, V&A Picture Library

held, Manuel Comnenus entered Antioch and married Maria of Antioch and an Orthodox patriarch was appointed again for Jerusalem in 1176, though he was unable to do more than visit the city for a year or so.[19] Against this, direct Byzantine rule in Bulgaria came to an end, and Italy continued to be a locus of rivalry between the Byzantines, the papacy and the German empire. Now, as on numerous other occasions, the problems surrounding possible alliances were compounded by the divide between the Eastern and Western Churches, and especially the Western claim of papal supremacy. Having achieved a difficult rapprochement with the papacy in the late 1160s, the Byzantines found, less than a decade later, that the pope and the German emperor Frederick Barbarossa had allied themselves after all.[20] The Byzantines failed as often as they succeeded, for instance in a joint expedition against Egypt with Amalric the king of Jerusalem in 1169 and a second abortive attempt in 1177. But Manuel I was not deterred from his attempts – promoted by a series of imperial marriages – to tie the crusader kingdoms to Byzantium. Imperial policy vis-à-vis the Seljuks had similarly mixed results. Campaigns against them in the late 1150s caused their sultan, Arslan, to come to Constantinople in 1162 as a suppliant. But when Manuel led an army to take Konya it was he who had to submit after suffering a major defeat at Myriokephalon (see p. 86).

Despite the many Latins at court and in the Byzantine armies, and the Western influences that were apparent in Constantinople, tensions rose between Byzantines and Latins. In the last decades of the twelfth century Byzantine writers often criticised Latin ways and Latin behaviour, while the Latins in turn suspected Byzantium and envied it for its legendary wealth. In 1171 Manuel expelled all Venetians from the empire, thereby providing ready ground for resentment. The Doge of Venice was one of the leaders of the Fourth Crusade, and according to Niketas Choniates he was determined to have revenge over the Byzantines.[21] The reasons why in 1204 the crusaders turned on Constantinople and looted its most precious treasures may be debated, but many factors combined to make it all too predictable. During a period of acute instability in Byzantium the crusaders had actually been called to help, while Pope Innocent III had made it clear for his part that there must be an end to Byzantine schism and that the Byzantines were expected to bear a large share of financing the Fourth Crusade. Not all the crusaders were in favour of diverting the crusade's target from Egypt to Constantinople. Further, there had already been assaults on the city by the crusaders in 1203. Alexius III had tried to stave off the danger, at the cost of raising large quantities of gold, but when faced with immediate danger he fled, and his murder left the city exposed. The Latin clergy justified targeting Constantinople on the grounds that the Byzantines had rejected papal supremacy, and both Western authors and Byzantines, including Niketas Choniates, describe the horrific scenes of desecration and looting, and the treasures seized and sold off.[22] The latter included not only the precious relics of the Passion and the Image or Mandylion of Edessa kept in the Pharos church of the palace, but also the countless classical statues which had adorned the city since the time of Constantine the Great.[23]

For a period of fifty-seven years there was no Byzantine emperor in Constantinople. The victorious Latins divided up their gains: Baldwin of Flanders became Latin Emperor, and part of Constantinople was allotted to the Venetians. Another lordship was established in Greece. Byzantines still held Epirus – where a court was established at Arta – and Nicaea, and a further kingdom at Trebizond on the southern shore of the Black Sea. Even before 1204 it would have been wrong to think of solid blocks of 'Byzantine' or 'Latin' territory; in many areas it was a matter of individual enclaves, towns and strongholds. The Turks were a constant danger and complication in Anatolia, and indeed Nicaea itself had been the Seljuk capital from 1081 until the successful siege of 1097. From 1204 onwards the former concept of a single Byzantine Empire ruled from Constantinople gave way to that of a number of separate but related duchies or princedoms, such as the 'Despotate' of Epirus (although the term itself was not yet used). The most important of these was at Nicaea, where a patriarch was established and to which many aristocratic exiles had fled; Theodore Laskaris, son-in-law of Alexius III, was crowned emperor in 1208 and set up a court there which sought to preserve continuity with the imperial past in Constantinople.[24] It was far from obvious at the time that this was going to end well, but the Byzantines at Nicaea obstinately held onto their vision of themselves, and, concertina-like, the 'empire' of Byzantium based on Constantinople was to have another two centuries of life yet.

Compared with the Byzantine Empire at its height the 'empire of Nicaea' is a misnomer, since it was in fact no more than a small principality; moreover it was in competition with other contenders for the role of Byzantine successor-state, especially the so-called Despotate of Epirus. The 'city' of Nicaea received new and impressive fortifications, but as before there were green areas within the walls. Nevertheless, the rituals of the court were maintained, as was the Byzantine system of higher education. Intellectuals such as Niketas Choniates went there from Constantinople, as did Nicholas Mesarites, and Theodore Blemmydes

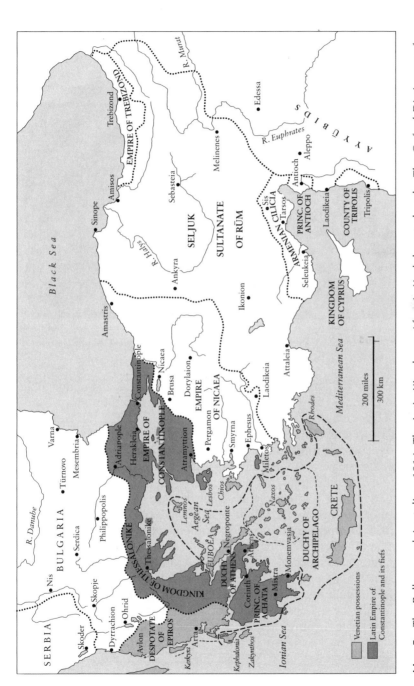

Map 5 The Balkans and Anatolia c.1214: The Latin Kingdoms. After A. Kazhdan et al., eds, *The Oxford Dictionary of Byzantium* (New York, 1991), p. 357

Fig. 8   Façade of S. Sophia, Trebizond (Trabzon, northern Turkey)

received most of his education there. Rhetoric flourished, and orators like Theodore Doukas Laskaris and later Theodore Metochites praised the city in elaborately traditional orations;[25] Nicaea had after all been the seat of two of the greatest ecumenical councils and had several major churches. Jousting and polo were also transplanted from the capital. The city's strategic position just across the water from Constantinople, and the successful campaigns and other policies of John Vatatzes in particular enabled it to emerge ahead of the other two successor states of Epirus and Thessaly (which at first formed a single large entity in the former European territory of Byzantium until it split into two in 1267),[26] and Trebizond.[27] Contrary to all that might have been expected, the Byzantines at Nicaea succeeded in returning and re-establishing Byzantine rule in the imperial city.[28] Michael Palaiologos, one of the generals of John Vatatzes, declared himself emperor as Michael VIII in 1259 alongside the heir, John IV Laskaris. Realising that the moment had come, Michael bought off the Venetian naval threat by giving generous concessions to the Genoese, but in the event his general, Strategopoulos, found the city undefended. Michael himself, still waiting across the Bosphoros, had to be wakened by his sister with the amazing news, and was thus was enabled to stage his entry to Constantinople for maximum effect on the feast of the Dormition of the Virgin, 15 August.[29] On Christmas Day 1261, after the return to Constantinople, Michael was to have John Laskaris blinded and imprisoned in a fortress on the shore of the Sea of Marmara.

Michael VIII had entered the city walking behind the great icon of the Virgin Hodegetria,[30] and he placed the Virgin in conjunction with the city on his coins, in an understandably symbolic claim to victory. Given the hindsight of historians and the almost mythical status attained by Constantine XI, the last emperor of Byzantium, and the moving story of the siege and fall of the city in 1453,[31] it is almost impossible not to regard the two centuries that followed as a story of inevitable failure. The territory and population of the Palaiologan state were very small, and perilously surrounded. There was also fierce internal opposition to Michael VIII and his infant son. The patriarch Arsenios who had crowned Michael excommunicated him for his action against John, and was himself deposed in 1265. However, a determined group in the Church (the Arsenites, named after Arsenios) continued to support the Laskarid succession. Constantinople itself was threatened from Bulgaria, from the Mongols, from the resentful Latins and from the jealous Venetians. Michael quickly found himself at war, and unsuccessfully, against Epirus and the Latin princedom of Achaea, and the ships of his allies the Genoese defeated by the Venetians. In addition, there was the problem of dealing with the papacy and the danger represented by Charles of Anjou, king of Sicily and Naples. The union of the Churches was again on the agenda as Michael VIII struggled to secure his position, especially after the various parties hostile to Byzantium allied themselves in 1267. Michael VIII was surrounded, and the position of the restored Byzantine state seemed desperate. The Mongols had retreated from the Balkans but now dominated Anatolia and had overcome the Abbasid caliph and taken Aleppo and Damascus.[32] After a Mamluk defeat in 1260 the forces allied themselves in 1263. Michael needed allies, above all to contain Hungary, whose ambitions extended to Constantinople, and he therefore allied himself with its king, Charles of Anjou, the Mongols and the Mamluks. Palaiologan princesses were married off to Mongol leaders. In dealing with Charles, the support of the papacy was critical. Michael was also prepared to agree to union, and at the Council of Lyons in 1274 his envoy George Akropolites – one of only three Byzantine delegates – swore loyalty to Rome. Although Joseph, the unwilling patriarch of Constantinople, was replaced and retired to a monastery, many clergy continued to share his views, and Michael had to work very hard to convince the doubters. The Union of Lyons was a personal initiative of the emperor and had not represented the views of the Byzantine Church. The unfortunate Michael was himself excommunicated in consequence of an alliance of the pope and Charles of Anjou in 1281, and saved only by the revolt in Sicily against Charles known as the Sicilian Vespers.[33] The attempt at union failed. Michael's son Andronikos announced the restoration of Orthodoxy in 1282, and a synod held in 1283 required Andronikos's mother, Theodora, to sign a written condemnation of her late husband's views; a purge of Unionist clergy followed. However, union was pronounced again by the Council of Ferrara/Florence in 1438–9, attended by the Emperor John VIII PalaIologos with a large retinue. At the time of the final siege in 1453 Byzantium was technically in union with the papacy, but George Gennadios, later the patriarch Scholarius, led a campaign of opposition which was only stilled by the very imminent danger; all joined together regardless of differences in the final liturgy and vigil in Hagia Sophia.[34] After the fall of the city Gennadios became the first patriarch appointed by Mehmet II, and wrote for him an exposition of the Christian faith; there was no longer need for union and it was quietly forgotten.

It is understandable that this period should be described in terms of fragmentation and that historians should be exhorted to have sympathy for the Palaiologans.[35] It is, however, the sheer longevity of Byzantine culture that needs to be explained. One factor was the symbolic importance attributed to the city of Constantinople itself; another was the attachment of the Byzantines to their own religious and political traditions. The latter enabled the cultural and religious traditions of Byzantium to persist through the Ottoman period, even in areas that were not part of the Palaiologan state. In modern Greece the legacy of Byzantium was a source of tension in the nineteenth century, but this very tension demonstrates how meaningful it was as a component of the new state. The resurgence of Orthodoxy in post-Soviet Russia and the hostility still felt by many Orthodox to the papacy cannot be understood if the Byzantines after 1261 are relegated to the margins of history as a pathetic remnant doomed to disappear.

Constantinople in 1261 was in need of restoration, and this was begun under Michael VIII. Culture also revived, and, according to Ihor Ševčenko, about 150 literati and scholars are known from the Palaiologan period, an impressive number in relation to the small population in the various centres.[36] Some of the wives and daughters of the leading men were as learned and as cultivated as their male relatives.[37] Intellectual elites existed at Mistra in the Peloponnese and Thessalonike as well as Constantinople, and fierce arguments took place as to the respective merits of Hellenism and of Orthodox spirituality contrasted with western Aristotelianism, even, as at Thessalonike, against a background of civil tension and unrest.[38] The scholars of the day engaged in intense study and editing of classical authors and it is impossible not to be struck by their extraordinarily energetic quest for learning, which led them to collect and rediscover classical works and manuscripts. The architecture of the Palaiologan period had a very distinctive style, with banded brick-work and tall domes, and many examples survive – hundreds, if we include the wider Byzantine sphere in Crete, Serbia and Bulgaria.[39] At Thessalonike several churches were built including the church of the Holy Apostles and those of the prophet Elijah and the Vlatadon monastery. From 1349 a further Despotate of the Morea in the Peloponnese was established by John VI Cantacuzene with its centre at the citadel of Mistra, near Sparta. Mistra had a central basilical church, the seat of the metropolitan, and other churches that mostly belonged to monasteries established within the town walls. The five-domed Paregoritissa church (1284–96), built by Nikephoros I Komnenos Doukas and his wife Anna Palaiologina at Arta, capital of the Despotate of Epirus, is equally impressive, and it was only one of many. Palaiologan architecture in Constantinople includes the Lips monastery (Fenari Isa Camii) and the *parekklesion* of Hagia Maria Pammakaristos (Fethiye Camii), both built as funerary churches. One of the masterpieces of Byzantine art also belongs to this period: the wall-paintings and mosaics that were part of the restoration of the Chora monastery, known as St Saviour in Chora or by its Turkish name, the Kariye Camii, by the prominent statesman and scholar Theodore Metochites in the early fourteenth century,[40] who had himself depicted in one of the mosaics wearing an extravagant turban and offering a model of his church to the seated Christ. In the same part of the city are the remains of the so-called Tekfursaray, also known as the palace of the Porphyrogenitus ('born in the purple'), a walled three-storeyed building with a courtyard in front and probably a throne-room, as at Mistra.

These buildings are indicative of a wealthy and educated, even learned, elite. How was all this afforded? Assessments of the economy of the Palaiologan period are only just beginning to move on from the negativity of previous scholars, and information is patchy. For the rural economy, more is known about Macedonia than elsewhere since the monasteries of Mount Athos had major holdings there. It is clear, though, that Constantinople, Thessalonike and, to a lesser extent, other cities were lively economic centres, and that trade and commerce were important.

In Constantinople there were substantial foreign concessions in the city, especially that of the Genoese on the north of the Golden Horn. Trebizond was well situated for the Black Sea trade; Thessalonike depended substantially also on sea-commerce, as did Monemvasia off the south-east coast of the Peloponnese. The central Byzantine world in this period consisted of a number of small cities with their rural hinterlands. The scale seems miniature by modern standards (typically less than ten thousand, with the exceptions of Constantinople and Thessalonike), but there seems to have been a distinct recovery in Byzantine urbanism after 1261.

Later, when the presence of Serbs and Turks made conditions in the countryside difficult and insecure, rich Byzantines moved their wealth to secure Latin colonies, and emperors were chronically short of money for defence,[41] but the ability of individual Byzantines to amass wealth remains striking. Nor was their commitment to secular learning diminished – indeed, it was stimulated further by the patronage offered at the several small courts that now existed. This enthusiasm was shared in imperial circles and fostered by inter-marriage with neighbouring and Western royalty.

By the early fifteenth century the Byzantine territory surrounding Constantinople comprised only two small areas on either side of the Bosphorus. The political contours of the world to which the 'empire' belonged had drastically changed: to the north and west of Constantinople, for instance, there was now a range of independent states, among which the second Bulgarian empire and the Serbia of Stephen Dušan (1331–55) were the closest. This raised complex issues of relationship and independence in respect of Byzantium.[42] Dušan, for example, had himself crowned emperor of Serbia at Skopje in 1346, and the title of emperor was further extended to the rulers of Bulgaria and Lithuania. Between 1204 and 1261 another force, the Mongols, had reached Poland, Hungary, Croatia, Serbia and Bulgaria. The story of the final years of Byzantium tends to be told in isolation when it should be set in the broader context of thirteenth- and fourteenth-century history, the relations between the Catholic and Orthodox states of central Europe and their confrontation with the Ottoman Turks. Already in the 1330s the latter had taken Nicaea and reached Nicomedia; they defeated the Serbs and others at Kosovo Polje in 1389, the Bulgarians in 1390 and the crusade from Buda at Nicopolis in 1396. In this context the fall of Constantinople was merely one episode, even if the most dramatic one, in a longer story that ended only when the Turks failed to capture Vienna in 1683.

Map 6   The Byzantine Empire c.1350. After A. Kazhdan et al., eds, *The Oxford Dictionary of Byzantium* (New York, 1991), p. 359

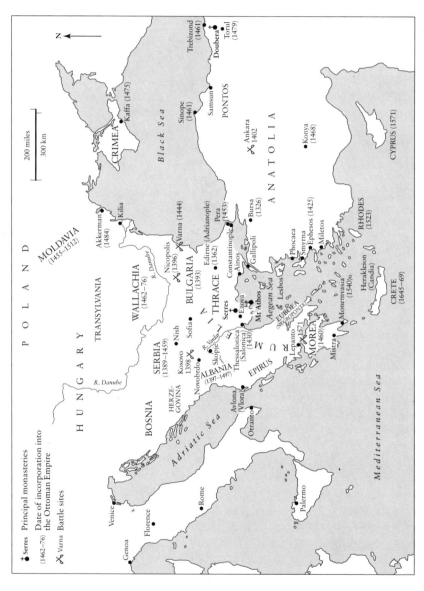

Map 7 The Roman Orthodox and Ottoman worlds in the fifteenth century. Anthony Bryer, 'Byzantium: the Roman Orthodox world, 1393–1492', in Christopher Allmand, ed., *The New Cambridge Medieval History VII, c.1415–c.1500* (Cambridge, 1998), p. 772

The Palaiologan period also saw intense internal division, struggles over the throne and even civil war. In the 1320s there was war between grandfather and grandson, Andronikos II and Andronikos III, and further civil war when John VI Cantacuzene was proclaimed emperor in 1341 alongside the young John V Palaiologos. In Thessalonike a group known as the Zealots had seized control and were besieged by John VI; the divisions were compounded by fierce religious disputes over the religious doctrine and practice of hesychasm, championed by the archbishop of the city, Gregory Palamas, and by the arrival of the Black Death in Byzantium. The same Gregory Palamas spent a not wholly unpleasant period as a captive at Nicaea, which had been in Ottoman hands since 1354, and wrote about his experiences among the Muslims there. The last phase of Byzantine rule was also played out against a background of turbulence among many surrounding groups and peoples including the Serbs, the Bulgarians and the Venetians, and the need to deal at the same time with Catalan mercenaries and Genoese. John VI was not the only emperor of the period to be faced with what seemed insuperable difficulties, and he spent the last thirty years of his life as a monk.[43] Even so, as Warren Treadgold points out in an even-handed assessment of the period,[44] the Byzantines showed a resilience that deserves more credit than they have usually received. Empires do not last for ever, and it is unreasonable to imagine that they can or should. The world had changed dramatically around them and the end was all too predictable. The Byzantines were vassals of the Turks long before 1453, and they had been forced to sue for union with a Catholic Church that most of them deeply rejected. But when the end was near they did not run away or plead for vassalage. They stood and fought.

Ottoman and recent Turkish tradition remembers the founder of the Ottoman Empire as Osman son of Ertughrul, who, at the beginning of the fourteenth century, built up a Turkish force inside the Byzantine province of Bithynia in Asia Minor and thus came dangerously close to Constantinople.[45] Bursa (Prousa) became the first Ottoman capital in 1326, and by 1346 Osman's son Orhan had become significant enough for the future Emperor John VI Cantacuzene to offer him his daughter in marriage in return for help in his campaign for the throne, and then to permit him to settle on the Gallipoli peninsula. By 1369 the forces of Murad I occupied Adrianople (Edirne), and soon the Ottomans began to advance north towards Serbia and south towards Epirus and even the Peloponnese. In 1387 they occupied Thessalonike; John V Palaiologos agreed to become a vassal of Murad and by the end of his reign in 1391 Byzantium was surrounded. Manuel II depended on Sultan Bayezid

(1389–1402) for his throne, and by 1394 Constantinople itself was besieged; outside help was vital, and a crusade was put together, led by Sigismund of Hungary, only to be defeated completely at Nicopolis on the Danube. This was the point at which the Emperor Manuel decided on the risky course of going personally to seek for Western help. Starting at Venice, he travelled to Paris and then to England, where he was entertained at Christmas by Henry IV, then returning via Paris and Italy again, with many promises but little aid. He arrived back at Constantinople only in 1403, by which time Bayezid had been defeated by Timur (Tamerlane) in central Anatolia and had died soon after. The Ottomans recovered to besiege Constantinople and Thessalonike again in 1421. A return to the policy of the Union of Churches seemed the best and, indeed, the only way out to Manuel's son, John VIII Palaiologos, and the emperor, the patriarch of Constantinople and several hundred other Easterners embarked for Italy in 1437, from where they returned only in 1440. John VIII was accompanied in Ferrara and Florence in 1438 and 1439 by intellectuals who included George Gemistos Plethon and Bessarion.[46] His striking appearance and his *capeletto greco*, a style also to be seen in the paintings of the Pantanassa church at Mistra, were recorded in medals, drawings and painting by Pisanello and Piero della Francesca, and in the Capella of the Palazzo Medici Riccardi in Florence by Benozzo Gozzoli. As for the policy of Union, it was successful in that it inspired a new crusade; however this crusade, known as the Crusade of Varna, was crushed there by the Ottomans.

John's brother, Constantine XI, the last emperor of Byzantium, came to the throne in 1449, only to find the young Mehmet II preparing for another attack on Constantinople as soon as he succeeded in 1451. To make ready, and to frighten the Byzantines, he built the great fortress of Rumeli Hisar on the European side of the Bosphorus opposite the equally imposing fortress of Anadolu Hisar; the Byzantines had four months in which to watch it going up and to think about what was likely to happen. Union had not saved them, and there was only very limited assistance from Venice and Genoa, so they did the only thing they could, which was to unite to face the onslaught.[47] It had been of no benefit to Byzantium that the Emperor John VIII had been willing to travel on papal ships from Constantinople to Florence in 1437 and to sign yet another declaration of religious union. After the Council of Florence the anti-unionist patriarch, George Scholarius, was deposed, yet at the end unionists and anti-unionists stood together as the last liturgy was celebrated in Hagia Sophia on 28 May 1453.

Fig. 9   Rumeli Hisar, Ottoman fortress on the European side of the Bosphorus

The last days of Constantinople were recorded by many historians on both sides. There were said to be 80,000 or more on the Turkish side to only 7,000 defenders of the city.[48] Many Byzantines refused to believe that Constantine XI had been killed during the siege, and indeed there were no eye-witness accounts of his death.[49] Mehmet 'the Conqueror' sealed his victory by riding his horse into Hagia Sophia, where the might of Allah was proclaimed from the pulpit and the Muslim Mehmet prayed at the altar. He allowed the looting to continue for three days and then set to work to rebuild and repopulate the city as the capital of the Ottoman Empire. In 1461 Trebizond also fell. Some managed to escape to Italy, especially Venice, or to the islands in Venetian possession, but the remaining Byzantines in Constantinople were organised into a *millet* under the new patriarch Gennadios. The Byzantine Empire was at an end.

It is very natural in these circumstances to regard the Palaiologan period as one of decline, and so it appears in many modern treatments. In addition to the loss of territory and the military threats, historians point to the preoccupation with religion, the reliance on mercenaries in the army, the disbanding of the navy, the vain attempts to deal with the economic imbalance of the empire, and even to natural disasters such as the earthquakes that struck Constantinople in 1296.[50] Certainly by the second quarter of the fifteenth century it seemed only a matter of time before the Ottomans would be successful in taking Constantinople. Yet the achievements of the Palaiologan period catch the imagination as much as the bravery and nobility of the Byzantines on that last day.

4

The Byzantine Mirage

Assisted by the praepositi, the emperor invests the newly appointed emperor with the robe and again the patriarch says a prayer over the crowns and the patriarch first crowns the senior emperor with his own hands and then gives the crown to the senior emperor and the senior emperor crowns the newly appointed emperor, and the two factions immediately cry out 'he is worthy!' . . . The cantors: 'Many years to you, God-crowned'; the people: 'Many years to you.' The cantors: 'Many years to you, emperors, with the empresses and the children born in the purple'; the people: 'Many years to you'. The cantors: 'And the Maker and Lord of all'; the people likewise. The cantors: 'Who crowned you with his own hand', the people likewise. The cantors: 'Fulfil the years for you and the empresses and the children born in the purple'; the people likewise. The cantors: 'For the complete establishment (*sustasin*) of the Romans'.

Constantine Porphyrogenitus, *Book of Ceremonies* Ch. 47 (38), protocol and *polychronia* for the crowning of an emperor

Byzantium lasted – on a generous view – for more than eleven hundred years, almost as long as Rome. No other medieval state could rival it in its longevity or its rich traditions, and the Byzantines themselves traded on this reputation in their dealings with others. Their elite literature imitated the classical authors, and they placed great emphasis on tradition and on their own past as 'Romans'. The apparent continuities in Byzantine history thus stressed by the Byzantines themselves have aroused both admiration and disdain in modern minds. It has also been extremely deceptive, influencing both older scholarship and popular views of Byzantium. It is one of the hallmarks of an orientalist conception of 'the other' to assume sameness for the purpose of denigrating: thus, while the West has been seen as developing, Byzantium has been traditionally consigned to the realm of the static, congealing in its own weight of tradition.[1] At the very least this Byzantine longevity raises serious questions about the extent to which a political system identified as 'Byzantium' could remain recognizably the same over so long a period.

Alexander Kazhdan, a Jewish Byzantinist who succeeded in leaving Soviet Russia and spent the rest of his life in America, argued vigorously against the too-easy assumption of Byzantine continuity.[2] This assumption conceals several questions: was there actual continuity over the whole period, and if so in what aspects? Did the Byzantines themselves believe that there had been such continuity? And finally, how have modern critics taken up the theme? As Kazhdan rightly said, only after confronting these separate questions is it possible to arrive at answers to the question of continuity in Byzantine culture and society. The previous chapters have already argued that Byzantium changed very considerably over its history, both for internal reasons and in response to the rapid changes going on all around it. But the issue has been an important one in Byzantine scholarship, and this chapter will take the argument somewhat further.

The argument as to continuity or discontinuity has focused on a series of particular phases or 'turning points'. The first such question relates to the transition from the 'ancient world' to 'late antiquity'. Kazhdan himself had earlier been one of the leaders in the earlier stages of the debate about the transition from the ancient to the medieval world, positing an almost complete collapse of urban life in the late Roman civic sense in Anatolia in the seventh century.[3] In broad terms this was undoubtedly justified, but the 'early medieval depression' did not affect only the eastern Mediterranean, and in contrast with Kazhdan, Christopher Wickham, for example, integrates Byzantium into the wider debate about Europe and the Mediterranean in the early medieval period. In the case of the urban society of the late antique East the changes had already been under way in many places for several decades, even if the principal reason for dramatic change in the seventh century was the effects of invasion, first of all by the Persian attacks on Asia Minor and their sack of cities such as Sardis, and then under the impact of the Arab invasions and many subsequent Arab attacks. The effect was to cause the economy and taxation system to collapse as well, and to remove the layer of civil administration and civic elites which had been central to the late Roman government. Cyril Mango has painted this period in very dark colours, and his analysis has caused others to claim that the Byzantine idea of continuity was no more than an illusion.[4] In fact, as we have seen, Byzantium reinvented itself. The loss of land and civic structures forced a move towards a more ruralised economy, a different mode of taxation, changes in the army structure and profound reorganisation of the administrative class.[5] All these changes were achieved in the period between the late seventh and the ninth centuries, and Kazhdan was right to insist on the vigour and energy with which a much reduced and endangered Byzantine state nevertheless went about ensuring its future. Other and later junctures also threatened Byzantine continuity, including periods of instability in the succession and, of course, the capture and sack of Constantinople by the Fourth Crusade in 1204. One can only be struck by the tenacity of the Byzantine system, which still enabled it to survive, and this chapter will look at some of the features which were integral to that survival.

One of them was the symbolic value attached to the city itself. Constantinople was the very heart of Byzantium. Renamed and rebuilt on ancient foundations by Constantine between AD 324 and 330, its population reached nearly half a million by the sixth century; at the other end of the Byzantine period, by the fifteenth century, the 'city' area included large open spaces. Constantinople survived a dozen sieges in the course of its history as well as the sack by the Fourth Crusade in 1204. Eusebius of Caesarea claimed that under Constantine it was a completely Christian city.[6] This was hardly possible at the time (it is contradicted by the pagan historian Zosimus), and it took time for the city that had begun as a monumental expression of Constantine's imperial position with palace, hippodrome, forum, main thoroughfare and imperial statue set on a great column, to be Christianised with churches and monasteries. Its partly surviving sea walls and its land walls, built in the fifth century by Theodosius II, were constructed to expand the area enclosed by Constantine's fortifications and match the increase in population. Excavation of the church of St Polyeuktos at Sarachane in Istanbul, built by Anicia Juliana in the early sixth century,[7] has revealed the wealth and ambition of the Constantinopolitan aristocracy, and their palaces in the city are known from the fifth century onwards; in later periods the city was also the site of great monasteries founded by aristocrats and members of the imperial family. The religious spectacles and processions of Palaiologan Constantinople drew Western travellers and pilgrims from countries including Spain, England and Russia. Under the Comnenian emperors in the eleventh and twelfth centuries it housed colonies of Italians from Venice, Genoa and Pisa along the Golden Horn, as well as slaves, freed slaves, Muslims and Jews, the last at Galata; the upper class lived in great houses and the poor in tenements cheek by jowl with their animals. Constantine had created a city based on the model of the administrative centres of his rival tetrarchs, but his successors filled it with churches and monasteries, which in the Palaiologan period

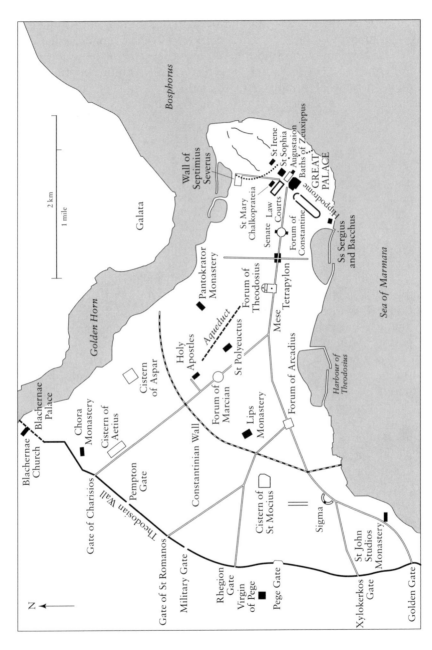

Map 8 Plan of Constantinople. After John Haldon, *Palgrave Atlas of Byzantine History* (Basingstoke, 2005), p. 40

Fig. 10   The Golden Gate, Constantinople, used for ceremonial entries and processions such as the triumph of Basil I in AD 879, when tents were set up outside the Golden Gate for the Arab prisoners and booty

were fortified enclaves set in a now ruralised environment. The Great Palace begun by Constantine (see further below) grew up near the ancient acropolis, which was later to become the site of the Topkapi palace of the sultans. This was the ceremonial heart of the imperial city until the Comnenian period. It was flanked by the ceremonial square known as the Augusteion and by Hagia Sophia and approached by the ceremonial route known as the Mese, and had its own passage to the Hippodrome for imperial public appearances and for the regular chariot races and displays. Most of the great buildings of Byzantine Constantinople have disappeared, and it requires an act of imagination to map the Byzantine city onto the modern one, but the sight of Istanbul continues to impress, especially when first seen from the Bosphorus, and the size and grandeur of Justinian's Hagia Sophia, as well as the sixth-century mosaic floors from the Great Palace, give an idea of what the Byzantine city must have been like at its height (see fig. 3 on p. 18).

Constantinople fell to the crusaders in 1204, and the Ottoman siege of 1422–4 left the Byzantines as tributary to the Ottomans. On several other occasions in the past the city had also come near to defeat, but had always escaped thanks, its inhabitants believed, to the intervention of the Virgin, who had been transformed in the popular imagination into a divine general who could be seen joining in the battle;[8] so strong was the sense that the city somehow belonged to the Virgin that it came to be believed that Constantine himself had dedicated it to her at its foundation. Constantinople's concentration of splendour and luxury as the seat of the emperor, and its remarkable survival over many centuries in the midst of dramatic external changes, placed it in a unique position in the eyes of its own people and of other powers in the medieval world. At the height of the 'Byzantine commonwealth', to use Obolensky's term,[9] it was the setting for the highly prescribed and formal etiquette of the court and the government, laid down in the Emperor Constantine VII Porphyrogenitus's *Book of Ceremonies* and various lists of precedence, and in the fourteenth-century treatise of Ps-Kodinos.[10] Between 1204 and 1261 the 'Empire' of Nicaea did its best to continue the practice and the ethos of imperial Constantinople, and it was assumed that the recovery of the city was critical to the very survival of Byzantium. In the last centuries of Byzantium Constantinople retained a mystique that was shared by Mehmet II himself. Constantinople was known as New Rome, and like Rome it changed over time. For the Byzantines the city was a constant and powerful constituent of their own sense of identity, but like all cities it had an organic development and responded to changing circumstances and needs.

Another element of continuity was the imperial office, yet here too one should take care not to be misled by appearances. The purpose of Byzantine ceremonial and of the Byzantine political theory, which remained essentially unchanged in the centuries following its formulation by Eusebius in the fourth century, was to give the impression of changeless verities, with the emperor as God's representative and the Byzantine system as the microcosm of heaven.[11] The reality was somewhat different. For one thing, as a Chinese traveller noted as early as the seventh century, succession to the Byzantine throne was seldom stable: there was no constitution to guarantee dynastic succession and no clear means of enforcing legitimate government. Several Byzantine rulers made sure that their own sons would not succeed by blinding them or making war against them, or had obtained the throne themselves by such means. Thus the Empress Irene had been regent for her son Constantine VI, but became 'emperor' herself by dethroning and blinding him in 797; after an earlier bid for independence by Constantine in 790 she had Constantine himself and all his entourage arrested and flogged.[12] Basil I had a hand in the murder of his co-emperor Michael III in 867, after having made war on him for seven years, and in 1382 Andronikos III forced his own grandfather, Andronikos II, to abdicate. Anna Comnena gives a remarkably candid account of how her father, Alexius I Comnenus, seized the throne in 1081.[13] The Empress Maria of Alania forced on him an arrangement whereby her own son Constantine became co-emperor, and after his accession Alexius himself deemed it expedient to ask for the forgiveness of the Church and to lead the court in penance for rebellion and civil disturbance. In Anna's view this settled the matter satisfactorily, and Alexius then 'turned his attention to the administration of the empire with clean hands'. Civil war between rivals for the throne was endemic in the Palaiologan period, especially in the fourteenth century. External military threats also sometimes provided an opportunity for an outsider to seize the throne, as in the case of Leo III, who was *strategos* of the Anatolikon theme and secured his place as emperor by successfully resisting the Arab siege of Constantinople in 717. Emperors were also vulnerable to the censure of the Church, represented by the patriarch of Constantinople. Sometimes this was connected with their private lives: Heraclius faced such problems when he married his niece Martina, and Leo VI when he married for a fourth time in 906, contrary to canon law, in order to legitimise his son, the future Constantine VII. After Heraclius's death Martina and her son were opposed by the senate and army and eventually both were mutilated; Leo VI obtained a papal indulgence for his marriage, and deposed the disapproving patriarch Nicholas, but the latter's successor imposed embarrassing penances on the emperor who was made to declare future marriages of the sort illegal. But the disputes could also be on matters of Church policy, as in the case of imperial willingness to seek unity with Rome in the later Byzantine period, and especially over the Union of Lyons in 1274. Though emperors could depose patriarchs, and indeed appointed them, this was far from being a one-way relationship and left open many possibilities for dissension, especially as not only was the emperor not the head of the Church but the authority of the patriarch could also be challenged by Church councils.

Just as Byzantine official society was characterised by the possibility of upward mobility, so the throne was open to the ambition of individuals; the stiff ceremonial and rules of etiquette and precedence laid down for the imperial court must be read as one way in which this threat of instability was tempered. Popular movements of opposition are not to be expected in such a society, and the system was hierarchical, with the emperor at the top; in such a system the removal of an individual emperor was not a matter of a different political or social programme but of rivalry between individuals and their supporters. Although in the sixth century Procopius maintained that if his *Secret History* became known it would endanger his life, when emperors engaged in persecution it was usually on religious rather than political grounds. Moreover they lacked the necessary state apparatus to justify the word 'totalitarian', which is quite often applied to Byzantium.[14] It is also anachronistic to imagine that a civil society could have developed in this medieval state: opposition or criticism tended to be expressed indirectly, as it was by several other writers under Justinian. Nevertheless, Byzantine historians seem to have enjoyed a remarkable freedom in their criticism of previous rulers, and, in turn, in the absence of modern public relations mechanisms, the reputation of individual emperors was subjected to ingenious manipulation in art and literature.[15]

'Theocracy' is another term much used of Byzantium, and *The Byzantine Theocracy* is the title of an elegant book by Steven Runciman.[16] The book argues that it was understood in Byzantium that emperors had the final authority over Church matters, but should an emperor abuse that authority or too openly flout the moral law, he would find himself in difficulty. In a subtle recent study Gilbert Dagron has also emphasised the ambiguities with which the imperial office was invested, and the clothing of Old Testament sacral kingship that Byzantine emperors were wont to assume, and which coloured their ceremonial.[17] This was another unresolved tension in the Byzantine system. In some respects, the emperors enjoyed a quasi-episcopal status, yet they remained lay persons, open to challenge, and only rarely did they attempt in practice to impose their supposed rights over the ecclesiastical establishment. Dagron brings out very clearly the extent to which another favourite among characterizations of Byzantium, the charge of 'Caesaropapism', or unjustified imperial control of the Church, was, in fact, an anachronistic slur born of Western ideas of separation of Church and state, as well as the lengths to which Byzantinists have had to go to explain that this notion of 'Byzantinism' was unfounded.

With the imperial role also went a framework of court culture that preserved the appearance of tradition and continuity to the end.[18] The Great Palace, the setting for centuries of this court culture, was extended and altered after Constantine the Great by nearly every other emperor, and its warren of rooms, reception halls and churches was the focus of imperial display and court life until the Comnenian emperors made the Blachernae Palace their centre in the eleventh wand twelfth centuries. Justin II (565–78) built a throne room known as the Chrysotriklinos or Golden Chamber, and Basil I (867–86) built the 'New' church and the Kainourgion. In the Pharos chapel within the Great Palace were kept the precious relics connected with the Passion of Christ, including the supposed crown of thorns, the lance used by the soldier at the Crucifixion and the sponge offered to Jesus on the cross, as well as the Image, or Mandylion, of Edessa; these were among the relics taken to the West after the sack in 1204 and made the centrepiece of the Sainte Chapelle in Paris.

In the many processions within Constantinople described in the tenth-century *Book of Ceremonies* the emperor and empress always set out from and returned to the Great Palace. It was here that they received foreign embassies and where the Byzantine officials and their wives presented themselves in an order of hierarchy that was laid down in scrupulous detail.[19] On the emperor's birthday those invited to dine dressed accordingly and entered the hall known as the Justinianos at the third hour; on the eve of an imperial reception formal acclamations were prescribed, beginning with the *polychronia* ('many years') to the emperor or emperors, led by cantors with responses from those present: 'many years to you, emperors of the Romans', 'many years to you, the servants of the Lord', 'many years to you, Augusti of the Romans', 'Lord, save the emperors with the empresses and the royal offspring', and so on. More elaborate *polychronia* accompanied the actual celebration on the following day, with the emperor seated on his throne, after which a herald of the imperial household read out the proclamation for the occasion. Sometimes there were special songs, or chants, and dance performances (not court balls, but ritualised displays).[20] The leaders of the ceremonial were the 'Blues' and 'Greens', originally the 'factions' or supporters of the chariot racing teams in the early Byzantine period. Official dress was prescribed, and girdles and insignia were handed out when new officials were appointed. A major object of this court life was also, however, simply to impress, and it was accompanied by a taste and requirement for luxury items of clothing, decor and *objets d'art* for gifts and display as well as a lively competition with other courts. Many of the ceremonies and processions were connected with the Church's liturgical year, especially at Christmas, Holy Week and Easter, and the reigning emperor and empress were required to attend many special services in Hagia Sophia. The patriarch also had a special place high in the hierarchy even on secular occasions.

Reading the *Book of Ceremonies* can lead one to conclude that the emperor and court led a stiflingly prescribed existence, especially if one calculates how many days of the year were taken up with these official duties. But appearances can deceive. Dress codes and seating plans at state banquets are not unfamiliar even today, and most states, even secular ones, have their rituals and their formal occasions. A monarchy such as the British monarchy still requires formal occasions with pre-scribed dress codes and rituals whose actual origin has sometimes been forgotten. Imperial ritual is also about the demonstration of royalty, and about legitimacy. In an intriguing comparison with Byzantium, where the Blues and Greens in a sense represented the people, even though the ceremonials might be taking place inside the palace where the 'people' never entered, the invitation lists, and even the seating plans of British state banquets are still published on the Gazette page of *The Times*. The *Book of Ceremonies* is in fact a book of protocols, not (except for a small number of sections) a description of what actually happened. Using it is like reading a book of menus or a guide to protocol, and we have little idea of how fully the protocols and the ceremonials were actually observed from year to year. Some emperors, for example Basil II and Nikephoros Phokas, were often away on campaign; nor did the ceremo-nial itself stand still, and new ceremonies and processions developed when in the Comnenian period the emperors used the Blachernai Palace rather than the old Great Palace. But the *Book of Ceremonies* is also about the symbolic meaning of Byzantine monarchy, for both internal and exter-nal consumption,[21] and this was how the ceremonies were perceived by the foreign ambassadors they were designed to impress; it is therefore interesting to find that this display, with the organ, the gold and the automata in the audience chambers, aroused powerfully conflicting re-actions in Liudprand of Cremona who made two official visits in the late tenth century as the representative first of Berengar II of Italy in 949–50 and then of Otto I of Germany in 968. Liudprand's missions and his experiences on these two occasions were very different, as were the two emperors then on the throne, Constantine VII Porphyrogenitus and Nikephoros II Phokas: on the first visit he was deeply impressed by the splendour of the court, but some twenty years later, after his second visit to Constantinople – this time as bishop of Cremona and the envoy of the German emperor – he reported back in extremely hostile tones about his personal treatment and the habits of the Byzantines and the Emperor Nikephoros himself.

The theory behind the *Book of Ceremonies* and the lists of precedence, as well as a similar surviving fourteenth-century treatise, emphasised the importance of maintaining established order. The opening of the *Book of Ceremonies* recommended to Constantine's son the solemn and time-consuming ceremonial round of the court as a means of maintaining *taxis*, order or harmony, in the state and the due observance of rank. Constantine's treatise *On Imperial Administration*, also addressed to his son, is as much a manual of kingship as it is of foreign relations, not meant for public circulation and with some outspoken criticism of his father-in-law Romanos I Lekapenos. The Byzantine emperor, in Constantine's words, was established by God: 'He sets kings upon the throne and gives them the lordship over all'.[22] In the Hippodrome the emperor was acclaimed by comparing him to David. But the extant *Book of Ceremonies* is now recognised as a dossier whose compilation still remains in many aspects unclear, while much of the contents of Constantine's treatise on administration have been described as 'hackneyed and inaccurate'.[23] The collection of protocols on ceremonial was put together in the wake of an extremely unstable period for the Byzantine throne, and Constantine VII himself had finally come to power only after great uncertainty and difficulty. Indeed, the same apparently high-minded Constantine sponsored a highly tendentious biography of his own grandfather Basil I (867–86), whose object was to justify the rise to power of the Macedonian dynasty. The complex balancing of power and influence expressed in imperial ceremonial, in which the emperor of the day found himself in a seemingly endless routine of asserting his own position in relation to the large and potentially dangerous group of officials and possible rivals with whom he was surrounded and with whom he lived in close proximity, was a mirror image of the balancing act that the Byzantines were forced to perform in relation to the outside world.[24]

The court culture of Byzantium had developed gradually since the days of the Roman Empire. Contemporary and later critics saw the reign of Diocletian (284–305) in the late third and early fourth century as marking a distinct move towards greater formality and pomp, and many modern accounts have repeated this, as well as accepting the claim made by contemporaries that the inspiration came from Sasanian Persia; in fact, however, the increase was incremental rather than sudden and there is no need to look outside the empire for an explanation. Although we have more evidence about later periods, imperial ceremony was already well developed in late antiquity and the early Byzantine period, as is amply shown in the long poem in Latin hexameters composed by the North African poet Corippus to celebrate the accession and crowning of Justinian's nephew and successor Justin II in 565, together with the ceremonials connected with his consulship on I January, 566.[25] We must suppose that this work was commissioned and recited very soon after the events it describes; Corippus names some of the high officials who were his patrons, and he clearly wrote to justify their political aims in supporting the new emperor, but in the course of the work he gives detailed and indeed unique accounts of imperial events in the sixth century including imperial receptions, the funeral of Justinian and the coronation of Justin II. Later literary works also frequently underlined continuity in their rhetorical descriptions of emperors and imperial events, yet, like the *Book of Ceremonies*, they did so in order to present an ideal rather than the reality – which was apt to be very different. Real-life emperors were neither imprisoned in this ceremonial nor restrained by the rhetoric that represented them as the representative of God on earth. Again, Byzantine emperors in visual art usually look stiff and stylised and wear state costumes that seem to a modern eye heavy to the extent of depersonalising the wearer.[26] Yet the individuals who wore these costumes were anything but subdued or lacking in individuality. Indeed, coexisting with the theory of Byzantine rulership and the weight of ceremonial was a tradition of literary invective against individual emperors that was just as well established as that of imperial panegyric. In the eleventh century Michael Psellus, author of a lively *Chronographia*, followed convention in his orations by imagining the emperor as haughty and impassive, but in his set of imperial biographies he did not hesitate to chronicle the infidelities and defects of the men and women who attained imperial rank in the late tenth and eleventh centuries, some of whom he knew well himself.[27]

Court culture was also a way of absorbing and neutralising some of the effects of the actual instability of the imperial throne, but a new direction can be seen in the late eleventh century when the emperor Alexius Comnenus introduced new titles and a much more family-centred imperial court. This was a period when great families, like the Doukai and the Comneni, the circle from which Alexius also came, had established themselves as landowners with great estates in Asia Minor. In an effort to consolidate his hold on the throne Alexius introduced a whole range of new imperial titles that he distributed among the members of his own family and the families that he wanted to secure as close allies.[28] We can see further evidence of this family-based rule in the middle and later Byzantine periods in the marriage alliances made with non-Byzantine ruling families, and the literary works produced to celebrate imperial marriages and funerals. Later Byzantium developed an aristocracy of noble families not so different from the noble families in the states of Western Europe, with whom they intermarried.

For many, Byzantium holds an intense fascination, associated as it is with luxury, gold and a sense of mystery. The last stanza of W. B. Yeats's poem 'Sailing to Byzantium' conveys a striking impression of the time-lessness of this imagined society:

> Once out of nature I shall never take
> My bodily form from any natural thing,
> But such a form as Grecian goldsmiths make
> Of hammered gold and gold enamelling
> To keep a drowsy emperor awake
> Or set upon a golden bough to sing
> To lords and ladies of Byzantium
> Of what is past and passing or to come.[29]

The title of a recent exhibition was 'The Glory of Byzantium',[30] and the objects on display there and in a more recent exhibition on the final phase of Byzantium undoubtedly dazzled the visitor with their richness and sheer artistic complexity. Both exhibitions concentrated on the luxury items with which Byzantium is always associated – ivory caskets, richly decorated manuscripts, icons, carvings, as well as silks, ecclesiastical embroideries and liturgical objects in gold and silver. Icon exhibitions, of which there have been several major examples in recent years, also feed this curiosity about the luxury of Byzantine religious culture, and the titles of two books on the subject by Robin Cormack, *Writing in Gold* (1985) and *Painting the Soul* (1997) point to the associations that commonly surround the subject of icons, even though the author himself is far from sharing them. Now, too, the monastic collections of St Catherine's on Mount Sinai and the monasteries of Mount Athos are becoming more widely known though exhibitions and publications, a development that gives great pleasure to many but that adds to the identification of Byzantium with luxury objects and especially religious art.

Nevertheless, it is necessary to mention some caveats. In the first place the items that have survived, and that arouse most interest, are precisely the luxury objects whose very value and status has given them a pro-tected history. Even when everyday objects survive they are much harder to appreciate, and when exhibited they do not draw in the crowds in the way that icons do. Some museums and some exhibition organisers have tried to find ways round this problem and to give the world of work and material culture an equal status with religious and luxury art, but there is still a long way to go. Secondly, medieval art is, for most people, hard to appreciate. It is undoubtedly true that a large propor-tion of the art of Byzantium was commissioned for religious purposes and destined for use in churches and monasteries. As in other medieval societies, the art that was produced was heavily dependent on patronage, and members of the imperial house and of the court were themselves eager patrons of religious buildings and religious art, just as they also commissioned items for court use and display. Many of the supreme examples of Byzantine art and architecture, such as Justinian's church of Hagia Sophia in Constantinople or the fourteenth-century decoration in the Kariye Camii (the monastery of St Saviour in Chora) commissioned by Theodore Metochites are examples of patronage of this kind. Other examples we know of only from descriptions in surviving written sources, like the 'New' church in the Great Palace built by the Emperor Basil I in the ninth century.[31] Some emperors, like Constantine VII Porphyrogenitus, took a well-informed and energetic interest in beautifying their own surroundings and restoring the imperial vestments and jewels.[32] Many of the icons and other objects known from the Byzantine world have no known artist or attested provenance, yet they too are the products of commissions by unknown patrons, as are the richly ornamented manuscript books which survive from most periods of Byzantium's history. The nature of artistic production also depends on the available skills and the way in which production is organised. Thus, Byzantine craftsmen were called upon to assist with the earliest great monuments of the Umayyad caliphate while the late seventh-century Dome of the Rock in Jerusalem and the Great Mosque in Damascus of the early eighth century use Byzantine motifs and Byzantine materials.

Byzantium's identification with the exotic and the mysterious, in fact the Other, is also demonstrated in other ways, for example in the name 'Byzance' given to a heavily oriental perfume. Julia Kristeva's novel, *Meutre à Byzance* (Paris, 2004) plays on this Byzantium of the imagination, and one of its characters, an academic in Santa Barbara, California, is revealed to have had a secret passion for Byzantium and especially for Anna Comnena – female, imperial, intellectual and somewhat mysterious – about whom he writes a novel. In the words of one reviewer, 'Kristeva's novel does not deal primarily with the historical Byzantium but with the imaginary Byzantium that the novel's characters all carry within themselves, or at least constantly yearn for.' The reviewer goes on: '[the name] Byzantium . . . [which] stereotypically brings to mind plots involving murder by poison and intrigues at a magnificent but dangerous court (whose main attributes in the French historical imagination are luxury and refinement), has gained a principally positive and abstract meaning: the dreamy and unreal, that which exists beyond time and space, which perhaps never existed at all.'[33] To this list of imagined attributes of Byzantium in modern consciousness I would add its association with the feminine, the accompaniment of its identification with the mysterious East.[34] The most familiar, and certainly the most commonly exploited, example of this exoticism is the Empress Theodora, constructed already as femme fatale by Procopius in the *Secret History*, with his description not only of the sexual exploits of her youth but also of her long toilettes, her white skin and her imperious manners.[35] This image of Theodora has been promoted in the popular mind by the famous mosaic in the church of San Vitale, Ravenna, traditionally dated to 546–8, and she has been the subject of countless plays and novels from the nineteenth century until today, and likened more than once to Eva Perón. The book about her by Charles Diehl, one of the founders of Byzantine studies as an academic discipline in France, invested her with a glamour that she has never lost; a very different picture can be gained from the contemporary non-Chalcedonian sources, where she is depicted as a loyal patron of an ill-used minority, but this has not found its way into general perceptions.[36] But Kristeva's Byzantium goes beyond the connotations of one or other of Byzantium's female characters, to encompass political and religious systems, and also the strangeness of a distant culture: as another of Julia Kristeva's characters remarks: 'C'est vraiment Byzance! Exoticisme des noms médiévaux, étrangeté de l'érudition . . .'

Byzantium was a society with a long history during which the world around it underwent many dramatic changes. It was also a society with an imperial court and all the rituals that went with it in the medieval world. Byzantium grew out of classical antiquity and lasted until the Italian Renaissance. Indeed, the intellectuals of the late Byzantine period were in many ways the precursors and the facilitators of that renaissance. Byzantium provided the Greek manuscripts and the intellectual tradition that fuelled Western humanism, yet it was itself very different from classical antiquity. After 1453 what had once been the Byzantine Empire was subsumed in, and in some Western imaginations identified with, Ottoman rule and the idea of the mysterious East. The idea of Byzantium as unchanging and static suited a Western European tradition that defined itself in contrast as innovative, forward-looking and, by the Enlightenment period, secular. The very term, 'Byzantium' was an antiquarian coinage of the sixteenth century, soon to be associated with decline and worse. The 'exotic' myth of Byzantium is also inextricably bound up with Western attitudes to Orthodoxy, both during the Ottoman period and also now. Not only is Byzantium defined in this myth as a quintessentially religious society; it is also Orthodox, and therefore different.

5

Ruling the Byzantine State

Plant trees of all kinds, and reed-beds, so that you may have a return without having a yearly worry, and thus have leisure. Get yourself live-stock, such as plough-oxen, and pigs, and sheep, and such other animals as will breed yearly, increase and multiply. For these will furnish you with a plenty at table. And so you will rejoice at all these things: in the abundance of wheat, wine and everything else, seed and livestock, edible and moveable. And if you lead this kind of life, do not relax and neglect it, otherwise everything will diminish.

Kekaumenos, *Strategikon*, cited by M. Hendy, *Studies in the Byzantine Monetary Economy, c.300–1450*

Transport and communication between Constantinople and other parts of the empire was difficult at best. Some highways were kept up, or at least had regular traffic and posting stations, such as the Via Egnatia crossing the Balkans from Dyrrachium, or the main imperial highway in Anatolia, of which we read in the *Life* of Theodore of Sykeon. The system was regulated by law and Justinian's legislation tells us about arrangements in the sixth century when roads were well kept up. Later, public routes were the responsibility of a special official, the *logothete* of the *dromos*, and public horses and carriages were both available, with regularly spaced stations and inns, though much less is known about their upkeep, or about road building generally. Even on the main highways travel was slow (twelve days from Thessalonike to Constantinople, for instance), and sometimes impeded for other reasons. Other inland routes were difficult and very slow; this had not changed since the late Roman period. Sea transport had always been quicker in the ancient world, and cheaper for large amounts of goods, but the speed and reliability for passengers varied with the route and size of the vessel. The availability of shipping also depended on political conditions, for example the presence of Arab shipping and the fleet of the Rus', and from the eleventh century the ships of the Italian trading cities reached the Black Sea.[1]

At its peak the territory of the empire stretched from one end of the Mediterranean to the other and beyond; at its smallest it was confined to a few small enclaves. For Procopius in the sixth century Britain represented a far-off semi-fabled land, yet in the seventh it had as Archbishop of Canterbury Theodore of Tarsus, born in Cilicia and educated in Constantinople. Constantine VII Porphyrogenitus in the tenth century saw himself as presiding over a family of nations outside the bounds of the empire; his successors, the Comnenian emperors, waged war simultaneously from the Adriatic to what is now eastern Turkey. Emperors and dynasties were often short-lived, and their ends violent. Yet the imperial ideology did not change, nor did imperial prestige; Byzantium remained in theory and in practice a centralised state under a monarchical ruler. From the late Roman period it inherited a bureaucratic style of government in which, even though patronage was always an important factor, offices were theoretically open. One of these officials in the sixth century was John the Lydian who wrote about his experiences working in the praetorian prefecture, complaining that knowledge of Latin had sadly declined and times were not what they were.[2] Entry to these careers required an elite education, always in theory and usually also in practice (the fact that John Lydian and Procopius complain of the boorishness of John the Cappadocian, one of Justinian's ministers demonstrates the level of expectation). This required training in Greek rhetoric and sometimes also law, though less often philosophy.[3] Bishops usually had a similar training, which was the pathway to success in the later Roman governing structure. Alongside this hierarchy of offices went a hierarchy of ranks and titles and this too was retained in later centuries even if the titles themselves changed.[4]

The changes in the seventh century resulted in the collapse of the traditional educational system, which had depended on the amenities and demands of civic life, and undermined both the supply of personnel and the need for so large an administration. In the eighth and ninth centuries, however, there was a gradual recovery from this very low base: the landowning elites had lost their influence, and service at court, imperial patronage and military rank became more important. Well before the seventh century, in fact, tax-raising had been taken out of the hands of the *curiales*, or local notables, who were replaced as leaders in civic government by the local bishop, an official called the 'father of the city', the provincial governor and an unspecified group of influential citizens,[5] but it is clear that the eighth and ninth centuries saw the rise of new elites and a new administrative system, which can be traced in part through the lead seals of officials, many of which have been published in recent years. Patient work on the collection and analysis of evidence about known individuals has pieced together what can be known of the careers of thousands of Byzantines from this period, both lay and ecclesiastical.[6] By the tenth century, but beginning earlier, family names appear in the sources, and this also points to the gradual growth of a new elite class and the beginnings of an aristocracy based on birth.[7] In this period of crystallisation there was a considerable degree of vertical mobility, and office-holders were highly-placed in contemporary characterisations of the elite; it was possible to rise to such positions from quite lowly origins, albeit via certain well-trodden routes, not excluding outright purchase. At the apex of the pyramid was the emperor, the fount of patronage. This was a system that offered, and sometimes explicitly encouraged, upward movement.

By the middle Byzantine period, in the eleventh and twelfth centuries, the issues were different again. A number of landowning families had by now built up great power and wealth, especially in Asia Minor,[8] and the Comnenian emperors evolved a new hierarchy of offices and titles for the highest appointees that was strikingly based on their own kinship relations (see Chapter 3, p. 42). It has been calculated that by the mid-twelfth century members of the Comnenian family and their relatives held almost 90 per cent of the highest military appointments. The interplay between the influence of powerful families and the traditional bureaucratic structure caused inevitable tensions, though there was less separation between the representatives of these groups than used to be thought. The 'magnate' families possessed lands in the provinces, but their influence and their wealth depended on their position at the imperial court rather than on bands of retainers on their estates.[9] Some imperial policies in this period worked in the favour of the 'magnates' by granting them rights over tax revenues. At the height of the earlier system, in the tenth century, both titles and offices were obtainable in return for cash, and holders of high offices received cash salaries from the emperor, a system that implied a high-cash state economy.[10] Patronage and connections were obviously important, but social class in Byzantium was never legally defined and status had to be sought afresh by each person. As we have seen, the middle Byzantine period saw the emergence of new and powerful aristocratic families, with estates, retainers and slaves, but middling provincial families with land also existed and are already attested earlier. In Late Byzantium members of the imperial family founded monasteries for their own salvation and that of their descendants, endowing them with estates and elaborate foundation rules.[11] Such monasteries occupied space in late Constantinople that in earlier centuries had been the site of dwellings or workshops. After 1204, and still more after the Byzantine return to Constantinople in 1261, the fragmentation of Byzantine rule was mirrored at local levels, and in the towns that had begun to revive from the tenth century in Greece and elsewhere, control was in the hands of the *archontes*, local bigwigs – a group to which the local bishop often belonged.

Surrounding the emperor were palace officials, including eunuchs, who had been an important part of the palace administration since the fourth century. In the Byzantine period eunuchs were not only of foreign origin but were sometimes the sons of ambitious families within the empire who hoped that if their sons were castrated they might reach high office.[12] Michael Psellus describes a famous and powerful eunuch who served under four emperors from Constantine VII to Basil II. This was Basil the *parakoimomenos*, or 'head of the bedchamber', the son of Romanos I Lekapenos by a concubine, and so the uncle of the emperor, who had been castrated in order to forestall any claims on the succession. In Psellus's words, 'actually, he was resigned to his fate and was genuinely attached to the imperial house – after all, it was his own family. He was particularly devoted to his nephew Basil, embracing the young man in the most affectionate manner and watching over his progress like some kindly foster-parent.'[13] Basil the *parakoimomenos* and his fine house in Constantinople were the subject of an epigram and an *ekphrasis* by the tenth-century poet John Geometres. Eunuchs were sometimes of slave origin, and the emperors and their richer subjects alike were served by slaves.[14] Constantinople had also had its own senate since the fourth century, in theory to rival that of Rome, and this continued to exist, although it had little political role in later centuries, and senatorial rank had been already opened very widely by Constantine.[15] The changes in the seventh and eighth centuries broke the continuity of senatorial rank, but the senate itself persisted, and those designated 'senatorial' (including high-ranking officials and some clergy) occupied a favoured place in the middle Byzantine hierarchy and retained some privileges and responsibilities; 'the sandalled senators', named from their distinctive footwear, formed a specific group on imperial invitation lists. The members of the court in the eleventh century perhaps numbered about two thousand persons. Also part of the ceremonial structure were the forementioned Blues and Greens, or 'factions', groups of organisers and supporters of the chariot races in the hippodromes who had been at the centre of the frequent urban violence in Constantinople and other cities in the early Byzantine period, and who retained a role in hippo-drome races and ceremonial;[16] the Blues and Greens still seem to have been playing these roles in the twelfth century. In the tenth century, based on the evidence of the *Book of Ceremonies*, they had an assigned place in the lists of precedence, drew salaries and had positions assigned to them along imperial processional routes. Surviving guest lists give a vivid insight into the official life of the emperor and the social hier-archies of the court. Those invited to imperial banquets included mili-tary officials and churchmen, and even some of the various categories of specialist staff and craftsmen in the palace were recognised with invita-tions or places in processions. The wives of officials took their rank from their husbands and had their own ceremonies, referred to in the *Book of Ceremonies* as 'the court of the women',[17] mirroring those of the men and led by the empress and female members of the imperial family; thus, for example, two state banquets were held for the visit of Princess Olga of Kiev in the tenth century, one for the women and one for the men. Life in the palace was also a matter of the constant exchange of money and gifts on appointment, on festive occasions and simply when receiv-ing the salaries due.

The Byzantine state inherited not only a system of bureaucratic gov-ernment but also a developed tax regime from the later Roman Empire. Any calculation of actual figures is dangerous, given the lack of hard evidence, but it is clear that the largest call on tax revenues, apart from the cost of maintaining the emperor and the court, maintaining the city of Constantinople and financing the imperial administration, was for the upkeep of the army and defences.[18] In the fifth and sixth centuries Anastasius (491–518). and Justinian (527–65) put a large amount of this resource into buildings and fortifications all over the empire. The basic late Roman and early Byzantine tax had been on land, calculated both on the extent of holdings and on manpower, to simplify a very complex subject, with calculations made centrally and payment exacted both in money and in kind or service, the ratio of money to kind vary-ing over time. A large paid army was maintained from this state revenue, for which the historian Agathias in the later sixth century gives us a paper figure of 645,000 for the whole empire and a real figure for the East under Justinian of 150,000.[19] The Byzantines produced several treat-ises on the art of war, and flexible cavalry tactics are stressed in the late sixth-century *Strategikon* attributed to the Emperor Maurice (582–602).[20]

Both the tax and the military system necessarily changed in the seventh century after the Arab invasions. The traditional view, based on the views of George Ostrogorsky, is that it was Heraclius who took the initiative in forming the system of 'themes', geographical areas whose commanders (*strategoi*) had responsibility for raising troops. The first four themes, dating from the later seventh century, were the Anatolikon, the Thrakesion, the Opsikion and the Armeniakon but the number grew later, especially when smaller units were created in a search for greater central control, and the developed system is described in a treatise on the themes commissioned by Constantine VII Porphyrogenitus in the tenth century. While the details remain extremely obscure, the new arrangements meant that army recruitment was decentralised, and a new class of soldiers was created with obligation to service. Ostrogorsky saw in this development a fundamental economic and military reform, related to the rise of a free peasantry and the distribution of lands, the so-called *stratiotika ktemata*, in return for hereditary military service. However the argument relies heavily on a document known as the *Nomos georgikos*, or 'Farmers' Law', which cannot bear the interpretation or the early dating placed upon it, and legal evidence for the *stratiotika ktemata* is not earlier than the tenth century.[21] The village unit and peasants in the early Byzantine period do seem to have included freeholders; however, the heavy emphasis placed in the Ostrogorsky thesis on a 'free' peasantry derives from two sets of ideologically charged ideas, first about the prevalence of slavery, or at least unfree status, among the rural population in the late Roman period, and second that of a linkage between the notion of a 'free peasantry' and the search for Slav origins. Difficult questions remain as to when and to what extent there was a deliberate reform of the military system involving territorial themes and military lands and how the theme soldiers were supported.[22] Large quantities of a new type of lead seal survive that had been used, beginning in the mid-seventh century, for documents issued by *kommerkiaroi*, who were apparently officials in charge of warehouses or depots in charge of supplying the soldiers with goods, whether levying them from the population as tax, or acting as private agents on behalf of the state. The soldiers still received some cash payment from the state, but at a far lower level than previously, reflecting the drastic drop in cash revenues in the late seventh-century state, and the eighth-century law-code known as the *Ekloga* and the early ninth-century *Life* of Philaretos assume that they owned their own weapons, armour and horse.[23] The *strategoi*, or theme commanders, acquired both civil and military power, a potentially dangerous combination, and the new system created localised provincial armies. The theme soldiers were assigned land on whose proceeds they supported themselves, but which carried the obligation of military service. As time went on the sale of such lands was controlled by

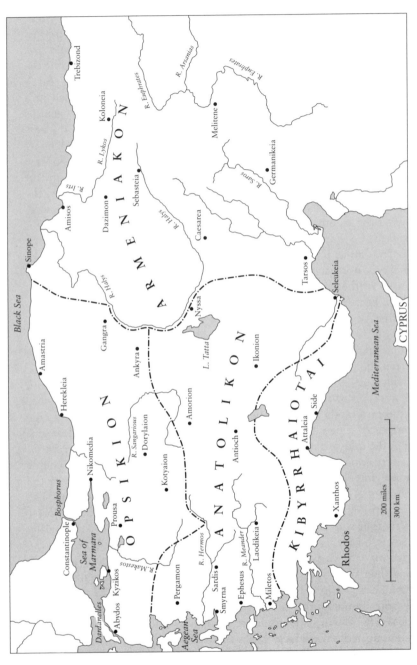

Map 9 Themes in Asia Minor in the later seventh century. After A. Kazhdan et al., eds, *The Oxford Dictionary of Byzantium* (New York, 1991), p. 2034

legislation, and there was an increased emphasis on heavy armed cavalry, which meant that soldiers required more to support them. The military emperor Nikephoros II Phokas (963–69) is credited in ways not altogether clear with a steep increase in the fiscal burden of the army costs while arguing in a military treatise of his own that soldiers themselves should be exempt from taxes.

Whatever the genesis of the theme system, it enabled Byzantium to maintain its role as a centralised state extracting taxes and maintaining an army. It also had the concomitant effect that military office became the route to power and influence. As the mistakes and pretentiousness of the late eighth-century set of semi-historical 'notes' on the city of Constantinople known as the *Parastaseis syntomoi chronikai* show, the secular education that had provided the pathway to office had all but disappeared, and though it began to revive from around 800 the new career structure that had meanwhile evolved had of necessity drawn on the military class.[24] The theme armies did not comprise the whole of the Byzantine army. In addition there were the *tagmata*, or guards units, who were theoretically more experienced and professional.

Byzantium in the seventh to ninth centuries was an early medieval state struggling for its own survival, but with the legacy of a strong imperial and territorial past that still influenced its organisation. It survived the Arab conquests by gradually regrouping and remodelling its army and its administration and by falling back to its core territories, the magnitude of which achievement is noted by Chris Wickham as 'the paradox of a crisis-ridden polity which managed to maintain a long-standing fiscal coherence'.[25] Over this transition period a different tax system was put in place, based on the *kapnikon* or hearth tax and the *synone*, or land tax in kind, and theme officials with new titles had already appeared as lay officials attending the Sixth Ecumenical Council in Constantinople in 680. The resilience of the state is impressive. Even if exaggerating, Oikonomides refers to the highly complex and monetarised system that operated in the ninth to eleventh centuries as a 'command economy', yet the concept of centralised government had not been lost even in the difficult earlier period.[26] This is indeed impressive, though it should not obscure the fact that the tax system was at all periods highly pragmatic, and admitted many anomalies. In theory, elaborate tax records were kept for every area, but judging from the little that survives, they may have existed more for show than anything else.[27] In practice the tax system was anything but fixed and allowed for widely differing degrees of implementation at local level – and this was no doubt one of its strengths.

Through a reorganisation of the army and its pay, a new and realistic base for the extraction of tax revenue and the transformation of the old administrative structure, Byzantium was able to adapt and survive as a centralised state through a time of profound change everywhere in the Mediterranean world. It also succeeded – if only with difficulty – in re-orientating itself towards the north after the Arab conquest of the eastern provinces and in finding new sources of the food for the capital after the loss of North African grain.[28] By the tenth century it was again able to challenge the Arabs in the east and claim a senior position in relation to the new kingdoms and peoples to the west and north. Although Basil II has gone down in history as the 'Bulgar-slayer', an image resonant in Greece to this day, he also fought a civil war in which the Anatolian themes were against him,[29] and by now the military and financial system that had served for three centuries began to show its age. The coinage was debased, and the Armenian theme army was released from duty by Constantine IX Monomachos (1042–55) in return for short-term gain in the form of payment of taxes just as the threat from the Seljuks began to be serious. Romanos IV Diogenes (1068–71) had to train soldiers and reconstitute the theme army before facing the Turks in the east, and was defeated and captured at Manzikert in 1071 at the head of a very mixed collection of troops.[30] This was a different world. Alexius I Comnenus had to allow Nicaea and Smyrna to be taken by the Turks while he addressed the Norman heavy cavalry at Dyrrachium in the west. Like his predecessor Constantine IX Monomachos, and faced with dangers from the Normans, the Pechenegs and Cumans, Alexius relied on mercenary troops from many different peoples, including Normans, Rus' and even Anglo-Saxons, a practice that was to arouse unfavourable comment from the French writer Odo of Deuil in the context of the Second Crusade. Emperors thus still depended on mustering armies centrally and could not rely on provincially based magnates to rally troops. Something of the flavour of these conditions is given by the fact that the victorious Pechenegs promptly took service on the Byzantine side after 1091. Ground was won back under Alexius's successors, despite the far more complex political world in which they now had to operate, but the attempt of Manuel I to break the Seljuk hold in the battle of Myriokephalon in 1176 failed completely; a huge army had been collected, stretching over ten miles with all its baggage train, but the emperor chose, or was forced, to attack at a location where the Byzantines were very vulnerable. After this there could be no further thoughts of removing the Turks from Anatolia.

Whatever the explanation for the debasement of the coinage in the mid-eleventh century, given the events of the 1070s Alexius I faced a crisis situation, and extreme measures were taken by the state to bring in more cash. Attempts to raise state income from the sale of titles, and the permissive attitude to the buying out for cash of obligations to military service that had already begun now increased; in the end the system of selling titles was given up altogether, and a useful source of state income lost, while the inflexible land tax gave way to special taxes and service requirements; at the same time privileges and special exemptions, in part for political reasons, benefited the powerful at the expense of the poor.[31] The results were a reduction in monetarisation and a potential threat to centralised government from the rise of powerful magnates, the very class to which Alexius himself belonged. What we see is a previously highly successful state, albeit with traditional and not very flexible structures, having to deal with dramatically changed circumstances: new political and military rivals in the Normans in the west and the Seljuks in the east, the growth of trading states such as Venice and Genoa, and, soon, the impact of the crusades. At the same time, parts of the empire, in particular Greece, shared in the urban growth that had begun in the tenth century.[32] In attempting to deal with these developments the state was conscious of the need to ensure the productivity of the rural population even while giving concessions to the privileged. Some of the results can be traced in contemporary monastic documents including those from Mount Athos, which in the absence of comparable state archives constitute one of the most important surviving sources for the later Byzantine economy. Similarly the financial administration became more centralised even as these concessions increased. Byzantine historians themselves always tended to personalise, and the twelfth-century historian Zonaras is sharply critical of Alexius's policies, especially the harshness of the tax-collectors.[33] Equally, the role of the emperor himself was always central, and the delay of fifteen years, for example, between Alexius's coinage reform in 1092 and his tax reforms in 1106–9 is attributed by Alan Harvey to the simple fact that the emperor was often away from Constantinople during this period.

From the end of the eleventh century the tax system depended more and more on the issuing of privileges. This took many forms, ranging from tax exemption to the granting of specific tax revenues to an individual rather than to the state. The emperors granted state lands or their revenues on a similar basis. This suited the state, given its shortage of gold, in that it largely replaced the cash salaries that had previously been paid to officials. The state grew smaller as a result, but the system was in theory more flexible since recipients could collect their taxes in a variety of ways, either in cash or in kind. From the twelfth century onwards the system, known as *pronoia*, became the main way of paying officials and soldiers, who were granted state revenues directly, most often from land, and would themselves collect the dues and services of the peasants (*paroikoi*) who lived on it and worked it. The value of the grant, and the number of *paroikoi* allowed for in the calculation, were set out in documents known as *praktika*, of which a large number, most relating to monastic houses, survive from the fourteenth century. These replaced the land tax register as the main tax records, and the surviving material shows that the calculations were drawn up by officials in great detail. The state was able by this system to reward individuals while relieving itself of the responsibility of large-scale tax collection and the need for paying salaries on a large scale in cash. It continued through the period of the Empire of Nicaea and after the Byzantine return to Constantinople in 1261. While it reduced any theoretical opportunities the state might have had to maximise production in a modern sense, since tenure was limited and conditional, this was a way in which the state could retain control of assets, which might comprise monasteries or fortresses as well as land.[34] *Pronoiai* eventually became hereditary, and dependent *paroikoi* came to constitute most of the peasantry; thus, in a gradual change from earlier centuries, dependent peasants became the norm.[35] 'Feudalism' is a term that has been much used in relation to Byzantium, for example by Ostrogorsky, and the date of its applicability debated, but the institution never existed in Byzantium in the technical Western sense. Wickham uses the term in the broader sense of a mode of production in which 'an agrarian surplus is exacted, by force if necessary, from the peasant majority'; this is compatible with a tax-based system in which the exaction may be made in cash or in kind, the essential element being the existence of exploitation and the predominance of peasant labour;[36] however this is not how the term is usually used in relation to Byzantium, and it is probably best avoided for that reason. The role of the state was also important throughout the Byzantine period, and while the revival of trade and commerce by the twelfth century was not driven by the state the latter nevertheless gained from it, partly by exacting duties on goods traded and partly also by granting privileges to foreign trading powers, especially the Italian city states – in the first place Venice, Pisa and Genoa.[37] But this was a difficult game, and the emperors were hard pressed to keep up with the Italians who exploited their concessions and undercut their charges.

The politics of late Byzantium were dominated by its military and naval weakness and the need for ships and assistance, which led both to repeated appeals to Venice and the papacy and to Byzantine willingness for religious union. The Ottomans had much larger forces and were far better equipped; the Byzantines could not afford to maintain a large land army or a navy, and by the second half of the fourteenth century they had lost most of their agricultural base and with it much of their population.

In particular during the period of the 'command economy', Byzantine emperors also tried to control the economy and trade. The *Book of the Prefect*, compiled under Leo VI (886–912), was one of a group of codes issued to cover various areas of the administration, including law, precedence and tactics. It apparently seeks to control trade and industry by affirming that trade guilds in Constantinople fall under the regulation of the *eparch* or prefect of the city, but it is, in fact, more a working document covering a group of particular trades, such as notaries, money-changers and personnel concerned with commodities such as gold, silk and leather, than a systematic set of regulations. There had been guilds since the time of the Roman Empire, and they had probably continued to operate during the seventh to ninth centuries, for which there is hardly any evidence. It is interesting to note that in the majority of cases slaves were allowed to be members of the guilds alongside free men. The prefect and his office belonged to the official bureaucracy and as such were included in the provisions for court ceremonial. However the document does not in itself prove that economic life in Byzantium was highly regulated and controlled, and its provisions in any case extended only to the capital. Artisans were recognised in this period as important in Constantinople, even though Byzantine writers tended to profess a haughty disdain for trade and traders. In the eleventh century, when the economy was expanding, tradesmen were even allowed to join the ranks of the senatorial order, calling forth predictable criticism from conservatives. Trade associations seem to have existed also in Thessalonike and in Athens, and in the changed conditions of the eleventh century onwards, as trade and markets opened up under the influence of the Italian city states, attempts to control them became anachronistic.

Urban production was largely artisanal, and often involved the work of slaves. Much of the evidence comes incidentally from texts such as saints' lives and mentions slaves as labourers, skilled workers or higher officials, depending on the trade, the wealth of their owner and the scale of the trade in question. At the other end of the scale, the workshops were often, in fact, owned by rich investors who did not work them themselves. Despite the *Book of the Prefect* it is possible to argue that the level of imperial control had actually been reduced in comparison with the period from Constantine to the Arab invasions.

Even before the sack of Constantinople in 1204 the economic life of the capital was deeply affected not only by the activity of the Italian city states but also by a rising population in both western Europe and Byzantium. Centralisation of government had been possible earlier, but the challenge in the much more fragmented and varied later medieval world was far greater.[38] Byzantine towns remained centres of consumption, but urban centres producing specialized goods such as silk began to develop outside the capital, including Thebes and Corinth. In late Byzantium economic life was increasingly privatised, and while towns were still centres of production and markets this activity was small-scale and many citizens were in fact peasants and small landholders. The rich in Constantinople had storehouses in their residences for produce and goods necessary in case of siege, and both there and also in Thessalonike, though on a smaller scale, a good deal of local economic activity clustered round the port areas, especially the Golden Horn; in comparison, inland late Byzantine towns had more the appearance of large villages. Settlements of non-Byzantines, especially Italians, were a major feature of the economic life of Constantinople in this period, as were Byzantine Jews and Jewish newcomers.[39] Late Byzantine cities, including Constantinople, had to function in a world in which the Western economic presence had increased and diversified, and many individual Byzantines involved themselves in financial and business relations with Latins. Many ways of accommodation could be found, even in the face of the Ottoman presence in the hinterland of Constantinople from the second half of the fourteenth century. But the small Palaiologan state could not in itself control or reverse these forces of decentralisation.

At all periods the basis of Byzantine taxation and of the economy in general was agriculture, and in the empire as a whole urban life on a large scale was the exception; the state was able to survive the transition from the late antique model because it found new ways to draw on its agricultural surplus.[40] For late Byzantium we have source material that can give a very detailed picture of peasant life, including the names, family structure and possessions of individual households. Self-sufficiency was the aim wherever possible, and polyculture was the rule, what we might now call market-gardening; the fact that the peasants in question were *paroikoi*, who could be assigned or given away to individuals or monastic houses, does not necessarily mean that productivity was essentially different from what it had been in earlier periods. Scholars debate both the level of monetarisation at different periods, including the amount of taxes paid in cash, and the extent of entrepreneurism or 'economic rationality' of the large landlords; current research tends to emphasise both, while allowing for the habit of non-monetarised exchange and the service obligations of the rural population.[41] We need to remember that most exchange was local at all periods, and that while artisanal products were always needed by peasant households, agrarian specialisation on a large scale was the exception rather than the norm.

The Church was embedded at every level in the economic and administrative life of the state. Ecclesiastics were included in the ceremonies of the court, which indeed had a strong religious component and often involved imperial processions through the city that halted at different churches on the way. The emperor was expected to observe the liturgical feasts of the Christian year, not only with services and processions but also with special banquets. Constantine also set a precedent for all later emperors in his church building, and it was part of the imperial image thereafter to found or refound churches. Later emperors also followed Constantine's example of providing for the upkeep of their churches, including their complement of clergy, as well as by making gifts of silver and precious objects.

Monasteries, including, for example, the twelfth-century Pantokrator monastery in Constantinople founded by John II Comnenus (1118–43), were the recipients of tax concessions and tax privileges in the same way as individuals. The Pantokrator monastery was given estates over a wide area ranging from Macedonia to the Peloponnese and Anatolia from which it could maintain its hospital, old men's home and leprosarium. Monasteries feature often in the evidence for fiscal arrangements in the middle Byzantine period, usually trying to appeal or protest against decisions of tax officials or in land disputes. An imperial ruling in the eleventh century tried to deal with this as far as Mount Athos was concerned by placing jurisdiction for all the Athos monasteries under the *protos*, or elected head. In late Byzantium monasteries owned land and *paroikoi* on a big scale. They often engaged in trade and some, like the Great Lavra on Mount Athos, the Kosmosoteira monastery in Thrace or the monastery on Patmos, had their own ships. The tax revenue of three of the Athonite monasteries in the early fourteenth century from *paroikoi*, excluding the value of tax exemptions, ranged from five hundred to four thousand gold coins per year.[42] In their capacity as property owners and holders of privileges monasteries also engaged in law suits: a famous case was brought by the monastery of the Great Lavra in 1196 against the office in charge of dues on maritime trade; after detailed hearings the monastery won.[43] In Constantinople and elsewhere, therefore, the great monasteries of the later period were a feature of urban life that the emperor could not control, yet that played a major role in the economy.

Emperors were also legislators and dispensers of justice. Appeal was still made to the two great codifications of Roman law of Theodosius II (AD 438) and Justinian (AD 529), and in the eleventh century Michael Psellus claimed familiarity with Roman law as 'the wisdom of the Italians', but the late Roman codes had by then been adapted and replaced by further codes in Greek, the *Ecloga* of Leo III and Constantine V (AD 741) and the *Prochiron* (AD 872), *Eisagoge* (AD 880) and *Basilika*, the latter based on the Justinianic code (AD 900). In addition, emperors issued individual laws, known as *Novels* ('new laws'), the 113 *Novels* of Leo VI being especially important.[44] Up to the sixth century there had been a highly regulated course of legal studies available at Berytus in Palestine, but the school there was destroyed in a major earthquake in 551, and specialised legal education was a casualty of the changes of the seventh century. Under the theme system fiscal and legal administration went closely together and provincial judges were not technically trained; the same official who had responsibility for getting in the state revenues also heard civil lawsuits, with any resultant fines also being due to the fisc. The fair dispensation of justice (not the same as legislating) was an important attribute of Byzantine emperors, and individual emperors from Basil I onwards took various initiatives to improve the legal system.[45] Another compilation, the *Peira*, based on actual judgements by one judge, Eustathios Rhomaios, marks the beginning of an academic revival of legal studies in the eleventh century when the future patriarch John Xiphilinos was appointed teacher of law in Constantinople by Constantine IX Monomachos. During the next century law and the courts seem to have been substantially restructured and fiscal justice made more specialised, and from that time on we hear of a series of distinguished and learned jurists and commentators. One of these, in the twelfth century, was Theodore Balsamon, who was commissioned by the emperor and patriarch together to write a commentary on the *Nomokanon*, the collection of the canon law from the earlier Church councils that was the basis of Byzantine ecclesiastical law; this had grown in several stages since the sixth century and had been revised in the late eleventh century. The patriarchal court and standing synod functioned alongside the imperial legal system from this time too. Ecclesiastical law and ecclesiastical courts existed alongside the civil law and each influenced the other; tensions were bound to arise at times, and challenges were made on the grounds

obverse   reverse

Fig. 11   Seal of Leo Areobindos, *spatharokandidatos, asekretis* and *krites* of Chaldia and Derxene, first half of the eleventh century. Paris, Bibliothèque Nationale, Cabinet de Médailles, Zacos Collection no. 651.

that a given case had been brought to the wrong court. Ecclesiastical and secular law were interwoven, and the jurists who wrote on law, who included several historians, were often themselves ecclesiastics. Like secular law, canon law needed to be studied, explained and interpreted and generated its own specialists; full knowledge of the law whether imperial or ecclesiastical was the preserve of the few.

Nevertheless, this picture of the Byzantine legal system must be qualified in several important ways. By no means all emperors were legislators, and even those who were also issued decrees or imperial orders that had the force of law as well. Concern for the law was important, but the sources also emphasise and cite in an approving way the personal dispensation of justice by emperors.[46] Emperors also bestowed privileges and issued chrysobulls, signed personally by them in red and named after the gold imperial seal. Even with all this legalism and specialist knowledge of law there was still a good deal of room for flexibility, so that decisions and arguments might rest more on ethical or other arguments than technical legal ones. Flexibility of another kind, called by the Byzantines *oikonomia*, was also built into the system. This principle, which was often explicitly invoked and applied, meant that, in view of man's fallen condition, excessive severity or rigidity could and should be tempered by charity, sympathy or a higher need. *Philia*, friendship and status, were other reasons for which judges were expected to moderate their severity. Thus a system which on the surface seems highly organised and defined by legislation was in fact anything but that, an apparent contradiction typical of Byzantine life. To this must be added the limited knowledge of the law on the part of the great majority of Byzantines, even extending to clergy and judges themselves, and the limited access to legal redress for ordinary provincials. This was true in the later Roman Empire when the civil administration of the provinces was somewhat more developed, provinces more urbanised and communications better, and it was far more likely to be the situation in Byzantium where few except landowners or rich monasteries would be in a position to conduct expensive and difficult lawsuits to protect their interests. It was always a good thing in such a system, as it had been in the Roman Empire, to have powerful connections, and if necessary to be able to travel to the capital to seek redress, but these paths were closed to all but a few. Furthermore, in many cases law was dispensed to suit the interests of the fisc, which were undoubtedly exploitative. Nevertheless, the conception of the legal system as fair and at least technically disinterested remained. The protection of the poor was a further part of the imperial image, proclaimed in the prefaces to imperial legislation and praised, when it happened, by historians. Justice was not only about equity, it also meant the protection of the poor against the rich, and the ideal emperor was one who heard cases himself and dispensed justice fairly and with a concern for the poor. Of course the reality might be otherwise, but this is a different image from that presented by the Roman law codes, and it speaks for the personal and Christian emphasis in the Byzantine system of justice.

There was a basic contradiction in the Byzantine system of rule. On the one hand, emperors were highly interventionist, not only making war and directing military and diplomatic policy but also issuing decrees, making law, appointing officials and Church dignitaries, summoning Church councils and intervening in doctrinal matters. However, with the exception of tax collection, provincial government was largely passive. Just as in the Roman Empire, the first priority was the collection of sufficient revenue to pay for the military needs of the state, which varied over such a long period, and to maintain the imperial court and the mass of officials and title-holders. The state did not interest itself directly in such matters as the development of towns and was content to leave most issues of provincial government to be handled at local level, so long as there were no military issues involved. Byzantium seems like the very model of a centralised state, yet the role of the state was extremely limited, even when its territorial extent and its prestige were at their height. Government in the provinces was based on the juggling act between finding ways to keep the taxes coming in and the local notables reliable.

Byzantium also possessed exceptional qualities of staying power and adaptability, in that it was able to maintain the key characteristics of imperial rule and the imperial office over a period of time that saw the transition from the ancient to the medieval world and from the early to the late medieval, a time during which other states and empires rose and fell and during which Byzantium had to deal with many new external challenges. Internally, the state took shape in the context of the urban society and culture of late antiquity, which was replaced by a typically early medieval village-based economy with a strong military organisation; in the ninth to eleventh centuries an elaborately reconstituted bureaucracy of ranks and titles gave the Byzantine court a unique prestige and influence, while in the Comnenian period the development of aristocratic government and social mores went together with a flourishing economic life and a return of Constantinople almost to the population level it had reached under Justinian in the sixth century. The shock of 1204, and the final conquest of 1453, as well as, it must be said, the aggressive expansionism of the West, denied Byzantium the chance of achieving some of the further developments that are now regarded as key stages in the triumphalist narrative of western Europe, but we need to look beyond the obstacles that this has put in the way of the reception of Byzantium in order to see this complex and highly distinctive state in a fair light.

6

An Orthodox Society?

He sent to the monastery of the Pantokrator for the venerable icon of the pure Mother of God, which it is said that St Luke executed from life when she was present; but the icon was later a gift to the Empress Pulcheria from Palestine from her sister-in-law the Empress Eudocia the Athenian, a truly wonderful gift. It was behind her as his guide, in whom he had trusted that it would be recovered, that he entered the city in the belief that this was fitting proof of his gratitude to her ... So the Golden Gate was re-opened after a long interval, and the bishop began to pray. As for the emperor, he entered the city with all his retinue, walking slowly, his thoughts raised aloft in fervent piety, walking on foot and leaving aside all his imperial pomp as not befitting such an occasion.

The entry of Michael VIII Palaiologos to Constantinople in 1261, according to George Pachymeres, *Relations historiques* II.31

Byzantium thought of itself as a Christian society, and it was certainly one in which religion played a very important role. Much – even if by no means all – Byzantine art is religious art, and Byzantine churches and monasteries dominate the surviving architectural remains. Even to-day it is churches rather than secular buildings that survive in the lands which were formerly part of the Byzantine Empire, and religious art dominates the artistic record. But this was, after all, a pre-modern society, and the real questions to be asked are not why religion was – as it seems to have been – so embedded in state and society but what difference this made in practice either to the workings of the state or to the lives of individuals. This chapter will argue that the still common view of Byzantium as a state in which the emperor controlled the Church is mistaken, and that we are mistaken if we assume that the Church always had its way, or that all Byzantines were religious.

Certainly anyone is likely to be struck at once by the importance of Orthodox Christianity in Byzantine life. The centrality, and indeed the economic and social importance of monasticism, as well as the degree of imperial and other patronage it received, is one sign of this. There were already monks on Mount Athos, the Holy Mountain, in the tenth century when St Athanasios founded the Great Lavra under the patronage of the Emperor Nikephoros Phokas. Athanasios's *typikon*, or founding document, explains how the inaccessibility of the Holy Mountain made it so suitable for monastic settlement:

> The mountain resembles a peninsula which extends towards the sea in the shape of a cross. The islands in the sea, Lemnos, Imbros, Thasos and the rest are a great distance away. Because of this, when winter comes, a ship is unable to sail from the mountain to the mainland to procure necessary provisions or to sail back from there to the mountain. It cannot find any sort of anchorage because the seashore on both sides provides no shelter. On the other hand, there is absolutely no way for a person to transport his own provisions by dry land, partly because the road is so long, and partly because the mountain is practically impassable for pack animals.[1]

Indeed, roads on Mount Athos are a fairly recent development; but despite Athanasios's description of monastic isolation, in late Byzantium the Athonite houses found ways of conducting business and owning commercial ships on a major scale. Several of the other great monasteries on Mount Athos were imperial foundations, as was the twelfth-century monastery of St John on Patmos and many others. Some emperors themselves became monks, like John Cantacuzene in the fourteenth century,[2] and many widowed empresses and unmarried daughters of emperors entered monasteries; it was not uncommon, either, for Byzantine intellectuals and teachers to take vows at the end of their lives.

Besides the prominence of the monastic tradition throughout the period (of which more later), much of Byzantine public life, including imperial ceremonial, had a religious aura and involved invocations and processions to and from Hagia Sophia and the other churches in Constantinople. Insofar as there was an official political theory underpinning the Byzantine state, it consisted of the Christianised-ruler theory worked out for Constantine the Great by Eusebius of Caesarea, according to which the empire was the microcosm of heaven and the emperor placed there by God to ensure the maintenance of true religion;[3] all emperors, whatever their worldly shortcomings, were therefore officially 'Christ-loving' and beloved by God and were acclaimed as 'orthodox emperors'. Church law and state law existed side by side, sometimes in uneasy juxtaposition, and the development and interpretation of Orthodox canon law was an important indicator of the symbolic as well as the practical impact of the Church on the behaviour of the population. At the same time there was no one undisputed authority, something that is even now a profound difference between Orthodoxy and Roman Catholicism.

According to Paul Magdalino, who is here following in the tradition already mentioned in Chapter 4, 'Byzantium is rightly described as a theocracy'.[4] Magdalino understands the term in the sense that all Byzantines, the emperor included, acknowledged that Christ was the supreme ruler, and talks of a fusion of Church and state. There was nothing in Byzantium like the Gregorian reform in the West, which asserted the superiority of the Church to the imperium, and in Magdalino's view the result of Byzantine Church reforms in the eleventh and twelfth centuries was that the emperor was recognised then, if not before, as the supreme regulator of ecclesiastical discipline. Both Alexius I Comnenus and Manuel I sought to regulate the Church by imperial decree, and the reign of Manuel in particular was a time of tension and struggle between emperor and Church. This is, however, indicative of an unresolved relationship between them, and indeed, the term 'Church' is itself misleading in that the members of the ecclesiastical synod did not constitute a single block but tended to disagree between themselves as much as with the emperor. Certainly emperors in this period felt no hesitation in taking a personal role in theological debate, and in 1147 Manuel I made official for himself the flattering title of *epistomonarches*, 'chief scientific adviser', in Magdalino's rendering. The same emperor's *Novel* of 1166, in which he laid down doctrine in relation to the latest controversial issue, and which was inscribed in red letters on white marble on the walls of Hagia Sophia, marked a high point in imperial interventionism.[5] As we shall see in Chapter 7, the Church was able in the same period to insist on tighter control of marriage. However, religious control was contested throughout the Byzantine period, and, indeed, religion in Byzantium was characterised throughout the empire's history by competition and fluidity. An overarching theory of rule under God did not prevent the salient features of Byzantine Orthodoxy at local level from being choice and privatisation, to quote a recent formulation.[6] Nor, despite its own claims, was Byzantium 'Orthodox' in any simple sense. True, many of the characteristics of modern Orthodoxy took shape in the Byzantine period, but crude assumptions of continuity must also be avoided. We will look in this chapter at the outward manifestations of Byzantine religion with these questions in mind.

The behaviour of Constantine I in relation to the first 'ecumenical' council of the Christian church at Nicaea in AD 325 is a good starting point. The emperor expressed great deference to the assembled bishops and did not preside at the council himself, yet he summoned it, issued official letters after its decisions were known and enforced penalties on those who refused to assent. Nor did he hesitate to use state powers or draw on the resources of provincial governors either in making travel arrangements for the attending bishops or in building churches. This was a powerful precedent for later emperors, who also involved themselves directly in Church affairs. However, while the creed of Nicaea was never rescinded and remains the basis of the Nicene Creed today, the council's difficult early reception demonstrates the fragility of the consensus that seemed to have been reached. Within a few years Constantine had restored those who had been exiled and in turn exiled Athanasius, Nicaea's most vociferous supporter. The reign of his son Constantius II (337–61) was punctuated by a series of further church councils that tended in a different direction from Nicaea as the emperor struggled to deal with continuing differences of view. These experiences in the early years of the empire set the pattern for all subsequent emperors, who, though they might select a patriarch or call a council, were rarely able to 'control' the Church. Many tried, like Theodosius II in the fifth century, Justinian in the sixth, Heraclius in the seventh and the various iconoclast and iconophile rulers of the eighth and ninth, but any success they achieved was usually temporary. The methods tried by Justinian, none of which was successful in the longer term, included holding talks with the non-Chalcedonian Syrians, issuing his own theological statements, keeping pope Vigilius under house arrest in Constantinople and doing his best to coerce him into accepting the council of 553, and deposing the patriarchs of Antioch and Constantinople. Most emperors found themselves alternating, like Justinian, between persuasion, threats and even, at times, persecution. The issues at stake changed over time but few if any emperors managed to avoid a clash with the Church or some elements of it.

At the same time, the emperor's own role was highly ambiguous. In their official lives emperors were certainly deeply associated with Christian ritual and ideology long before the detailed protocols in the tenth-century *Book of Ceremonies* were established. Yet a religious coronation ritual had been surprisingly slow to develop, and some of the military elements of Roman imperial succession long remained in place, such as raising the new emperor on a shield in the Germanic manner. Emperors were always liable to be challenged, especially by patriarchs who disagreed with or disapproved of their actions. The patriarch Germanos resigned rather than accept iconoclasm, and, as we have seen, Heraclius's marriage to his niece Martina and Leo VI's uncanonical fourth marriage aroused the opposition of the Church. However, patriarchs of Constantinople also frequently found themselves removed by emperors. Thus, when the patriarch Constantine II (754–66), appointed by the Emperor Constantine V, was accused of treason he was scourged and publicly beaten before being made to ride round the Hippodrome and be spat upon while sitting backwards on a donkey, and was finally beheaded. Ignatius (847–58, 867–77), who was himself the son of an emperor (Michael I Rangabe, deposed 813), was made patriarch by the Empress Theodora in 847 but had to resign when she was exiled in 858, only to be restored by Basil I in 867. Of course politics, personalities and religious affiliations tend to go together. But what is striking in the case of Orthodox Byzantium, with its insistence on precedence and protocol in lesser matters, is that these relationships were not in fact governed by constitutional protocols. In his sixth-century verse panegyric on the restoration of the dome of Hagia Sophia the poet Paul the Silentiary presented emperor and patriarch as twin poles of authority in total harmony with each other. In later Byzantium, emperors found themselves in what were effectively power struggles with the Church hierarchy. After the return of the Byzantines from Nicaea to Constantinople in 1261 Michael VIII Palaiologos was subjected to intense opposition from the Church for his deposition of the patriarch Arsenios, as well as to his policy of seeking union with Rome. 'The Church' in Byzantium did not speak with one voice. Patriarchs came and went and at times of acute controversy members of the synod in Constantinople often disagreed with each other. In some matters, such as marriage law, it was expressly confirmed that emperors might appeal to the very Byzantine principle of 'economy' (*oikonomia*) in order to set aside canon law in the interests of state or for other good reasons, but the use of such a right was itself open to challenge.[7] Whatever the theory or the display of harmony between emperor and Church, this remained one of the main points of instability about the functioning of the Byzantine state.

Councils, or synods, of bishops were the main official way of deciding matters both of doctrine and of Church discipline. Though not all of them by any means had equal or even reasonably equal representation from both East and West, seven councils came to be recognised as 'universal' ('ecumenical', from *oikoumene*, meaning the whole world): these were held at Nicaea (AD 325), Constantinople (AD 381), Ephesus (AD 431), Chalcedon (AD 451), Constantinople (AD 553), Constantinople (AD 680) and Nicaea (AD 787). Another council held in Constantinople in AD 691–2 is referred to either as the Council in Trullo (referring to the room in the palace where it was held) or the Quinisext, since it supplemented both the Fifth and Sixth Councils by issuing canons on matters of church discipline. An element of reinvention was at work in the way that these councils were remembered. The acts of the Council of Nicaea (AD 325) do not survive, and for its crucial proceedings we rely on the partial witness of contemporaries like Athanasius of Alexandria and Eusebius of Caesarea, or later writers. The first council was soon also remembered as having been attended by 318 bishops, certainly too high a figure, and based on the scriptural number of the servants of Abraham (Gen. 14:14). The seven councils were also depicted in visual art as a symbolic statement of orthodoxy. The Council of Chalcedon in 451 is remembered in the West as having settled important doctrinal matters, but in the East it led, in the sixth century, to the formation of separate churches by the many who could not accept it. The authority of a council depended in practice on whether it was accepted and whether its decisions stayed in force. Thus the Council held at Hieria by the icono-clast Emperor Constantine V in 754 was overturned by the Second Council of Nicaea in 787, which extracted formal recantations from the bishops who had participated. Most of these councils issued canons, or regulations, which, when collected, became the basis of Eastern canon law, and formal records ('acts') also survive in most cases. However, recent scholarship has demonstrated beyond doubt that these are far from objective records; some were even composed in advance of the council itself, or by groups with particular agendas, and the appended lists of signatory bishops are notoriously untrustworthy, especially in troubled times when many bishops whose sees were insecure or occupied by in-vaders held purely titular appointments. Besides the seven ecumenical councils there were many lesser and local ones, which varied in complete-ness of attendance and official or unofficial or regional status. Many of them, such as the Lateran Synod held in Rome in 649, at which Maximus Confessor was the guiding spirit, resisted official religious policy. At the other end of the scale, at the end of the Byzantine period the Emperor John VIII Palaiologos personally attended the Council of Ferrara-Florence in 1438–9. The Byzantine emperor sitting in state in a synod with his bishops, as John VI Cantacuzene is shown in a manuscript illustration, also made an impressive sight. However the reality was by no means as clear as the official image suggests.

The period of the iconoclastic controversy in the eighth and early ninth centuries shows us the extent and also the limits of imperial influ-ence over the Church. Leo III (717–41) and particularly his son Constantine V (741–75) tried to push through a purge of the religious

images and icons that had been growing in popularity at least throughout the previous century or even longer.[8] This was a movement driven
from the top. Some mosaics in churches were destroyed or whitewashed,
and some images destroyed, but there is little sign of popular support,
or of a reformation driven from below, although many of the bishops
were willing to go along with imperial policy. This was not a movement about corrupt clergy or the abuse of ecclesiastical office, and the
arguments on both sides focused closely on the religious status of
images themselves. The iconoclasts, including the Emperor Constantine
V himself, argued that the veneration of icons was an abuse amounting
to idolatry, but the iconophiles mounted a strong theological defence,
protesting that icons were not worshipped as divine but merely venerated. The lack of Scriptural authority for image veneration was dealt with
by appealing for justification to an 'unwritten tradition'. In the first phase,
culminating with the second Council of Nicaea in 787, the most important defence of images was contained in the three *Orations against those
who attack the holy images* by John of Damascus, writing from the
monastery of St Sabas near Jerusalem, and thus within the Umayyad
caliphate and outside the empire. The iconoclastic policy was reversed
by the Empress Irene at the Second Council of Nicaea in 787, when
repentant iconoclast clerics were received back into the Church, but a
further iconoclastic council was held in 815, and the arguments now
shifted away from the earlier charge of idolatry towards the theology of
the image and highly complex theories of representation.[9] However,
the force of iconoclasm died away with the waning of the military and
economic crises that had given rise to it, and in 843, under the Empress
Theodora, the widow of Theophilus (829–42) and regent for her young
son Michael III (842–67), images were permitted once more, without
resort to a formal synod.

The end of iconoclasm was presented as 'the triumph of Orthodoxy'.
An official document was drawn up known as the Synodikon of Orthodoxy ('statement of the synod on orthodoxy'), which was to be read out
in churches on a newly established Feast of Orthodoxy; it condemned
the 'heresy' of iconoclasm; in later centuries, from the Comnenian
period onwards, additions were made to it. An energetic propaganda campaign also followed, in which a concerted effort was made by pro-image
writers to blacken their opponents and magnify the extent of persecution and of actual iconoclast damage. In several iconophile sources interested in creating iconophile martyr stories pious women are said to have
tried to stop the removal of the Christ icon on the Chalke Gate of
the Great Palace under Leo III, and to have been martyred as a result.[10]

Fig. 12   Feast icon of the 'Triumph of Orthodoxy', c.1400. The Empress Theodora, the young Michael III and the patriarch Methodius flank the icon of the Mother of God Hodegetria attributed to St Luke, with iconophile saints below. Copyright the Trustees of the British Museum

One of our main narrative sources, though a highly one-sided one, is the iconophile chronicler Theophanes, writing in the early ninth century before the controversy had ended. His account of the death of the iconoclast Emperor Constantine V in 775 shares in the general iconophile vilification of their rivals, and especially of Constantine himself. Theophanes points out with relish that Constantine developed a very unpleasant disease, saying 'he became sorely afflicted with carbuncles on his legs, and was, on account of the extreme inflammation, seized by a violent fever of a kind unknown to physicians', and makes an explicit comparison between Constantine and the manner of his death and the accounts by Christian writers such as Eusebius and Lactantius of the deaths of earlier persecuting emperors: Constantine V was 'polluted with much Christian blood', and 'in all manner of evil he had reached a pinnacle no less than Diocletian and the ancient tyrants.'[11] The result of the intense literary and editorial activity that the iconoclastic controversy inspired was that a high proportion of the surviving sources present an extremely distorted and even deliberately falsified version of events; elaborate rules of evidence had to be laid down in the preparations for the council of 787, which involved checking the texts against copies held in the patriarchal library of all books produced that allegedly contained supporting passages from the Fathers. During the proceedings of the second Council of Nicaea, called by the Empress Irene and the patriarch Tarasios in 787, it was alleged that the iconoclasts had falsified the record by removing offending pages from volumes containing references to religious images.[12]

Iconoclasm had been an imperial initiative, and its failure meant that the Church and the monasteries emerged as the winners. The charge that image-veneration was an abuse that needed to be reformed was successfully refuted, and it had been shown that while emperors could manipulate politics and influence high-ranking clergy, they could not dictate the religious sensibility of the populace as a whole. Hundreds of letters survive written in the early ninth century by Theodore, the abbot of the Stoudite monastery in Constantinople, who was imprisoned as a defender of religious images during the second phase of the iconoclast period. Among his correspondents were well-placed lay persons, both men and women, who clearly sympathised with his views. Devotion to icons has sometimes been attributed to the sphere of private religion, in which female piety was an important factor. However, given the fact that the sources for iconoclasm are so biased and also so unrepresentative of Byzantine society as a whole, it is difficult to estimate the beliefs and practices of ordinary Byzantines, still less to ascribe a special role to women in their veneration, but hagiographic and other sources do contain stories of icons kept at home and specially venerated. Relics of saints were also important in Byzantium, and frequently formed the focus of pilgrimage to healing shrines both near Constantinople and all over the empire, but with the ending of iconoclasm in 843 the way was opened for a passionate devotion to religious images both in the home and in public, and late Constantinople and other centres such as Arta and Thebes were famous for their public processions of Marian icons, each of which had its confraternity of the faithful.

With the ending of iconoclasm in 843 monastic life flourished. According to Theophanes, monks had been made particular targets by Constantine V and had been publicly humiliated in the Hippodrome at Constantinople. Now monasteries flourished, new monasteries commissioned service books and other texts and their churches were decorated with ambitious pictorial schemes. Byzantium never had the kind of distinct monastic rules found in Western monasticism, but the Stoudite approach to the monastic life influenced others, and a series of foundation documents (*typika*) survive from monasteries established in the succeeding centuries.[13] New areas, especially mountainous regions, were colonised by monastic complexes, among them the peninsula of Mount Athos in northern Greece, Mount Ganos in Thrace on the western shore of the Bosphorus, and Olympos, Latros, Auxentios, south of Chalcedon, Kyminas and Galesion in western Asia Minor. Bulgarian monasticism was also well established by the middle of the tenth century, and there were new foundations in southern Italy and Sicily in the late ninth and tenth centuries. In mainland Greece the first church at Hosios Loukas in Phokis dates from the tenth century. This spread of monasticism went hand in hand in such areas with Byzantine political and military influence, as it did in Cyprus, reconquered by the Byzantines from the Arabs in 965; however, the tenth-century foundations in Constantinople, such as the Myrelaion and the monastery of Lips, show that this was in fact a general development. For every great imperial or aristocratic foundation from the eleventh century and later, such as the Theotokos Kosmosoteira in Thrace or the Theotokos Kecharitomene and the Theotokos Bebaias Elpidos in Constantinople (fig. 21), there were literally hundreds of less pretentious establishments all over the Byzantine Empire. The eleventh-century monastery of the Theotokos Evergetis outside the walls of Constantinople was a model for several of these later monasteries and was also at the beginning of a reform movement in Byzantine monasticism.[14] Ironically, in view of the opportunities for abuse that it offered, the practice of *charistike*, a kind of monastic privatisation whereby temporary ownership of and privileges over a monastery would be granted to an individual in return for the restoration or improvement of its buildings, also flourished in the eleventh and twelfth centuries; this was advantageous to the individuals, and encouraged the development of monasteries and aristocratic investment in them.

The characteristics of Byzantine spirituality developed in the monasteries can still be observed in monasteries of the Orthodox world today. This is best known in the case of the monasteries of Mount Athos, which despite the introduction of some modern technology preserve an unbroken tradition of monastic practice (together with important libraries and archives), but there has also been a continuous tradition since the Byzantine period in other monasteries, including the twelfth-century monastery of St John on the island of Patmos where the book of Revelation is traditionally believed to have been written. The monastery of St Catherine on Mount Sinai, founded by Justinian and Theodora in the sixth century, is also still very much a living community. Palestine was the site of several important monasteries in the fifth and sixth centuries,

Fig. 13   The burning bush, courtyard of the monastery of St Catherine, Mount Sinai

and a large number of monastic foundations in the Judaean desert have been identified, some of which still had monks until not long ago.[15] Having survived iconoclasm, Orthodoxy has not had a Reformation, and even modern Orthodox churches are still decorated with frescoes and icons of fourth-century Fathers of the Church such as Gregory of Nazianzus and John Chrysostom, and of Byzantine saints of all periods both male and female. From the ending of iconoclasm onwards, elaborate schemes of decoration evolved in the churches of Byzantine monastic complexes, with rows of saints, fresco or mosaic cycles of the life of the Virgin and the life of Christ, and usually the Virgin, known to Byzantines as the Theotokos, or Mother of God, in the apse and Christ Pantokrator, or Ruler of All, in the dome. The worshippers were surrounded by a comforting array of heavenly protectors, with the sense of an enclosing womb; the feeling of mystery was enhanced by the smell of incense and by impressive music and liturgy. The Syriac writer Ephraem in the late fourth century, and later writers in Syriac, composed elaborate liturgical hymns, but in Greek the highpoints in the development of Byzantine hymnography were the elaborate *kontakia*, verse homilies, of Romanos in the sixth century and the elaborate hymns and canons by eighth-century poets such as Andrew of Crete, Cosmas and John of Damascus. Many musical manuscripts survive from the later centuries of Byzantium, and these preserve a rich and complex repertoire, precursor of the 'Byzantine' chant used in contemporary Orthodox churches. A series of commentaries on the liturgy beginning in the seventh century expressed the emotional and symbolic meaning of the church and the services; these were not mere theological exercises, and as in the Orthodox tradition today, the church itself was taken as a symbol of heaven and religious belief expressed in the liturgy. It was fully in keeping with this attitude that the icons that hung on the walls and on the iconostasis (the screen in front of the sanctuary) seemed like familiar presences and were greeted by the faithful on entering the church with a bow and a kiss.

At the heart of Byzantine spirituality was the ascetic, the holy man or woman who had rejected society in order to devote him or herself to God. Again this was a development of late antiquity, beginning with the early hermits and ascetics like Antony in Egypt and Syria. The stars of Byzantine asceticism included stylites like Daniel, Symeon the Elder and Symeon the Younger, all of whom spent years living on top of pillars; equally famous were legendary women saints who were believed to have spent many years disguised as men and living as hermits. Later the style of sainthood changed to admit married women and domestic virtue; in

Fig. 14 Pillar of Symeon the Elder, stylite at Qalat Seman, Syria

a similar trend, the mothers of famous monks and ascetics were themselves presented as paragons of religious virtue. In the tenth century Luke the Younger of Stiris in Greece was the founder of the monastery of Hosios Loukas, which still stands as one of the major Byzantine monuments in Greece, and in the eleventh century St Lazaros (originally called Leo) was the founder of the monastic centre on Mount Galesion, just north of Ephesus in Asia Minor. Lazaros imitated the famous stylites of the fifth and sixth centuries by living for many years on top of a pillar, on which he also died in 1053; as often happened, the monasteries that sprang up on the mountain were the result of groups of followers collecting around the holy man and forming themselves into monastic communities; in turn these communities attracted imperial patronage from Constantine IX Monomachos.

Lazaros/Leo was the fifth child in his family and had been entrusted by his parents to a monastery at only five or six years old. He later succeeded in his ambition to travel to Jerusalem, where he spent some years at the famous monastery of St Sabas and was a witness of the destruction of the church of the Holy Sepulchre by the Caliph al-Hakim in 1009. He returned on foot to Asia Minor to avoid the persecution of Christians that was causing even some monks of St Sabas to convert to Islam.[16] The pattern whereby a holy man like Luke of Stiris or Lazaros of Mount Galesion settled in a particular place, living in a cave or on a

Fig. 15 Hosios Loukas, monastery and pilgrimage centre associated with St Luke of Stiris, Phokis, Greece

pillar, and gradually attracted a following of disciples that grew into an organised monastic community with its own rule was followed in Cyprus by St Neophytos the Recluse, whose painted cave near Paphos can even now be seen beside the still-functioning monastery (fig. 20). Neophytos was also a prolific writer and his output is discussed further in Chapter 8. In later Byzantine times monasteries were often founded by members of the aristocracy or the imperial family to house themselves, their relatives and their tombs. These too had strict rules, though it is clear that the high standards laid down by the founders were not always attained in practice, and a certain accommodation might be made for the aristocratic ladies, widows and unmarried daughters who retired to live in them. Their founders laid down elaborate rules and requirements and in both their buildings and their organisation these great monasteries were in many ways like fortified estates.

Byzantine monasteries were highly diverse. The fourth-century rule of Basil of Caesarea was important, but eastern monasteries were not organised according to particular rules or groupings as happened with the Benedictine tradition in the West, and individual monasteries had their own rules and service books. Moreover, the Byzantine monastic tradition accommodated not only large monasteries with a strongly communal life and others with looser structures but also individual holy men and ascetics. Pachomius had founded the cenobitic (communal) monastic tradition in early fourth-century Egypt, and in the fifth century the famous abbot Shenoute ruled a large monastic complex of monks and nuns at Atripe in Upper Egypt and wrote extensive rules for them in Coptic. But the eremitic tradition of solitary retreat into the desert was also strong. Monasteries might be organised as *lavras*, in which the monks lived in their own dispersed cells and came together only for the more elaborate Sunday liturgy. This was common both in Palestinian monasticism and on Mount Athos, and it can still be a stated ambition of Orthodox monks to be allowed to live in the outlying cells or *sketes* on the surrounding mountain. A tradition of contemplation and self-examination was set by early monastic writers such as Evagrius Ponticus, and major monasteries had collections of spiritual writings that were read out for the improvement of the monks or nuns. Some monastic figures also became controversial, especially in relation to Orthodox mysticism. In the tenth century Symeon the New Theologian taught that Christians could experience the divine through the uncreated light of the Transfiguration; the goal of this spiritual journey was *theosis*, or participation in the divine life. Although Symeon himself aroused opposition, his teachings represented a strain in Byzantine spirituality that can be recognised throughout its history, and which contrasted strongly with the Western concept of original sin; similarly the doctrine of purgatory was a Western idea that Byzantines included in their lists of the 'errors' of the Latins.[17] In late Byzantium the spiritual trend set by Symeon was represented by the hesychast ('quietist') movement, an ascetic style of spirituality based on inner repeated prayer, which was associated especially with Gregory Palamas the archbishop of Thessalonike. 'Hesychasm' – which was neither a movement nor a doctrine but a range of spiritual practices whose followers placed an emphasis on mystical inwardness over rationalism – had its roots in the prayer of the earliest eastern monastics, but in the fourteenth century it became a conduit for other profound divisions in intellectual and political life, and 'Palamism' was at first officially condemned and then officially approved by councils in Constantinople in the middle of the century. *Parrhesia*, 'outspokenness', was the hallmark and privilege of the awkward holy man in all periods of Byzantium. With this diversity and these individualist traditions, monks were at some periods difficult for emperors to control and were often a source of disruption. This had been especially true in the fifth century when both individual monks and groups such as the so-called Tall Brothers, four monks from Egypt who had gone to Constantinople to further their dispute with the Alexandrian patriarch, played a key role in the tensions of urban politics.

In literature, and in the inscriptions in Byzantine churches, holy men and women are called *hagios* ('holy'), which is often translated as 'saint'. However there was no formal process for canonising saints; what mattered was recognition, and this sometimes required considerable effort on the part of their supporters and biographers. The lives of saints, of which very large numbers survive, are effectively eulogies, and some are carefully constructed so as to present their subject in the most favourable light. The pattern for all subsequent hagiography was the *Life* of Antony, who died in AD 356, traditionally attributed to Athanasius, bishop of Alexandria and champion of Nicene orthodoxy.[18] Whether Athanasius was actually the author is still a matter of dispute, as are the Greek and Coptic elements in its composition; the *Life* also survives in a later translation into Syriac, in an interplay of languages that is entirely typical of the early Byzantine period. It presents Antony as a holy man and solitary, not highly educated yet able to debate with pagan philosophers, a figure of authority and charisma among the monks of Egypt, but above all a defender of Nicene orthodoxy like St Athanasius himself. During Athanasius's exiles he had had to take refuge with the monks of Egypt, and the presentation of Antony in the *Life* is deeply coloured by this set of events. The work immediately became a classic, especially in the Latin translation that was quickly made, and St Augustine writes in the *Confessions* about the important role it played in his conversion.[19] In the Byzantine Empire it was a model followed in one way or another by nearly all later hagiographers. Some lives of saints read like novels, for example the lives of Pelagia, a famous courtesan who lived for years disguised as a male monk, or Mary of Egypt, who was believed to have lived as a male hermit in the Judaean desert for forty-seven years,[20] and yet acquired an enormous devotional significance for later generations.[21] Similarly the collections of tales and sayings of the monks of the Egyptian desert, the desert fathers, again circulating in several languages, formed the basis of Orthodox spirituality throughout the Byzantine period; in later Byzantine monasteries like that of the Theotokos Evergetis in Constantinople, as in the monasteries of Mount Athos, monks would listen to readings from their own collections of extracts based on early ascetic literature. Ascetic spirituality played a major part in the consciousness of Byzantine Christians. But some saints' lives also presented highly tendentious versions of their subject, like the *Life* of St Stephen the Younger, who was imprisoned, tried and put to death by the iconoclast emperor Constantine V (741–75).[22] Hagiographers, like other religious writers, engaged in ideological battles over beliefs, personalities and religious practice.

Not all was benign about Christianity in this society in which everyone claimed to be orthodox. According to Orthodox belief the true faith is revealed gradually in response to error (heresy); the alternative view, of course, is that the successive struggles over right belief themselves determined what was to be deemed orthodoxy, that is they constituted a search for orthodoxy, not a series of challenges to an original given.[23] What is clear is that attaining right belief, whatever it might be, was taken extremely seriously. At what point this sense of orthodoxy – right belief – became Orthodoxy in the later sense is a difficult question. The Council of Chalcedon in 451 is advanced in the West as a key moment, and the West did not accept the Fifth Council in 553; however, several popes in the seventh and eighth centuries were of eastern origin themselves, and they took the side of the iconophiles during the iconoclast controversy. Nevertheless the two churches gradually grew apart and developed separate and distinct practices that differentiated them from each other, though there is ample evidence that the events of the 'Great Schism' of 1054 were not in fact regarded by contemporaries as marking a final break.[24] In the Palaiologan period several emperors were prepared to agree to union with Rome from political and military motives, and this gave rise to bitter internal disputes within the Church in Byzantium; but the Eastern Church itself had not been united even formally since the sixth century. Even in the New Testament period there were competing versions of Christianity and a very important part of the history of the Church thereafter consists in the often unsuccessful attempt to impose unity.[25] This continued throughout the Byzantine period. Already in the late fourth century heresy attracted penalties in law under the legislation of Theodosius I, and other mechanisms were also in place at various levels for controlling religious dissent. There was the possibility of the exile and deposition of bishops by emperors and punishments including mutilation could also be inflicted. In the seventh century Pope Martin I and St Maximus Confessor both died as a result of their treatment. Theodore of Stoudios was exiled more than once for opposition to the imperial line. In the early twelfth century the Emperor Alexius I Comnenus had Basil, the leader of the Bogomils, publicly burned.[26] But in contrast with the West, there was no Inquisition in Byzantium. The Byzantines were surprisingly tolerant in practice of religious minorities in their midst, and for the most part sought out heterodox individuals or groups for punishment only in the context of the policy of particular emperors. Antagonisms and rivalries within Christianity itself often tended to find expression at local level as ecclesiastical leaders, usually bishops, condemned each other, pronounced anathemas (curses and excommunications) on their opponents in synodical letters and removed or inserted names in the official diptychs (the lists of orthodox bishops). At some periods this quite frequently led to religious violence, as when under John Chrysostom, bishop of Constantinople in the late fourth century (who was twice sent into exile himself), there were scuffles in the streets and alleged arson in the city over the issue of Arianism. From the sixth century onwards the city of Antioch not infrequently had more than one bishop at a time, each claiming to be orthodox. Byzantium had inherited from the Roman Empire the assumption that religion was a matter of public policy, on which emperors were entitled to legislate. However, it was a matter of local rivalries and personal ambition, as well as private devotion and spirituality, and neither the emperor, nor, certainly, the patriarch of Constantinople, could guarantee conformity. Furthermore, while the Byzantines were good at religious polemic and hostile rhetoric against deviants of all kinds, they were not consistent or successful persecutors. Justinian and his successor Justin II failed when they attempted to force the Eastern non-Chalcedonians to conform, and Heraclius and his grandson Constans II were equally unable in the seventh century to impose Monotheletism, which like most doctrinal initiatives by emperors had started as a well-meant compromise. The Byzantines developed a fierce rhetoric for dealing with heretics, and had to deal with dualists within the empire in the form of Paulicians and Bogomils – but they were not faced with local movements of protest and opposition to the organised Church such as developed in the West in the later medieval period, and the episodes in which Bogomils were sought out in the twelfth century were an aberration.[27] It is an interesting question, therefore, whether Byzantium was really a repressive society or whether it is more a matter that it presented itself as such.[28] Magdalino invites us to compare the Church in Byzantium with the position of the established church in England or the Orthodox Church in modern Greece. Laws requiring all Jews to convert to Christianity were also passed at different times in the seventh, eighth and ninth centuries in Byzantium, and anti-Jewish writings in the name of Christian apologetic were an established form in Byzantine literature, but there is little evidence that the laws were seriously enforced.[29]

Byzantine Christianity was also exported beyond the boundaries of the empire. A succession of foreign rulers accepted Orthodox Christianity along with alliance with the empire – the kings of Lazica and the Tzani in the Caucasus in the sixth century, the kings of Axum and Ethiopia,[30] Vladimir, prince of the Rus' and the tsars of Bulgaria. In the thirteenth and fourteenth centuries Serbian rulers replicated Byzantium in their dress, liturgy and ceremonial.[31] Already in the fourth century Constantine I had written to the Shah of Iran to protest about the latter's treatment of Christians in Persia, and religion, including the position of Christians in Persia, was a constant factor in relations between the two empires, in particular during the Byzantine-Persian wars of the late sixth and early seventh centuries. Heraclius's wars are presented by his poet and publicist George of Pisidia as holy wars and in Old Testament terminology, and following Constantine's precedent in his campaigns against Licinius the Byzantines continued to think of their warfare as divinely ordained and protected, even if without the specific connotations and rewards attached to the Muslim idea of *jihad*. The importance of Orthodoxy in the histories of Greece, Russia, Bulgaria, Serbia and elsewhere is a direct result of Byzantine influence, which extended at different times to many other countries from Hungary to Albania, and the continued existence of a Greek Orthodox patriarchate in Jerusalem even today, with large numbers of Arab Palestinian Orthodox, is part of the same phenomenon. The remarkable willingness of the Byzantines to allow the development of Christianity in the vernacular in the context of its Slavonic missions met with opposition in the Catholic West, with its insistence on only three sacred languages – Latin, Greek and Hebrew – but it laid the foundations for several national churches. The patriarch in Constantinople was, of course, regarded as both senior and influential, but never took on the position of the pope, and the concept of national churches was already established in Serbia and Bulgaria well before the end of the Byzantine Empire.

In Byzantium, therefore, there was instability among the leadership of the Church, just as in the imperial succession. Bishops and patriarchs might be deposed, imprisoned or sent into exile by emperors; but equally, they engaged in rivalry with each other and some opposed the emperor. The very figures who fell foul of the imperial will, like Severus, patriarch of Antioch in the early sixth century, sometimes went on to acquire immense prestige with their own supporters; Severus himself, if unwillingly, was one of the founding fathers of the separatist anti-Chalcedonian movement.[32] There was no firmly established or centralised ecclesiastical hierarchy, and religion for the Byzantines was about much more than high politics. The ordinary Byzantine was as likely to frequent a holy man, resort to the use of amulets or pray before the domestic icons as to listen to the strictures of a bishop. It would also be a great mistake to think that every Byzantine was intensely religious. The personal lives of individuals were indeed affected by the controls of Church legislation and practice, as we shall see in the next chapter, but throughout the long history of Byzantium bishops had to work hard to keep their flocks from distraction and temptation, and the sheer energy with which they went about the task suggests that they found it an uphill task.

7

How People Lived

The city of Constantinople is eighteen miles in circumference, half towards the sea and half towards the land ... The Greeks who live there have a wealth of gold and jewels. They walk about dressed in silk, with patterns of gold sewn or embroidered on their garments. They ride their horses like princes.

Benjamin of Tudela, Jewish traveller from Spain, late twelfth century, trans. A. Sharf, *Byzantine Jewry*, p. 34

It is difficult to convey the flavour of ordinary life in a society whose surviving material is dominated by luxury items. This is as true in religious matters as in secular society; while Byzantine churches in the medieval period were often unimpressive from the outside, all were richly decorated inside with mosaics, frescoes and icons on the walls and gold and silver ornaments, and the complex Byzantine liturgy was performed by clergy in fine vestments. Surviving church treasures indicate the investment that went into ecclesiastical life, as does the *katholikon* or main church of St Catherine's monastery at the foot of Mount Sinai, which, with an uninterrupted history since the sixth century, is still in use. The *Book of Ceremonies* is full of references to magnificent objects, imperial and foreign gifts, court costumes and items used in the rituals of the imperial palace and Hagia Sophia.[1] Even the landed aristocracy of the Comnenian period still derived a significant proportion of their income from holding offices, and were thereby required to spend a considerable amount on keeping up the dress and everything else that went with the lifestyle of living in Constantinople and attending the imperial court, and in the Palaiologan period there was a similar taste for expensive display.

Nevertheless the vast majority of the population lived very differently. Saints' lives from all periods of the empire give pictures of ordinary life that are sometimes rhetorical or fanciful but that can also tell us about life at different levels of Byzantine society. Modern scholars have recognised that hagiography does far more than that, indeed that saints' lives can be highly sophisticated, and frequently controversial and biased, literary productions; far from being straightforward records they invariably have a message and sometimes multiple messages. Even so, they are often an invaluable source of information. At one extreme is the eighth-century *Life of S. Stephen the Younger*, a tendentious piece of iconophile propaganda complete with an interrogation scene in which the saint appears before the wicked iconoclast Emperor Constantine V.[2] But also referring to the eighth century the *Life of Philaretos* depicts a well-to-do provincial family in rural Paphlagonia, in northern Asia Minor, which had owned a substantial house, enough land to have on it fifty or so *proasteia*, or dependent units, and many animals and slaves. His is not an ordinary family: it was destined to produce an imperial bride, and Philaretos had lost much of this property to the greed of rival families during the upheaval of the Arab invasions. This *Life* is important for what it tells us about agrarian history in Asia Minor.[3] In an earlier period, also in Asia Minor, St Nicholas of Sion struggled to break the attachment of villagers in Lycia to tree-worship.[4] In contrast, the *Life* of St Symeon the Fool by the seventh-century Cypriot writer Leontios of Neapolis, a highly rhetorical work with a dramatic setting in sixth-century Emesa in Syria, is full of vivid details of urban life.[5]

Another early seventh-century holy man, Theodore of Sykeon in Galatia (d. 613), was born to a local girl who worked with her mother and sister in an inn on the main highway and who had slept with a customer, a former hippodrome performer then serving as an imperial courier.[6] Sykeon was attacked by the Persians in AD 622 (and is now submerged under the waters of a dam); the *Life of Theodore*, written early in the 640s by his disciple George (who says he had obtained information from Theodore's schoolfellows and contemporaries) is particularly rich in circumstantial detail and is therefore much used by historians.[7] The mothers of holy men feature prominently in such texts, and, if we are to believe the author, Theodore's mother had ambitions for her son. She prepared to send him to Constantinople at the young age of six, hoping that he could enter the imperial service; this required a gold belt and expensive clothes, which she had ready, and she was only deterred by a dream in which St George explained to her that her son was destined for God. By now the three women had gone up in the world and were leading a more respectable life: instead of offering their personal services to their customers they now employed an excellent cook and relied on their cuisine for business. The *Life* contains many other details, for instance that Theodore was able to go to school while still a child; the village was visited by plague; it had several shrines and churches as well as holy men living nearby; despite his piety Theodore wore a gold belt, necklace and bracelet as a boy; white bread, boiled and roasted fowl were among the delicacies that his family could provide. Theodore was able to travel to Jerusalem and see the holy places, and there became a monk at the monastery of the Virgin Mary at Choziba, but he returned to lead the life of a holy man at Sykeon. According to George, his mother did not appreciate spiritual matters, and married an important person at Ankyra; however, Theodore's sister became the head of a convent, also at Ankyra, and his grandmother also adopted the life of a nun. Like many of the heroes of saints' lives, Theodore adopted various ascetic practices, performed cures, cast out evil spirits and was able to guarantee good crops – for this he became famous and was in much demand from surrounding places including Ankyra, the major town in the area. His monastery grew, and he sent his archdeacon to Constantinople to buy silver vessels to replace the marble ones that they were using for the Eucharist. Some of his disciples founded monasteries of their own in different places, and Theodore and two of his monks went on a second journey to Jerusalem, where his prayers caused it to rain after a serious drought – George notes that Jerusalem was dependent for its water supply on pits and cisterns. When Theodore returned he was visited by the general Maurice and told the latter (correctly, as it turned out) that he was destined to become emperor. Theodore himself eventually became bishop of Anastasioupolis, where he intervened on behalf of the peasants who were being treated unjustly by one of the leading citizens. Theodore successfully petitioned the patriarch of Constantinople to allow him to resign his bishopric, supposedly on the intervention of Maurice, who was now on the throne, and was later summoned to Constantinople where he was entertained to dinner by the patriarch, the emperor and the senate and was honoured by all the officials of the imperial bedchamber. He was later summoned again, this time to Hieria, and again entertained by the emperor and empress after he had cured their child. He travelled to other towns in Asia Minor including Sozopolis and Amorium, and performed many miracles, including curing the children of two senatorial ladies from Ephesus. A further powerful patron was the general Domnitziolus, who had benefited from Theodore's prayers as he left for the war against Persia; so great were his gifts that the monastery was able to re-roof the church with lead tiles and acquire many treasures. Later, Domnitziolus also presented a gold processional cross made in Constantinople, which contained precious relics of Christ and the Virgin, the gift of the new patriarch of Constantinople.[8] After further visits in the reign of Phocas (592–609), during which he visited Domnitziolus, now patrician and curopalates, at his residence at Arcadianae, and caused him and his wife to be blessed with three sons, and in 612, when he cured Niketas the patrician and cousin of Heraclius, Theodore died in AD 613, the third year of the Emperor Heraclius.

From this rich text we learn all sorts of details about life in the provinces before the Arab conquests, albeit from an area on the main thoroughfare from Constantinople to the East. Holy men like Theodore interacted with every social class from slaves to emperors. Theodore became famous and extremely well connected, and maintained his prestige through four reigns that included the murder of Maurice, the usurpation by Phocas and the latter's fall and succession by Heraclius. The *Life* tells us about women,[9] about family life and about the fluid network of monasteries and holy men's cells that existed in Asia Minor. Travel was possible for pilgrims, monks, members of the upper class and military and lay officials. Rich gifts were made to churches and monasteries, some of which, like that at Sozopolis, already possessed icons.

The *Life* of Theodore of Sykeon depicts a household of strong women, with no male head, who converge to spoil and promote the one young male child in the family. The women have some choice in their lives, they are able to make a living through the proceeds of the inn, and, later, Theodore's grandmother chooses the religious life while his mother marries into a prominent family. However, she must still have a dowry, and when she dies without further children the dowry is returned to Theodore as the eldest son. His aunt leaves him her property when she dies, and Theodore also acts as head of the family when he places his twelve-year-old sister in a convent. His grandmother is praised for her care and concern for the girls who entered her convent. The general picture is of male prestige and even authority, combined with a limited degree of female independence. Households were not infrequently headed by women, and women controlled their inheritance. By the ninth century the model for Byzantine female sanctity included married women, such as St Anastasia of Aegina, from the first part of the ninth century. According to her hagiographer, she had been married twice at her parents' instigation but managed to persuade her second husband to enter a monastery so that she could do the same. She built three churches on the island during her life as an abbess, but even before that she had been notable for her piety and her charity, which the *Life* tells us even extended to heretics: 'once after a famine arose and everyone was reduced to destitution, she generously donated food not only to her fellow believers, but also compassionately distributed [food] to the so-called Athinganoi'.[10] Byzantium had several powerful empresses, including Irene, who ruled alone from 797 to 802 after engineering the blinding of her son Constantine VI, for whom she had been regent;[11] Zoe, the second daughter of Constantine VIII, had an extraordinary imperial career (1028–50), being the wife of two emperors, then ruling briefly with her sister Theodora and finally deposing Theodora and marrying Constantine IX Monomachos, in a marriage of which Michael Psellus suggests the patriarch disapproved;[12] she is depicted with her third husband, Monomachos, in a mosaic in Hagia Sophia. Despite the influence of the Church and its attempts to control morals, she and other empresses were also able to take lovers, just as some emperors had mistresses; Constantine IX's mistress Skleraina lived openly at court with Zoe's knowledge, and did not conceal her ambitions. According to Psellus, who admits that he was 'bewitched' by her conversation, there was even a formal contract that was ratified in the presence of the senate.[13] Theodora made a comeback after the death of Constantine Monomachos in 1055 and, as Psellus put it, began to behave ruthlessly and like a man.[14] Many empresses wielded power as regents if their husband died leaving a young son. One example was Eudokia Makrembolitissa, the second wife of Constantine X Doukas and mother of a large family. Feeling, in 1067, that his death was near, her husband was anxious to secure the succession for his two sons Michael and Constantius; while he was still alive Eudokia swore an elaborate oath in the presence of the patriarch, the synod and the senate never to remarry. Copies of the oath (which runs to 102 lines of Greek text) are still extant; it was signed by Eudokia herself and by the patriarch John Xiphilinos, who also swore that if she reneged on her oath he or his successors would anathematise her and remove her name from commemoration in the liturgy. Her sons were still under age and on her husband's death Eudokia reigned as if she were the emperor, though she was probably never acclaimed as such. But soon enough she did renege on her oath (from which the patriarch released her) and married a general, Romanos Diogenes. It was the same Romanos who was captured by the Turks at the battle of Manzikert a few years later, which event enabled the family of her first husband to reassert itself. Eventually the Caesar John, brother of Constantine X, proclaimed the latter's son Michael emperor and had Eudokia and her two infant sons by Romanos deposed and sent to a monastery.[15]

However, there were more forceful imperial women in the Comnenian period from 1081 onwards, in particular Anna Dalassena, the mother of Alexius Comnenus, his adopted mother Maria of Alania and his wife Irene Doukaina, who was still very young when Alexios gained power. Alexius gave his mother extensive powers while he was away on military campaign during his early years, and his daughter Anna gives a vivid picture of the relationships within the family. When Alexius died Anna hoped that her brother John could be ousted in favour of her husband Bryennios, and insists in her history on the fact that she herself was crowned before John had even been born; however, in this contest, Irene Doukaina supported her son, the scheme was foiled and Anna had to retire from public life. Comnenian and Palaiologan imperial women also founded monasteries and acted as patrons. The foundation charter of Irene Doukaina's convent of Kecharitomene explicitly ruled that after her death it would be led by her daughters, then her granddaughters and in perpetuity by the descendents of her eldest daughter, the historian Anna Comnena. Women were excluded from official positions in both state and Church, and in the books of ceremonial, while the wives of important officials are included, they take their rank and precedence, as mentioned earlier, from their husbands. But these and many other examples show Byzantine women at the top levels of society exercising both leadership and power.

Of course, imperial women were in a class apart, and the nature of the surviving evidence along with the general lack of documentary sources makes them an easier subject to study than the Byzantine family in general. In Byzantine society the nuclear family was the normal but not exclusive pattern. One would not expect a medieval society to have other than patriarchal family structures, and indeed fathers and husbands could exercise control in Byzantine families in both formal and informal ways. For instance, marriages were often arranged at a very young age, well in advance of the statutory minimum marriageable age of thirteen, as families sought to make advantageous alliances; in the Comnenian period early betrothal was used in this way by the upper classes who had most at stake. Judith Herrin has recently argued that in comparison with other medieval societies the Byzantine family 'may have had a potential for slightly more toleration', and Angeliki Laiou describes Byzantine society as one that 'looks patriarchal on the surface'.[16] There is a good deal of surviving evidence on matters of marriage and sexual relations in the writings of the jurists of the eleventh century onwards and in the eleventh- and thirteenth-century collections of legal cases. Laiou expresses well the complex relationship in Byzantine social practice between the attitudes of the Church and the civil law and the jurists:

Fig. 16 Gold marriage belt, Constantinople, late sixth to seventh century, probably a marriage gift. Dumbarton Oaks, Byzantine Photograph and Fieldwork Archives, Washington, DC

in some respects, the church was more sophisticated than the civil law, for it was willing to go beyond appearances and face the issues of internal, subjective consent or absence of consent. On the other hand it stated the fear of pollution which other sources may hint at, and at that level responsibility, intentionality, consent are less relevant. The end result is that women were less protected by ecclesiastical law than by civil law.[17]

By the time of Justinian the influence of Christianity had somewhat softened the legal position of women inherited from earlier Roman law,[18] but the ideal of Christian marriage was surprisingly slow to develop, and Church blessings were required only in the reign of Leo VI (886–912), under whom concubinage was also abolished. Splendid gold marriage belts and other jewellery from the sixth century demonstrate that marriage was a matter for rejoicing and celebration, and John Chrysostom complains of the suggestive songs sung at wedding receptions. The gold marriage belt in the Dumbarton Oaks collection combines both Christian and pagan symbols on its twenty-one small and two large medallions. Despite this evidence for the celebration attached to marriage, female saints' lives, especially in the early period, emphasise the late antique Christian ideal of sexual renunciation, and great stress continued to be laid on the desirability of celibacy. Among the familiar characters in hagiography of the earlier period are those of the young woman who becomes an ascetic to avoid an arranged marriage, or who disguises herself as a man to conceal her female sex, or the married couple who agree not to have sexual relations. Marriage is depicted as an obstacle to sanctity, and wives, like St Matrona, are presented as having to flee from their importunate husbands.[19] From the ninth century, however, an emphasis for women on Christian marriage and sexual relations can be seen in hagiographical sources and correspondingly in the increasingly maternal way in which the Virgin Mary is depicted in contemporary art. Marriage and inheritance feature prominently in Byzantine legislation from this point on. The message of the prevailing ideology was that women should stay at home, be good mothers and confine their activity to acts of pious charity.

Yet the reality was somewhat different. For example, women could inherit, and the dowry system was a protection for them. Angeliki Laiou has studied the epithalamia written for imperial and aristocratic marriages in the eleventh to thirteenth centuries, as well as funeral orations and literary sources, which even in a society of arranged marriages nevertheless dwell on the themes of conjugal love and domesticity.[20] Many non-aristocratic women also found ways of exercising influence outside the home, and at the lower levels, as in all agrarian societies, and in pre-industrial towns generally, their labour was essential. The evidence is skewed by the assumptions made in many of the contemporary sources, which tend to remove working women from view: we know about women's activity in spinning and weaving because this was part of the expected activity of a Byzantine woman, and we know about dancers and performers, who constituted a kind of counter-culture. The Virgin Mary was imagined as spinning in Byzantine art, and her spindle was one of the Marian relics in Constantinople; in the fourth century the imagery of spinning and weaving had even been applied in a homily delivered in Hagia Sophia to the conception and gestation of Christ in her womb.[21] But Byzantine women also worked in the fields, in the marketplace and in manufacturing, invested in trade and managed shops.

The presentation of Christian marriage as a positive ideal was accompanied by increased attempts by the Church to regulate it. In Roman law, and even as late as the eighth-century *Ecloga*, marriage was essentially a civil contract, but the influence of the Church gradually began to be felt, for instance in matters of divorce. A *Novel* of Leo VI (886–912) and a *Tomos* issued by the patriarch Sisinnios in 997 both recognised marriage as positive, but sought to regulate it. Imperial marriages were especially likely to cause contention. When, in the seventh century, the Emperor Heraclius married his niece Martina the marriage lasted, despite strong protests at the time, but Martina's attempt to rule after Heraclius's death in 641 led to a revolt, as a result of which she was deposed and banished to Rhodes with her tongue slit. The Emperor Leo VI contracted a fourth marriage to his mistress Zoe Karbonitsina in 906 against his own legislation but in the interests of securing the succession. His second marriage had been to another mistress, also by the name of Zoe, and he had then married a third time, against Church law and his own enactment. This fourth marriage went much further and led to a major crisis in relations between emperor and patriarch. Nevertheless, the outcome was far from predictable and in this case Zoe herself managed to rule as regent between 914 and 919/20, before she was forced to enter a convent and the marriage was anathematised. The son born to Zoe and Leo VI in 905, who had been legitimized by the notorious marriage, was to succeed eventually in coming to power as Constantine VII Porphyrogenitus (945–59), one of the most notable of Byzantine emperors. Marriage was prohibited for Christians with persons defined as Jews, heretics, clerics, guardians, rapists, adulterers or those who had been married twice or three times already. Strict rules also prohibited endogamy, and this was extended by the *Tomos* of Sisinnios, with prohibitions on marriage extending to those defined as connected to the seventh degree of consanguinity.[22] The contention on this subject in the Comnenian period between the emperor, the Church and the aristocracy is revelatory for understanding the complex and shifting interests on the part of the emperors and the Church.[23] Alexius I Comnenus ruled on several occasions on questions of marriage and betrothal, ostensibly taking a severely moral line, yet his daughter Anna's account of his seizure of power makes it quite clear how much questions of marriage alliances between powerful families now mattered. His young wife Irene Doukaina was not crowned with him – she was only crowned seven days later after the intervention of her powerful family. In the meantime the widowed Empress Maria of Alania, mother of a young son, remained in the palace, and it had been suspected that Alexius intended to try to marry her.[24] Alexius later claimed imperial 'economy' in order to bend the rules. His grandson, Manuel I, the son of a Hungarian princess, legislated to confirm the Church controls while himself intervening vigorously to control aristocratic marriages, and also promoting foreign marriage alliances and invoking Western practice as justification for legal change.[25] The self-interest of the Comnenian aristocracy, including the imperial family, tended in the direction of arranged marriages and early betrothal, and placed a great emphasis on family and family alliances, and they resorted to some ingenious expedients for evading the rules. It was also important to be able to dissolve marriages, and the jurists of the twelfth and thirteenth centuries were also much engaged with decisions on canonical and uncanonical marriages. Imperial marriage policy involved a delicate balancing act with the Church, but the Church's control of marriage continued to be asserted and, after 1204, to grow in relation to that of the emperors.

The Church also attempted to intervene in matters such as dress. Surviving textiles, mainly from Egypt, show that clothing was often decorated with patterns and even pictorial motifs. Women wore make-up and jewellery, as we see from mosaics and surviving jewels and make-up articles such as pots, jars and perfume boxes, while the condemnation heaped on this by Church fathers such as John Chrysostom and the rhetorical trope whereby fine clothes and jewels are equated with falsity and deceit that we find in many saints' lives prove just how widespread the habit was. In order for the description of female saints as truly beautiful through their unadorned virtue in opposition to worldly women decked out in fine silks, make-up and jewels to work, the latter has to have been, in fact, the common form for women wealthy enough to afford it. It is true that nudity is not a feature in Byzantine art, and dancing was condemned in Church literature, and public dancing forbidden by the Council in Trullo in the late seventh century, yet, even so, dancers continue to feature as a motif on many kinds of artefact, from textiles to ceramics, silver and ivories. In the sixth century the Empress Theodora had been a performer in the hippodrome and the law had to be changed to permit her marriage to the Caesar Justinian. Procopius makes the most of this background in his *Secret History*, but Theodora was able to rise above it and take on all that the imperial role demanded; she was even remembered as a saintly protectress in non-Chalcedonian Eastern tradition.

A fairly well-to-do family like that of Philaretos included husband and wife, children and slaves. Danelis, a widow from Patras in Greece in the ninth century, allegedly had 3,000 slaves, whom she left with all her property to Leo VI; the emperor is said to have freed them and settled them in southern Italy.[26] There are many issues surrounding this story, and the number of slaves is no doubt suspect, but the matter-of-fact way in which they are mentioned shows that domestic slaves were taken for granted. The writers of three eleventh-century wills, two of them an aristocratic husband and his widow in Constantinople, the other a lesser official, Eustathios Boilas, from Cappadocia, all list slaves among their possessions; under the terms of Boilas's will those of his slaves who had not already been freed were given their freedom and provided for with money and other gifts. The generosity of Boilas included legal marriages for his slaves, and he decreed that all male children born of his freed family servants and slaves should be 'brought up in the church of the Theotokos in the learning of the holy letters and shall be made clerics, being provided for by the church'.[27] The holy man Andrew the Fool, probably in the tenth century, was bought as a slave and then put in charge of the other slaves in his master's household.[28] Slaves had access to such rights as asylum in the Great Church, and a case in the *Peira* records a judgement in a private case brought against such a slave by the victim's family that he should be sold and his price handed over to the victim's wife. It was laid down by Alexius I Comnenus that slaves should marry in church, but that this would not bestow freedom on the couple, as had evidently been assumed by some.

As we have already seen, eunuchs were also accepted as part of the households of rich Byzantine families, a practice that went back to the late Roman use of eunuchs in official posts, especially in the imperial household. Some were bought from outside the empire, but others had been castrated by their own parents as a means to a career, even though this was forbidden by law. There was a long tradition of hostile attitudes to eunuchs in high offices in the palace, which only proves that they did achieve distinction. This hostility was strongest in the early period, especially at the end of the fourth century, particularly when the eunuch Eutropius acquired excessive power and was the subject of a devastating attack by the poet Claudian and others. But in the sixth century two eunuchs, Narses the Armenian and Solomon, were second only to Belisarius among Justinian's generals. This pattern continued to be followed. In the early ninth century a prominent eunuch was Leo the Sakellarios, a conspirator against the Empress Irene in 802, and another eunuch, Theoktistos, combined civil and military roles as the close advisor of Michael II, Theophilus and the Empress Theodora and the leader of military expeditions against the Arabs in the 840s. The role of eunuchs in the hierarchy was regularised in the ninth- and tenth-century lists of precedence, which divide court dignities and offices into those held by the 'bearded' and those held by the 'beardless', i.e. by eunuchs.[29] Some high churchmen were also eunuchs, even patriarchs, including Germanos (715–30), Niketas (766–80), perhaps Methodios (843–47) and Ignatius

(847–58, 867–78), though the latter was a special case in that he was the son of an emperor, Michael I Rangabe and had been castrated when his father was deposed in 813. It is interesting in view of the prominence given in Byzantine polemical writings against the Latins to the complaint that Latin clergy are clean-shaven to find eunuch patriarchs depicted in art as beardless.[30] Some ambivalence remained, and differing interpretations were placed on Matt.19:12 ('For there are eunuchs who have been so from birth, and there are eunuchs who have been made eunuchs by men, and there are eunuchs who have made themselves eunuchs for the sake of the kingdom of heaven')[31] and the story in Acts 8:26–40 of the eunuch servant of Queen Candace of Ethiopia who receives baptism from Philip. This ambivalence is expressed in a treatise *In Defence of Eunuchs* written by Archbishop Theophylact of Ochrid (d. after 1126), which takes the form of a discussion between a monk who puts the case against them, and a eunuch who justifies their contribution to society.[32] Eunuchs feature often in hagiography, and the conventional prejudice against them did not prevent them from being employed in Byzantine families – indeed, some came from prominent Byzantine families themselves. Eunuchs were also commonly held to be libidinous; it would be interesting to know what effect their presence had on family dynamics.

Except for the rich in their mansions in the capital, life in Byzantium was no more comfortable than it was in the medieval West. By the late sixth century, the large porticoed houses of the wealthy in the late Roman period, with their mosaic floors and internal atrium, were giving way in most parts of the empire to more modest dwellings, or were themselves being divided up for multiple occupancy. Bryan Ward-Perkins refers to this kind of change as 'the disappearance of comfort'.[33] It is recognised that in some places in the eastern provinces, for instance at Scythopolis (Bet Shean in modern Israel), urban life continued vigorously into the Umayyad period, but this was unusual even for the East. Much less is known about housing during the difficult period of the seventh and eighth centuries, but the few known churches dating from the seventh century are small and unprepossessing when compared to the large imposing edifices of the late antique period. Later Byzantine housing that has been excavated is less imposing and less architecturally refined than that of late antiquity; store-rooms and workshops were built into the complex and the ground plan is often irregular. The houses of ordinary people in the countryside were, of course, liable to be very modest indeed.

Byzantium inherited from the Roman Empire an organisation of society, culture and economy based on a network of cities – though most of

Fig. 17 Scythopolis (Bet Shean, Israel), a centre of late antique urban life until the mid-eighth century

these 'cities' were extremely small. In the sixth century Justinian founded a new city at his birthplace in Illyricum, which was known as Justiniana Prima, that, according to Procopius's description, had many of the standard characteristics of Roman cities since the High Empire, and which can be seen on ancient urban sites all over the empire, from Jerash in Jordan to Butrint in Albania: public buildings, open spaces, large dwellings, an aqueduct, baths and fountains and, by the sixth century, substantial churches.[34] Justiniana Prima is probably to be identified with the excavated site of Čaričin Grad south of Niš in Serbia. Its building was a prestige project, but the ideal of civic life expressed in its planning was already out of date, especially in the West, and its location in the heart of the Balkans is ironic, given that it is precisely in the Balkans where there is the most marked difference between the classical city model and the early medieval settlements that succeeded it, clustered round defences and ecclesiastical centres and lacking the spacious open plan of late antique cities.[35] The transformation of urban life between late antiquity and the medieval period is one of the great themes of recent scholarship.[36] Towns did not disappear in the Byzantine Empire, even in the 'early medieval depression' of the seventh to eighth centuries, but they changed their form, and, as Chapter 5 showed, the nature of the tax system needed to change in response. The reasons for the rise of a new kind of town in western Europe, and in parts of the Byzantine Empire, from the tenth or eleventh centuries are equally disputed, but the role played by trade and production in this development distinguishes it from the classical model of the city. Meanwhile villages (concentrated settlements) had become important units of organisation, though in many areas villages are more difficult to trace archaeologically than late antique cities; in Byzantium, villages became the main units for tax assessment, and even in the late period when *paroikoi*, or dependent peasants, worked large estates, the village pattern was kept.[37]

As the saints' lives demonstrate, Byzantine villages were likely to possess several shrines and churches, and monastic dwellings often grew up round a particular holy man like Theodore of Sykeon. Some of the precious gifts to these local churches have survived and their value and quality tell us about the priorities of the donors, but many of the local shrines will have been extremely modest. In the countryside the Church's influence was probably felt mainly through contact with holy men and monasteries, but bishops were important people in urban contexts. Again, for all the complications involved in using them as historical evidence, saints' lives present a picture of ordinary Byzantines of every social level

Fig. 18 Silver paten showing the Communion of the Apostles in repoussé, from Riha, Syria, AD 565–78, with an inscription in niello reading 'For the peace of the soul of Sergia (daughter) of John, and of Theodosius, and for the salvation of Megalos and Nonnous and their children'. Dumbarton Oaks, Byzantine Photograph and Fieldwork Archives, Washington, DC

going to holy men for aid with their ill-health or domestic problems, and of family members who themselves went into the religious life. What people actually believed is of course hard to say. But one area in which the Church did affect the lives of ordinary people was in terms of charity. Giving to the poor was one of the fundamentals of early Christian ethics, and this continued in Byzantium. Again, saints' lives are full of stories about the generosity of their subjects – this was Philaretos's claim to holiness and to the epithet 'the merciful' (in the sense of being generous in giving). The patriarch of Alexandria in the early seventh century, known as John the Almsgiver, from the Greek term *eleemon*, earned the epithet by building seven hospitals and feeding the refugees from the eastern provinces overrun in the Persian invasion.[38] From an early date the Byzantine world had hospitals, or, rather, hostels for travellers offering care and nursing for the sick, old people's hostels, orphanages, homes for the poor and other charitable foundations founded by rich individuals, bishops or indeed emperors. The canons of Church councils laid down such foundations and their maintenance as a religious duty, and or *philanthropia*, philanthropy, counted as an important imperial virtue.[39] Church fathers from the fourth century onwards, such as Basil of Caesarea, preached on charity and founded institutions for the poor and the sick, and emperors such as Justinian followed their example; Constantine VII Porphyrogenitus, who especially directed his attention to lepers, and Romanos Lekapenos (920–44), were only two out of the many who receive particular praise for their charitable actions. At the same time, healing was also the business of holy men, and rich and poor alike visited the many healing shrines such as those of SS Cyrus and John in Egypt, SS Cosmas and Damian, the Virgin's shrine at Pege in Constantinople, which claimed cures for many members of the imperial family and their children, or the pilgrimage site of Germia in western Galatia. In the collections of stories of miraculous cures attached to some of these shrines, a sense of competition with 'Hellenic medicine' is evident, and the superior healing power of the local saint is asserted. The saints had their own specialities, SS Cyrus and John being especially proficient at curing eye diseases, and St Artemius at Oxeia in Constantinople being recommended for diseases of the genitals. Thousands of pilgrim tokens, lamps or *ampullae*, small bottles, testify to the numbers of travellers to healing shrines. Driving out demons was another function of holy men that was much in demand to judge from the miracles recounted in hagiography. Many people also turned to magic spells and amulets, of which a large number survive. Often these amulets carried Christian images of saints or the Virgin, but amulets for women facing childbirth also refer to the evil eye, the demon Gylou, enemy of newborns, or depict the womb itself, seen as dangerous and 'wandering', as in classical medical theory. Surviving examples on papyri and other materials show that incantations and spells were used alongside Christian prayers. But were the people who bought them and used them really any more superstitious than people now who wear jewellery with lucky charms or the like?

In his book *People and Power in Byzantium*,[40] Alexander Kazhdan set out his theory of what he termed *homo byzantinus*, 'Byzantine man'. According to Kazhdan, Byzantine man was an individual without power, in a society with weak vertical and lateral social ties, confined within a nuclear family in an autocratic state. His final aim, Kazhdan says, was, 'in principle, a solitary, eremitical life, free from any form of social relationship' (p. 33). Kazhdan's bleak vision has much to do with his view of Byzantium as totalitarian and centralised, its powerless citizens 'alone and solitary in a dangerous world, naked before an incomprehensible, metaphysical authority' (p. 34), and indeed with his own experience of modern authoritarianism. Cyril Mango's view of 'Byzantine man' is also negative, at least in cultural terms: the 'average Byzantine' inhabited a world dominated by superstition, in a society whose literature appears deficient to a modern observer, and which was opposed to such pleasures as the theatre, bathing, music and dancing; his thought-world had 'the peculiar imperviousness of the medieval mind'.[41] In the qualities that Norman Baynes attributed to his 'man in the East Roman street', 'the faith of humble provincial folk' ranked foremost.[42] However, value judgements and generalisations of this kind are not a helpful way forward. A high proportion of the source material we have is normative, and therefore hard to interpret. Leaving aside some intellectuals and higher churchmen, 'Byzantine man' and 'Byzantine woman' were probably not very different from medieval people anywhere.

8

Education and Culture

I have passed over in this work many facts worthy of mention. The years have not been numbered by Olympiads or divided into seasons (as Thucydides divided his), but I have simply drawn attention to the most important facts and all the things which I have been able to recollect as I was writing this book. As I say, I am not making any attempt at the moment to investigate the special circumstances of each event. My object is rather to pursue a middle course between those who recorded the imperial acts of ancient Rome on the one hand, and our modern chroniclers on the other. I have neither aspired to the diffuseness of the former, not sought to imitate the extreme brevity of the latter; for fear that my own composition should be over-burdened, or else omit what was essential.

Michael Psellus, *Chronographia* VI.73, trans. Sewter, p. 191

Cultural histories of Byzantium are not hard to find, and come in many different guises.[1] In the case of literature, should one try to describe the works of the major authors, or the preferred literary genres, or somehow to encapsulate the 'essence' of Byzantine literature? Should artistic production be contextualised or judged in its own right? How should this complex culture be evaluated by a modern reader?[2] This chapter will concentrate on written and artistic culture, and will need to be partly descriptive, but it will also attempt to show the developments that took place over time and to confront the difficulties that scholars have found in arriving at fair judgements, or in finding appropriate methodologies.

There was a learned elite in every period of Byzantine history, although as in any pre-modern state it was always restricted and the numbers varied. Literary production of any kind required a level of education available only to the few, and, with the exception of some women of high status, mostly to men. Most of the female saints recorded in hagiography are praised only – though perhaps predictably – for their knowledge of the Scriptures and the Psalms, which they often received from their mothers at home. Elite education was dominated by the study of the technicalities of Greek rhetoric; even specialised fields such as law, philosophy and theology assumed a thorough grounding in rhetoric, which Paul Magdalino has called 'the vital lubricant for the entire machinery of government'.[3] Every educated Byzantine had been trained in the basic rules of rhetoric, established centuries before, and this had a profound effect on Byzantine literature; indeed, a very high proportion of Byzantine poets, historians and authors generally, if they were not churchmen, were themselves teachers of rhetoric. John Geometres for example, one of the best Byzantine poets, author of poems praising the Emperor Nikephoros Phokas, of outspoken criticism of his murderer and successor John Tzimiskes and of verses commenting on the civil war of 986–9, was also the author of commentaries on two classic rhetorical textbooks. Much of this training consisted of ingenious exercises on themes or classical topics, and had been preceded by 'grammar', detailed study of the ancient authors. The language of high style was itself artificial, based on the style and vocabulary of the authors studied, which was very far from the Greek actually spoken – indeed, 'imitation' (*mimesis*) was stated as an explicit aim in Byzantine education and Byzantine literature.[4] In ecclesiastical writing, too, while large quantities of pedagogic and catechetical material were produced for lay and monastic use the more ambitious works of churchmen required the same rhetorical background as secular writing. Huge numbers of Byzantine homilies, or sermons, have survived, and these have recently begun to be studied more systematically for their literary and cultural value;[5] but here too a thorough grounding in rhetoric was a prerequisite for any but the least pretentious, and the results – often far too artificial for modern taste – can be seen in examples from every period of Byzantium.

Visual art in Byzantium was not exempt from this intellectual and classicising approach. Both literary and artistic production in this society depended on patronage, and the concept of the artist was yet to develop;[6] furthermore, the relation between patron and artist is not something on which there is usually any information. Finally, Byzantine artists worked within established technical and iconographic frameworks. Byzantine icons, for example, far from arising from the personal and spontaneous inspiration of the painter, often convey a highly complex iconographic and doctrinal message. Art and literature also came together in the highly evolved literary genre of description and praise, in prose or verse, of works of art and notable buildings. *Ekphrasis*, or vivid description, was a feature inherited from classical rhetoric and taught within the Byzantine educational system. Not only was this technique used within literary works of every kind, but it also took off as a literary mode in itself. Byzantines wrote literary descriptions of religious images or buildings, especially churches, and indeed some notable buildings such as the sixth-century churches of St Polyeuktos and SS Sergius and Bacchus in Constantinople had laudatory verses inscribed on them. A famous early tenth-century *ekphrasis* by Constantine the Rhodian combined as its subject matter the seven wonders of the world and the church of the Holy Apostles. Literary *ekphraseis* complemented the classical and late antique habit of inscribing buildings and the bases of statues, and the dedicatory verse epigram continued to be an important form in Byzantium. Other literary descriptions of buildings were not inscribed but delivered orally on a celebratory occasion, like the long poem in Greek hexameters on the rebuilt Hagia Sophia by the official Paul the Silentiary, delivered in the church in the presence of Justinian in the Christmas and Epiphany season of 562–3.[7]

In the ninth century, after the ending of iconoclasm, the patriarch Photius delivered a homily containing a famous description of the restored image of the Virgin and Child in St Sophia in which he praised it for its lifelike qualities, but Byzantine ideas of realism differed from ours. In their icons, the saints were each identifiable by their special appearance or dress. In the tenth century, the abbess Irene of Chrysobalanton saw Basil of Caesarea appearing to her and recognised him from his icons, and numerous other stories told of saints appearing in dreams and being recognized in this way.[8] But so that no mistake would be made, the images of saints in Byzantine churches, whether in panel-painting, mosaic or fresco, also carried verbal identification, their names appearing alongside their figures. Even the Virgin was labelled as *Meter Theou*, the Mother of God.

On the surface, then, this was a highly structured society in which the available forms of expression were limited and mostly formal. One of the most characteristic Byzantine literary productions was the rhetorical letter, and large numbers of letter collections survive. Byzantine letters tend to be seen by modern readers as artificial, or valuable simply as sources of historical information, but they were in fact the expression of a society that valued friendship and connections, and in which the members of the intellectual elite, especially churchmen, might be living far apart.[9] The exchange of letters was another habit that flourished in late antiquity and that the Byzantines had inherited. Books are often mentioned in Byzantine letters, and were highly valued and difficult to obtain. There were no public libraries, and books were expensive, each

Fig. 19   The restored Virgin and Child in the apse of Hagia Sophia, AD 867.
Dumbarton Oaks, Byzantine Photograph and Fieldwork Archives,
Washington, DC

one having to be hand-copied. Book production depended on supplies
of parchment, which was expensive; paper, an invention believed to have
been brought from China by the Arabs, was known in the ninth
century, but it did not come into significant use until later, nor did it
displace parchment. In the eighth century, when culture was at a low
ebb, the availability of books declined sharply and there was also concern about the authenticity of evidence cited at the Church councils of
680 and 787.[10] Knowledge of secular and classical texts diminished, but
the patriarchal library in Constantinople (see Chapter 6, p. 104) held
patristic and other Christian material against which texts could be
checked, and a wider range of manuscripts began to be sought out and
copied again as culture revived from about 800. Photius (b. c.810) wrote
a work known by the title *Bibliotheca* ('Library' – not his own title) and
addressed to his brother, consisting of 280 chapters describing the many

works that he says he had read over many years. They included classical, technical and theological works, though no poetry. In many cases Photius's summaries give precious information about works now lost or preserved only in part. He also compiled a lexicon of vocabulary suitable for use by ambitious authors. In the next generation Arethas, who was to become archbishop of Caesarea (d. after 932), commissioned manuscripts, added learned notes (*scholia*) of his own and was a prolific author; we still have some of his manuscripts, including an important manuscript containing twenty-four of the dialogues of Plato and another of Aristotle's *Organon*.[11] Every monastery also needed at least a few books, and important monasteries had very significant libraries of their own. One that has survived to the present day is that of St Catherine's monastery on Sinai, knowledge of whose already rich library was greatly enhanced by the unexpected discovery during restoration work in 1975 of several thousands of hitherto unknown manuscripts or parts of manuscripts. The monastic library at John of Damascus's monastery of St Sabas near Jerusalem was still rich enough in manuscripts in the nineteenth century for antiquarian travellers to remove them in significant numbers to St Petersburg and elsewhere. A high proportion of the surviving Byzantine manuscripts, especially the most richly decorated examples, are Gospel books or psalters, but secular studies also went on even inside monasteries and convents: Anna Comnena wrote her history of her father's campaigns in the monastery of Kecharitomene where she had lived for thirty years. While living there she was at the centre of an intellectual circle interested especially in the works of Aristotle. The books collected and copied by Byzantines included large numbers of classical works, as the library of Photius shows (see above). Michael Choniates, archbishop of Athens in the twelfth century, brought his books with him from Constantinople. He was unimpressed by the cultural resources of Athens, and his correspondence often concerns exchanges or acquisitions of books; among his library were copies of works by Euclid, Galen, Thucydides and Nicander, and even the Hellenistic poet Callimachus.[12] In the twelfth and thirteenth centuries Byzantine scholars like Tzetzes and Planoudes collected and edited classical texts, and in the last half-century of Byzantium Italian collectors sought out the Greek manuscripts that had been preserved by the Byzantine bibliophile tradition, while the manuscripts taken by émigrés from Constantinople to Italy before and after 1453 played a key role in the development of humanism.[13] Some of these collectors were aristocratic women, like Theodora Raoulaina (c.1240–1300), niece of Michael VIII Palaiologos, patron of Planoudes and protégée and correspondent of the patriarch Gregory II of Cyprus.

Theodora herself copied surviving texts of Aelius Aristides' orations and Simplicius' commentary on Aristotle's *Physics* and is the author of a surviving *Life* of two ninth-century iconophile saints. Theodora was deeply involved in both ecclesiastical and secular politics. She was clearly exceptional, but other noble Byzantine women also entered convents on being widowed and continued the learned pursuits of their secular lives.

The literary interests of a limited elite are, of course, no index of general literacy, and the elite itself was small at all periods, especially in the last period of Byzantium, when, paradoxically, intellectual activity was probably at its height. The number of highly educated persons varied at different periods. In the sixth century office holders and civil servants were capable of writing the classical epigrams collected in the *Cycle* of Agathias; the literary interests of later Byzantine elites are also demonstrated by the fact that these and other poems including verse inscriptions and contemporary poems were included in the ninth-century anthology made by Constantine Cephalas and in the tenth-century Palatine Anthology, and that high-style Greek epigrams continued to be written. In the early ninth century there were even iconoclast epigrams, which evoked a response in similar vein from Theodore the Studite.[14] But in the difficult period between the Arab invasions and the revival of learning from about AD 800 few had access to the secular education that had until then been available in all the larger cities of the empire. The bulk of the population at all periods were occupied in agriculture, and the majority will have been illiterate.[15] Letter-writers and notaries are well attested in early Byzantine Egypt where the evidence is most plentiful and where in fact the level of literacy is likely to have been higher than in most Byzantine provinces then or later; exercise-books for learning Greek and Latin also survive among the papyri of this period, which show that pupils were still reading – or trying to read – Homer and Virgil. In late antiquity elementary education was widely available in towns, and the grammarian, who taught at the next level, was an important figure in all parts of the empire.[16]

Saints' lives are full of stories of young men or boys from poor and uneducated families who learned their letters when they went into monasteries. A notable example was the Cypriot St Neophytos the Recluse (d. after 1214); he learned to read and write only when he entered a monastery, but was later the author of voluminous writings that include his comments on events in the contemporary Mediterranean world. Neophytos eventually settled near Paphos and lived as a recluse in a cell he decorated himself with his own paintings. A monastery developed around him for which he wrote a *typikon* consisting of a

Fig. 20 Neophytos's cell near Paphos, Cyprus, with wall paintings by Neophytos himself

Testament and twenty canons. Some books were clearly available to Neophytos, but his library of ecclesiastical and patristic works also had some large gaps, and indeed the level of literacy could vary as much within monasteries as in the secular world; this has been shown in a study of the documents from the monasteries of Mount Athos.[17] A rather different example, also from Cyprus, is that of the future patriarch Gregory II of Constantinople (1283–89), who wrote an account of his early life as an introduction to his collected letters in which he recounts his resourceful quest for an education in Greek in Latin-ruled Cyprus. After sixty years of Latin rule no one in Nicosia could provide it and he was forced to go to 'Roman' schools where the teaching was in Latin. He eventually found his way to Nicaea and his ideal teacher in Constantinople, 'which God had given back to the Romans', in the person of George Akropolites, from whom he learned Aristotle's logic, Euclid and arithmetic. From this idyllic existence he was eventually 'dragged' into Church politics and unwillingly made patriarch; he earns our sympathy when he says that this is why he has not written much, for in such circumstances, with so many duties and demands on him, no one could possibly produce good work, and eventually he stopped.[18]

At the higher level, the Emperor Theodosius II is often credited with founding a University of Constantinople in 425. The term is misleading, and nothing like a modern university came into existence either then or later; the basis was still personal, in that students went or were sent by their families to study with individual teachers. However, Theodosius's initiative was still remarkable in that thirty-one teaching positions or 'chairs' were set up at state expense covering both Greek and Latin, and including rhetoric, philosophy and law. This made Constantinople more than competitive with the other late antique cities that had clusters of teachers, such as Athens, Alexandria and Antioch. It also indicates the high level of rhetorical education and the importance of rhetorical skill in public life in the early Byzantine period. Ambitious students would travel to find the best teachers, and a vivid picture of student life in Alexandria in the late fifth century is given in the *Life* of Severus, the controversial patriarch of Antioch, by Zacharias of Mytilene. Christian and pagan students studied together, but evidently student life could give rise to brawls and incidents between them. One of the most interesting discoveries in recent years is the group of lecture rooms at Alexandria, each seating about thirty students with a larger auditorium nearby, excavated by Polish archaeologists in the area of the modern city known as Kom el-Dikka.[19] This points to a considerable degree of organisation, or at least cooperation, between the teachers. Specialist teaching in law was to be found at Berytus (modern Beirut) and Gaza was also a centre of rhetorical education in the sixth century. At Athens, under Proclus in the fifth century and Damascius in the sixth, Neoplatonic philosophy was taught at the Academy, which traced its origins to Plato himself; archaeologists believe they have identified the site of this school on the north slope of the Areopagus. Neoplatonic philosophy was also taught, for instance, at Apamea in Syria, but Justinian's legislation against pagan teaching in 529 made its continuance untenable, and a somewhat romantic account describes how seven philosophers from Athens left the Byzantine Empire for Sasanian Persia in the hope of finding Plato's philosopher king in the young king Chosroes I, a hope in which they were disappointed.[20] However, of the seven, Simplicius, at least, continued his philosophical activity, possibly in Syria, with important commentaries on Aristotle.

Intellectual life in sixth-century Constantinople showed many signs of a society in transition. Latin was still studied, despite the complaints of John the Lydian that no one knew Latin any more. Priscian the grammarian wrote in Latin in Constantinople at this time, the Code of Justinian was issued in Latin, which was still the language of the law until Justinian started issuing his new laws in Greek (see Chapter 5), and formal imperial occasions still required speeches to be made in both Latin and Greek. Corippus, a grammarian who had come to Constantinople from North Africa, composed a long Latin poem celebrating the accession in 565 of Justinian's nephew and successor, Justin II (see Chapter 4). Justinian's attempt to win back Italy and the Western empire posed some interesting linguistic and cultural issues. Cassiodorus was among the Romans from Italy who came to Constantinople after 540, and the future pope Gregory the Great was a papal legate there in the 580s. But for someone to be skilled in 'both languages' was already a matter for comment, and Gregory protested about his own lack of skill in Greek. Procopius of Caesarea wrote about Rome and Italy as if he were a tourist, and Romanos the 'melode', author of nearly sixty surviving *kontakia* or poetic homilies delivered during the night vigil service in a church of the Theotokos in the north-east quarter of Constantinople, inserted gratuitous attacks on classical culture into his compositions. Romanos wrote in Greek, but of a vernacular kind and using a stress accent. His elaborate *kontakia* reflect on mainly New Testament themes and employ refrains in which the congregation joined. They also seem to be influenced by the themes and techniques of liturgical poetry in Syriac. The Antiochene chronicler John Malalas produced a world history starting from creation with a very unclassicising emphasis, and this was followed by many others, for instance the so-called *Chronicon Paschale,* or Easter Chronicle, which went up to AD 628 and the *Chronicle* of Theophanes produced in the early ninth century. If there was not a 'closing-in', there was certainly a more religious emphasis in late sixth-century culture. The history of Theophylact Simocatta, which covered the Byzantine-Persian wars of the late sixth century, was – as far as we know – the last high-style secular history in Greek to be written until the revival of history writing several centuries later, and the two other major historians of the late sixth century, John of Ephesus and Evagrius, both wrote histories focusing on religious affairs.[21] From the reign of Heraclius, Greek took over formally as the language of state, leaving Latin to survive in military and some ceremonial contexts, while the loss of the eastern provinces and contraction in Byzantine urbanism led to a dramatic drop in the availability of civil education.

After the very obscure period in the seventh and eighth centuries, higher education began to be available again, though now focused even more heavily than before on Constantinople. Teaching started up under imperial auspices in the Magnaura, a basilical hall on the edge of the Great Palace, and the subjects taught included philosophy, astronomy, mathematics and grammar. Some individuals in the ninth century, such as Leo the Mathematician, a student of Ptolemy and Archimedes and an inventor in his own right, who became the first head of the Magnaura school,[22] and Photius, were also clearly able to acquire an extensive education through their own initiative. Leo had evidently been giving private lessons in his house in Constantinople; called 'a truly renaissance man' by Paul Lemerle, he attracted the attention of the caliph Mamun and was metropolitan of Thessalonike from 840 to 843.[23] Ignatius the Deacon had been taught by the patriarch Tarasios (784–806), who had supported the Empress Irene at the iconophile council of 787. Michael Syncellus wrote his guide to syntax in Edessa c.811–13, before he came to Constantinople. He had been a monk of St Sabas and *synkellos,* or advisor, of the patriarch of Jerusalem, but ended his life as a monk at the Chora monastery in Constantinople. The patriarch Photius, the author of the *Bibliotheca,* had received his elementary education at a local monastery, and says that John Mavropous, to whom he owed much at a later stage, had been taught by his uncles.[24] The latter became metropolitan of Euchaita in Anatolia, and was later a monk of the Prodromos monastery in Constantinople. By the eleventh century formal provision of higher education in the capital was extended by a further imperial initiative. By a statute issued in 1046 or 1047 by the Emperor Constantine IX Monomachos new posts were established in law, rhetoric and philosophy. Mavropous's pupil Michael Psellus became 'consul of the philosophers', in which he was succeeded by his pupil John Italos. The emperor's prime aim was no doubt the training of bureaucrats, so it is striking that Psellos's friends John Xiphilinos, the new *nomophylax*, or teacher of law and head of the school, and Constantine Leichoudes, another of the circle and minister under Constantine IX Monomachos, both later became patriarchs, though Psellus typically goes out of his way to praise the latter for his combination of political and philosophical skills.[25] In 1107 Alexius I Comnenus established three posts for the teaching of the Gospels, the Epistles and the Psalter, which were all held by deacons of Hagia Sophia. There were also teachers in the twelfth century attached to other churches, including the Holy Apostles, but these seem to have been mainly concerned with what the Byzantines called 'grammar' and part of a kind of private network of schooling that existed below the official state positions.[26] Theology as such was not taught, which in itself accounts for the highly rhetorical nature of much Byzantine theological writing; but neither was philosophy taught as philosophy – indeed, one of the key questions about Byzantine philosophy in the past has been how far it was, in fact, separable from theology.

State support (which included imperial salaries and a place in the official hierarchy) and the involvement in higher education of men who held religious office are key features of the middle Byzantine system. After 1261 and the return to Constantinople from Nicaea higher education in the capital needed to be reconstituted. Michael VIII Palaiologos founded a school of philosophy under George Akropolites, but Maximos Planoudes seems to have taught in a monastic environment at the Chora and Akataleptos monasteries. As we have seen, one of Akropolites's students was another future patriarch, Gregory II of Cyprus.

At no point, however, did these initiatives resemble what was already happening in the West as universities with their own statutes, curricula and regulations began to develop in Paris, Bologna, Oxford and elsewhere. The number of pupils in Constantinople (the word 'student' gives the wrong impression) was tiny in comparison with that in the larger Western centres, and while there were regular subjects covered this was not the same as the regulated curricula such as were prescribed for Paris in the thirteenth century, and the organisation of teaching was still very much in the hands of individual intellectuals. It is not perhaps surprising that of the educated elite in late Byzantium several were churchmen or monks, like George Pachymeres and Thomas Magister, but this does not seem to have been the case with Demetrios Triklinios, the editor of

Aristophanes and the Greek tragedians, who lived in Thessalonike. Theodore Metochites, minister of Andronikos II Palaiologos, commented on Aristotle and wrote on classical literature and astronomy. He had to leave Constantinople when Andronikos was forced out in the civil war of 1328 but eventually entered the Chora monastery. Metochites built up an extensive library at the monastery and is responsible for the restoration of the church and thus for the masterpieces of fresco and mosaic which make this one of the most visited of Byzantine monuments. Metochites himself is shown wearing a dramatic turban, with saints in the dress of aristocrats.

The intellectuals of the Palaiologan period were not only philologists who collected and edited classical texts but also polymaths who studied and wrote on mathematics, astronomy, natural science and many other subjects. By the second half of the fourteenth century they were also making translations from Latin – Ovid, Boethius, the *Somnium Scipionis*, Augustine and Aquinas' *Summa*. Some now started to emigrate to Italy and to teach there, as did Manuel Chrysoloras and John Argyropoulos, who taught at Padua, Rome, Milan, Pavia and Florence. In the last half-century of Byzantium George Gennadios, the future patriarch Scholarios, taught logic and physics in Constantinople and attended the Council of Ferrara-Florence as a Unionist. The aged George Gemistos ('Plethon'), exiled to Mistra in the Peloponnese by the Emperor Manuel II, also attended the Council and gave lectures in Florence and wrote on the comparison of Aristotle and Plato, preferring the latter. It is often stated on the basis of a comment by Ficino in his preface to Plotinus that Plethon's lectures gave Cosimo de' Medici the idea of founding a Neoplatonic Academy but in fact there were a number of such learned groups.[27] Nevertheless, the comparison between Plato and Aristotle was a topic that preoccupied the intellectuals of the day, and Plethon and Scholarios engaged in a battle of words on the subject, each composing treatises against the other. Plethon's last and unfinished work, the *Laws*, based on the *Laws* of Plato, was burned after his death and after the fall of Constantinople by Scholarios, but before that others in Scholarios's circle had also joined in the controversy. Bessarion, bishop of Nicaea, a truly great intellectual of the period who had studied with Plethon at Mistra, was offered a pension by the pope and made a Roman cardinal for his services at the Council.[28] He was a Platonist like Plethon, but a comparative moderate in this controversy. Bessarion lived until 1472 and spent the rest of his life in Rome and Bologna where he compiled a great library; nearly five hundred volumes were handed over by him to Venice in 1468 and eventually became the core of the Bibliotheca Marciana.[29]

Bessarion also had a major impact on Greek studies, both personally and through his own scholarly activity. He annotated many of his manuscripts and translated Greek works into Latin, including Aristotle's *Metaphysics*. Books and translations were very important, but so were personal contacts and intellectual activity, and in the last half-century of Byzantium there was an extraordinary two-way traffic with Italy.

These men were the cream of the Byzantine intelligentsia. However, alongside the secular education system, which in one way or another maintained a learned tradition for most of Byzantium's existence, went the religious education associated with monasteries. Very little is known about the training of clergy as such before Alexius I established the three teaching posts, and much of it must have happened in monastic settings. The earliest monasteries from the fourth century onwards produced a range of monastic literature, including saints' lives and didactic texts. Monastic establishments needed liturgical texts and copies of the Scriptures. They also developed collections of their own with the readings for the liturgical year and extracts from ascetic writings for the edification of the monks.[30] Associated with the eleventh-century monastery of the Theotokos Evergetis in Constantinople, whose buildings have not survived, is a collection of such material that is currently being studied.[31] Besides both liturgical and administrative documents it had its own collections of liturgical and ascetic material; the latter is known as the *Evergetinon* and contains extracts from patristic and later writers. Several later monastic foundations took the Evergetis *typikon* as their model. The original *typikon* of c.1300 of Theodora Synadene, niece of Michael VIII Palaiologos, for her foundation of the 'Virgin of Sure Hope' in Constantinople, survives in a fourteenth-century manuscript in Oxford containing miniatures of Theodora and her large family. Among the earliest monastic texts are those associated with Pachomius and Antony, the founders of monasticism in Egypt, and the sayings and the lives of the desert fathers in Egypt were already being collected and circulating in the fifth century.[32] Also in the fifth century, Theodoret, bishop of Cyrrhus in northern Syria, wrote a series of lives of Syrian ascetics. Early monasticism crossed linguistic boundaries. There are *lives* of St Symeon the Stylite the Elder, who occupied the top of a pillar at Qalat Seman in Syria for forty years (see fig. 14), in both Greek and Syriac; one of the two Greek *lives* is by Theodoret. In late antiquity many such writings, including apocryphal literature, circulated in translations – Latin, Syriac, Georgian, Armenian and Arabic, and they sometimes survive only in a translated version. Very little is known about how such texts were used

Fig. 21   The foundation document of the convent of the Virgin of Sure Hope, portrait of Theodora (Theodoule) and her daughter Euphrosyne. Copyright Lincoln College, Oxford, Ms Gr. 35, fol. 11r.

and how they circulated, and it is clear that travellers, many of them monks themselves, played an important part in their dissemination. The same stories turn up in widely different contexts, and can only be explained by a theory of oral transmission,[33] but some saints' lives also circulated widely and were translated into different languages.

Theological works were composed in enormous quantities. Most of the leading bishops from the fourth century onwards were themselves prolific authors, turning out Scriptural commentary, exegesis, homilies, letters and theological treatises – John Chrysostom wrote two series of over seventy homilies on the Book of Genesis alone, and the manuscripts of his genuine works run into thousands. Together with the three Cappadocians, Basil of Caesarea and the two Gregorys – Gregory of Nazianzus and Basil's brother Gregory of Nyssa – Chrysostom produced an enormous corpus of writing that was fundamental for later Byzantine theology. This theological production must be included in any judgement of Byzantine literary activity. The three Cappadocian fathers were all highly educated men who could write in excellent classicising Greek, and Gregory of Nazianzus has been compared with Demosthenes for his skill as an orator; his masterpiece was his funeral oration on Basil. Homilies and saints' lives could be composed in a variety of literary registers, but many were highly rhetorical. In later Byzantium it was taken for granted that churchmen would also be authors, and, as we have seen, many of them were also classical scholars, but those who rose to be bishops in the fourth and fifth centuries were pioneers. As Peter Brown has argued, their command of a literary education, *paideia* in Greek, gave them prestige and enabled them to hold their own in the secular society of late antiquity.[34] But, in addition, their writings were staking out the ground for a Christian system of knowledge capable of matching the thought-world of classical antiquity. The synthesis produced by John of Damascus in the eighth century demonstrates how thoroughly this was achieved.[35]

The study of Byzantine philosophy on its own merits and not merely as transmitting ancient texts now lost, or as part of the history of reception, is only now beginning to be taken seriously.[36] A recent study of Theodore Metochites begins by asking 'Is there Byzantine philosophy?'[37] Philosophy could also be a dangerous activity: John Italos was condemned ostensibly for taking Plato too seriously, and the Platonic theory of forms was officially condemned in the additions that Alexius I ordered to be made to the Synodikon of Orthodoxy. Psellus' generation in the eleventh century had found ways of combining an enthusiasm for Plato with a prudent observation of limits. Psellus himself was the leading intellectual of his time, historian, philosopher, essayist, letter-writer and author of an imperially commissioned work on religious and other questions, yet he remains a puzzling and contradictory figure. His historical work, the *Chronographia*, brings a new and personal note to Byzantine historiography, with its surprisingly outspoken judgements and sharp psychological observations on imperial rulers in the late tenth and eleventh centuries, but it is difficult to discern Psellus's own philosophical or indeed religious beliefs. Psellus had a low opinion of the intransigence of the patriarch Michael Keroularios in 1054, and had to accept the habit and retire for a time to a monastery, but he was soon back, and he and his friends on the whole managed to balance their Platonism with the demands of an Orthodox society, and perhaps to convince any doubters that their study of Plato was a literary enterprise rather than something that affected their own beliefs. Under Alexius I Comnenus Psellus's pupil John Italos was specifically accused of failing to make this distinction, and the trial and condemnation of Italos for heresy in 1082 must have come as a shock, especially as Italos was in fact more of an Aristotelian than a Platonist. Nevertheless, Michael Italikos and Theodore Prodromos were keen Platonists under Alexius I's successor, and the works of Aristotle were read by many as serious objects of study, including the group around Anna Comnena. Psellus says he himself started with Plato and Aristotle and moved on to the Neoplatonists, Plotinus, Porphyry, Iamblichus and Proclus.[38] The works of Aristotle continued to be read by generations of Byzantine intellectuals. In late Byzantium a series of Church councils in the fourteenth century condemned the Aristotelian opponents of Gregory Palamas, including George Akyndinos and the intellectual and historian Nikephoros Gregoras, author of a history in thirty-seven books of the period since 1204 and of a dialogue with Barlaam of Calabria; the controversy culminated in 1351 when Palamite hesychasm was finally affirmed as official Orthodox doctrine by John VI Cantacuzene in a council held at Blachernae with a document signed in Hagia Sophia. Philosophy was always regarded as an essential part of higher education, but it led at times to deep controversy, and in any case was always in danger of being outflanked or unfavourably compared with rhetoric. It has often been held that Byzantine philosophy was unable to achieve more than a scholarly response to ancient writers, but this limited view stems from prejudice against Byzantium, and there are signs that it is changing, though the work is made more difficult by the fact that many texts are still unedited or even unpublished.

Modern judgements of Byzantine literature tend to be extremely negative. A recent verdict has called it 'humorless, boring and dogmatic', while the late German Byzantinist Paul Speck described the much-vaunted ninth-century 'revival' of letters as 'cultural suicide'.[39] It is a curious feature of the academic study of Byzantium that even notable scholars of Byzantium have gone out of their way to denigrate their subject, and judgements on its literature are particularly prone to be negative. It is not easy to deal with this prejudice given the inaccessibility of this literature to the majority of people. Hostility to Byzantine culture is longstanding. It rests on two main factors: an unfavourable comparison with classical literature, together with the assumption that this is the appropriate starting point for any assessment of Byzantine literature, and an anachronistic expectation in relation to the writing of a medieval society. Contemporary criticism finds it difficult to deal with the high value placed on rhetoric by Byzantine authors and its deep influence on their writing. Characterisations of the Byzantines as 'snobbish', based on the culture of the elite, and, to be fair, their own often expressed opinions, forget or fail to capture the functional role that intellectual life and rhetorical skill played in this society.

We can at least try to be more realistic in our assessments. High-level literature in Byzantium was the product of a society that valued rhetorical skill as an essential part of the intellectual equipment of the elite, which included high churchmen. The persistence of this ideal and the consciousness of a great intellectual past that stretched back to the classical antiquity were high among the values that enabled Byzantium to maintain itself for so long. Alongside high-style literary production went a huge output of technical writing that included treatises on military matters and diplomacy. In the tenth century Constantine VII Porphyrogenitus directed a massive encyclopaedic initiative that pulled together extracts from earlier writers and was designed to cover the whole of human knowledge. The influence of rhetoric can be felt in the openings of the *Book of Ceremonies* and the *Geoponika*, extracts dealing with agriculture, and all these works need to be approached with care as sources of information; after all, these are compilations of earlier material, not modern textbooks. Also from c.1000 comes the so-called Souda, an enormous Greek lexicon, a combination of dictionary and encyclopaedia. The Byzantines cannot be blamed for the fact that their learning was so much based on classical antiquity (though, indeed, this also presented them with some problems when it seemed to clash with the necessary profession of Orthodoxy), and it is not surprising if they felt superior in culture to their Western contemporaries.

But if literary culture was the domain of the elite, and a large percentage of the population at all periods was illiterate or at best barely literate, how was opinion formed in this medieval Christian society? It was formed in many ways: through the liturgy, through family life, through oral communication, through visual art and through preaching (though there was no organised parish system). Stories circulated and were collected, for example the stories of the miracles that were believed to have occurred at holy sites such as the shrine of St Artemius in Constantinople, SS Cyrus and John in Egypt, or the healing shrine of the Virgin of Pege ('the Source') in Constantinople. Apocryphal texts about the descent of Christ into Hades or the Dormition ('falling asleep') of the Virgin, which perhaps circulated through monastic contacts, found their way into popular consciousness. There was an efflorescence of such stories in the early Byzantine period, which existed in different versions and in several languages, and they made their way into visual art as well as literature. Another field where the imagination ran riot was the apocalyptic – prophecies and imaginative stories about the world to come. In the seventh century Christians reacted to the capture of Jerusalem by the Persians (AD 614) and its surrender to the Arabs (AD 638) with a renewed anti-Jewish literature in both Greek and Syriac that looked to an apocalyptic future in which Christianity would triumph. One of the key examples, known as the apocalypse of Pseudo-Methodius, has survived in Syriac, Greek, Latin and Old Slavonic. Different examples are the popular legends about the Emperor Constantine and his mother, Helena, or about Constantine and Pope Sylvester, which replaced actual historical knowledge about him. In the Christian imagination Constantine and his mother Helena formed a pair who were envisaged in disputation in which they defeated eminent Jews, and, together with the True Cross (whose finding was attributed to Helena), they became signs of Orthodoxy. In these stories, Constantine did not fight against his rival Maxentius but against giants called Byzas and Antes, and his victory took place in Constantinople, not in Rome. Again in the popular imagination, he was believed to have buried a full set of relics of the Passion under his column in Constantinople; the base survives until today. Some of this network of ideas is already found in the sixth-century *Chronicle* of Malalas, and can be seen again in the *Parastaseis Syntomoi Chronikai*, the compilation of notes about Constantinople dating from the late eighth century, and in the imaginative and legendary 'Lives' of Constantine that circulated when real historical knowledge of the foundation of Constantinople was at a low ebb.[40] After the ending of iconoclasm a further collection of stories developed and found its way into various written works of wonder-working icons and their exploits – hitting back at their attackers, bleeding when wounded by a Jew or a 'Saracen', or even shooting back the missile, or flying over water to escape the iconoclasts.

Even high-style Byzantine literature belonged in a context of orality and performance. Gathering in groups of friends, Byzantine intellectuals formed reading groups, and the standard way of 'publishing' a (hand-written) book was to hold oral readings. In intellectual circles patrons held semi-public book readings. Under Manuel I, during the twelfth century, oral performance was the norm, whether in the salons of members of the elite or before the imperial court or in Hagia Sophia. Patrons like Eudokia the *sebastokratorissa* gathered intellectuals round them, and for a writer a connection with such a patron was an important way to preferment, even if it also gave rise to tensions and competitive anxiety. One writer complained of the 'thousand and myriad sophists' in Constantinople vying with each other to gain the attention of patrons.[41] Speeches were also delivered, and sometimes poetry declaimed, on formal public occasions. Private or public commissions included *epitaphioi*, funeral orations, and *epithalamia*, wedding eulogies, written for members of the imperial circle and others.[42] The mention of sophists, and the fact that writers from the so-called Second Sophistic such as the second-century author Aelius Aristides were highly valued by Byzantines as rhetorical models, invite a comparison between rhetorical culture in middle and late Byzantium and in the Greek East in the early Roman Empire.[43] There are many similarities, including the high value placed on rhetoric, the self-conscious but complex reference to the past, and (at first sight, at any rate), the emphasis on performance. Some orators of the Second Sophistic were famous performers and affected a delivery that attracted crowds, and they too had their detractors. Byzantine intellectuals modelled their oratory on just these examples, but the context was very different. The focus on Constantinople in the eleventh and twelfth centuries was intense, and the patronage relations more intimate and personal, part of an aristocratic network that was in sharp contrast to the civic setting of oratory in the Greek east in the high Roman Empire.

Until the twelfth century nearly all Byzantine literature was composed in a kind of literary Greek that approximated to that used in antiquity. Some works, for instance chronicles and some saints' lives, were simpler, and lacked the pretensions of high-style compositions, but in general it was taken for granted that literary composition required a special language that had to be learned and that was equally difficult to appreciate. In the tenth century this principle was applied to saints' lives, in a massive rewriting of existing hagiography into a more acceptably 'high' style. But in the innovative literary context of the twelfth century some authors, such as Theodore Prodromos and Michael Glykas, began to use the vernacular for some of their writings. There was also a middle register, more functional than the high style but more elevated than the vernacular. To complicate matters still further, the twelfth century also saw the appearance in Greek of heroic poetry at a time when similar sagas were also appearing in the West, and there was a revival of the immensely popular romance narratives ('the Greek novel') of the Hellenistic period. The vernacular epic poem *Digenes Akrites* tells of stirring exploits on the eastern frontier of Anatolia in the period before the Byzantine defeat by the Seljuks at Manzikert.[44] Four romances also date from the twelfth century; one, *Hysmine and Hysminios*, is in prose, but the other three are in verse, in accentual iambics, in sharp contrast with the classical quantitative metre. Like *Digenes Akrites*, the fragmentary twelfth-century *Aristandros and Kallithea* by Constantine Manasses used the fifteen-syllable 'political' verse that was later to become standard. There seems to have been a gap in the thirteenth century, but more romances survive from the early fourteenth century onwards, and these are all in political verse and in the vernacular. Five were originally composed in Greek but six others were translated from Western originals in Old French or Italian. Sharp controversies surround much of this literature. Scholars disagree about the debts of the Byzantine romances to their Hellenistic originals, the influence of Western romances and the dating of individual works. The case of *Digenes Akrites* is particularly fraught, in that the 'original' version has not survived, and the two main manuscripts, one of which dates from the fifteenth century, differ substantially from each other. Similarities between the fifteenth-century E (Escorial) version and later oral poetry have suggested that the poem derives from oral 'lays', but according to Roderick Beaton the original version came into being in Constantinople early in the twelfth century as a result of a single act of literary creativity, albeit drawing on oral stories, and the two main manuscript versions each in different ways developed this 'core'.[45] The twelfth-century romances are a self-conscious revival of the Hellenistic genre, but the later vernacular examples do seem to relate to a broader background, and in some aspects reflect the world of Western chivalry translated to a Greek context. The texts, which cover a spectrum from early fourteenth-century Constantinople to mid-seventeenth century Crete, have been hailed as marking the emergence of modern Greek literature.[46]

This is to go beyond Byzantium, but the very complex and still only partly understood phenomenon that these texts represent raises important questions both about orality and about narrative fiction in relation to Byzantine literature. Why romance narratives re-emerged in the twelfth century is a question that relates to the highly innovative and creative literary environment of the time, but there was no lack of fiction or narrative as such in Byzantium. For example, while Theodora Synadene exhorted her nuns at Bebaia Elpis to read the lives of woman saints for their personal edification, fictionality had from an early date found a place in hagiography, and saints' lives covered the whole spectrum not only from the simplest to the most rhetorical but also from the more sober to the most fanciful. Fictional tales of martyrdoms in the days of persecution in the Roman Empire continued to be written when the idea of such persecution was completely anachronistic. They fulfilled a desire for stories, and especially for stories that reinforced the popular impression of the heroic past of Christianity. Such stories were written down, and some had considerable literary or intellectual pretensions. The *Life* of St Catherine of Alexandria envisaged the saint as highly born, even imperial, and as debating with pagan philosophers in Alexandria in the presence of the very Maxentius who was defeated by Constantine in AD 312. Such was the appeal of the story that at some time in or after the ninth century the monastery on Mount Sinai took her name and has retained it to this day. Martyr-acts also tended to circulate in different versions, which indicates a fluidity of the text as well as the popularity of the story.

Byzantium was a medieval society, and its literary and artistic production needs to be judged accordingly. But it was a highly unusual medieval society in that – while obviously with varying success at different times – it had a living and sophisticated literary tradition that in real ways derived directly from classical antiquity. No other medieval society could claim as much. In its heyday it also held a hegemonic position among the emerging peoples of central and eastern Europe, such as the Bulgarians, the Serbs and the Rus'. To the east, the brilliant cultural achievements of Baghdad under the Abbasid caliphate also drew on the classical and early Byzantine tradition, and there was some interconnection: according to several accounts the Emperor Theophilus appointed Leo the Mathematician to the post in the Magnaura after he had been was courted by the Caliph Mamun. A learned milieu continued to exist in Syria and Mesopotamia after the break of the Syrian Orthodox church with Constantinople and after the Arab conquest, and produced extensive literatures in Syriac and Arabic. But, in contrast with Byzantium, the Abbasid flowering did not last.[47]

From the perspective of the medieval West, Byzantium seemed exotic and, in cultural terms, intimidating, while central and eastern Europe looked to it as a model for their own literary and artistic, as well as religious, development. It was not surprising if in some Western circles, especially in the crusader period, the Byzantines acquired the reputation of being arrogant and unreliable; such a reaction betrayed an underlying suspicion of cultural inferiority that was certainly part of the response of the Latins to the intellectual and other riches of the empire. All these factors have led to an equally problematic response to Byzantine literature on the part of modern scholars. Byzantine literature has not made it into the western canon, and the emergence of a more literary approach among Byzantinists that is willing to take Byzantine writing seriously as literature is very recent;[48] only a few would now question the appropriateness of applying the techniques of modern literary criticism to the literature of classical antiquity, but this is a question still debated in relation to Byzantine literature, and its appreciation presents the problems of relative inaccessibility, an adverse comparison with the classical and a deep-seated tendency, even by the best scholars, to read it primarily as a source of information for historians. In this context the unusually large amount of literary analysis devoted to the romances of the twelfth century and later is very striking. A major factor is clearly the interest of scholars in other fields – classics, comparative literature and modern Greek – who have seized on this material and brought to it techniques developed in their own fields. In contrast, the few scholars who are attempting to develop a genuinely literary approach to other kinds of Byzantine literature are clearly not yet comfortable with what they are trying to do, and no established methodology as yet exists. We frequently encounter in the scholarly literature on Byzantium words like 'renaissance' and 'humanism' on the one hand, especially from Greek and Orthodox scholars, and on the other denials that such positive vocabulary is applicable. Against a long line of predecessors, Ihor Ševčenko, who is perhaps the most senior and distinguished Byzantinist still active today, contends that the Palaiologan literature and learning deserve neither term;[49] Paul Magdalino, one of the most intelligent Byzantine historians, concludes that while there was a potential in the twelfth century for Byzantium to equal or share in the twelfth-century renaissance that was taking place in the West in practice it fell behind; its undoubted 'flashes of style and consciousness' were insufficient to counteract its tendency to be inward-looking and esoteric;[50] Cyril

Mango, another extremely eminent scholar, is uniformly hostile to Byzantine culture.[51] What is the problem? Why does it seem to be impossible to judge Byzantum without the tendency to over-compensate or to denigrate?

Much more than the study of Byzantine literature, Byzantine art history has flourished in countries associated historically with the Byzantine religious and architectural inheritance, whose scholars often saw it as part of their own Orthodox tradition.[52] It has also been slow to emerge from a concentration on style and on patronage. Finally, the aesthetic appreciation of Byzantine art may in fact be even more difficult than that of Byzantine literature, in that many people are drawn to Byzantine icons or Byzantine churches without realising that Byzantine art and architecture were also bound by contemporary conventions and played a very specific role in Byzantine society. Byzantine art appeals on a very straightforward level as an art of beauty, luxury and spirituality, as is shown by the popularity of Byzantine exhibitions in Europe in recent years, especially icon exhibitions. A trawl through the library catalogue of Princeton University, where this book was finished, came up with forty-three catalogues of such exhibitions; but the very strength of this response demands that Byzantine art is presented in a way that makes clear that it did not only consist of icons, highly decorated and illuminated manuscripts and other precious objects. Byzantine art is an art that needs explanation, sometimes highly complex explanation, and the aptly-chosen title of Robin Cormack's book, *Writing in Gold*, of 1985, points to both these key features. More so than Byzantine literary studies, art history specialising in Byzantium is a highly developed academic field, probably the most critically aware area in Byzantine studies. In addition, and in reaction against the earlier importance placed on stylistic analysis, some of the best current work on Byzantine art history is now highly contextualised; that is, the objects of analysis are placed in a deep context of historical information. The 'art historian' has become the historian, and conversely, historians need to be far more aware of visual material if they are to do justice to the 'new Byzantine art history'. A new generation of art historians has grown up who emphasise the function of artistic production within Byzantine society, the material conditions for that production and the ways in which its messages were understood by contemporary viewers. They want to stress that Byzantine art was secular as well as religious,[53] and they are sometimes impatient of 'historians of text' who they believe have not yet caught up with these sometimes very sophisticated approaches to Byzantine culture, and some art historians correspondingly represent themselves as historians of Byzantine culture *tout court*.

Some older questions nevertheless remain important, among them that of patronage. Byzantine art is late ancient and medieval art, not produced in order to satisfy the creative urge of the individual artist, but in response to commissions. It is only with the twelfth century that artists' signatures become more common. One who did sign his work, but at the very end of our period, was Domenikos Theotokopoulos, who began as an icon painter in Crete, and was transmuted into El Greco, 'the Greek', as he later signed himself, using Greek characters, only by learning new techniques and finding new subjects in Italy and Spain. It is the patrons who are known: we know of a few Byzantine architects, such as the famous sixth-century Isidore of Miletus and Anthemius of Tralles who were the architects of Hagia Sophia, a few pieces of early silverware are signed, and the mosaicists who made the floors in synagogues and churches in the eastern provinces sometimes included their names, but the vast majority of Byzantine painters and craftsmen are anonymous.

Like Byzantium itself, Byzantine art grew out of late antique art and classical art. Byzantine art history has been a discipline of its own for generations, yet Byzantine art developed within a tension with classical art, even while transforming it. Byzantium's rich visual culture emerged from, but is different from, the rich visual culture of antiquity, while at the same time it faced the acute dilemmas of identity and reference that characterised Byzantine literature. Because of this uncertainty of identity, some objects are hard to date: the so-called Trier ivory, for example, depicting the arrival of relics in Constantinople and their imperial reception, has been placed both in the fifth century and in the ninth.[54] Even the mosaic of Theodora and Justinian at Ravenna, so well known as to be ubiquitous as a modern symbol of Byzantium, lends itself to disagreements about dating, even if within a narrower range.[55] Dating is still a key activity in Byzantine art history, though it nowadays tends to rely on a wider range of contextual evidence than style alone. Some objects, again, especially ivories, were created in a highly classicising idiom, such that the scholarly literature abounds with attempts to identify 'renaissances' or revivals. Even allowing the appropriateness of the term, these, however, depend heavily on the identification and dating of specific objects; some venerable concepts such as the 'pagan revival' in late fourth-century Rome or 'the Macedonian renaissance' of the tenth century (the former has as much or more to do with literature as with visual art) have been knocked from their pedestals by the redating or re-interpretation of central items. It does not follow, for example, that the

Fig. 22 Ivory depicting the reception of relics in Constantinople, attributed to either the fifth or the ninth century, Trier, Cathedral Treasury

owner of a classically decorated piece of ostentatious silverware was himself not a conventional Christian – he may have admired the object and the style as a sign of the contemporary good life. Later Byzantines could, equally, enjoy classical authors, or write in the classical manner, without feeling that they had to identify with the views expressed. Our own culture draws eclectically on a huge range of sources, and this was also true for some periods of Byzantium, especially in the areas most open to Sasanian, Eastern or Islamic motifs and traditions. The combination was different at different times and in different works, and the creativity of the artist lay exactly in that variation.

A central problem in Byzantine art history has been the identification of Byzantine – as distinct from classical – art, with the idea of increased spirituality, seen as both a stylistic and an interpretative feature; on this reading, icons as such the sixth-century icons of Christ, the Virgin and St Peter now at Sinai become the quintessential expression of Byzantine art and of Byzantium itself.[56] Later periods when work of such high quality was produced can then be described only in terms of revival or renaissance. Equally, the 'spiritual' quality of such works is allegedly what marks off Byzantine from classical antiquity, while, conversely, late antique as opposed to classical art has been seen as representing decline, and thus its evaluation is deeply implicated in the discussion of periodisation and the transition from antiquity to medievaldom. To place the Trier ivory, for example, in the fifth century would be to accept that foreshortening and loss of perspective were already a feature of late antique or Byzantine art. The Arch of Constantine, erected in Rome in AD 315, is a set-piece of the late antique use of *spolia* – elements from earlier monuments – that is characteristic of the late antique period, and has consequently been written off in the past as indicating decadence.[57] Yet the same Emperor Constantine adorned his new city of Constantinople with famous classical statues taken from pagan temples, and their number was vastly increased by the additions of his successors. How, then, to understand the aesthetic appreciation of those who sat in the seats of the Hippodrome in Constantinople and saw these statues crowded together on the central *spina*, or who walked past the Senate House or the Baths of Zeuxippus, both of which were also repositories of ancient statuary? The same statues, or at least those that had not been destroyed during the Nika riots of 532, were still there to be looted by the crusaders in 1204, with the horses from the façade of San Marco in Venice as a reminder of the statuary that adorned Constantinople for so many centuries.

Byzantium was an intensely self-reflexive culture, and there were also deep problems for Byzantines in religious art. According to Orthodox thinking, there could be no innovation in the depictions of divine and holy persons because their images were believed to represent them as they actually were. Byzantine writers such as John Malalas in the sixth century were also interested in physiognomy, and this is the background for a ninth/tenth century text ascribed to 'Oulpios [Ulpius] the Roman' that was in the past taken as a manual for painters. During the iconoclast period the exact manner in which the divine could or could not be represented in art was hotly debated and became the subject of highly complex theoretical discussion. Defenders of images argued that while words could lie, pictures spoke the truth. The Emperor Constantine V himself joined in the attack on images with his *Peuseis*, or 'Enquiries'. The iconoclasts argued that the Eucharist was the only true image of Christ, and in some key places, including Hagia Sophia, mosaics were destroyed and replaced with a plain cross, and religious images were condemned as an innovation. Against this it was argued that they represented genuine though unwritten tradition, equal to the written tradition contained in the Scriptures and the writings of the Fathers. The second phase of iconoclasm in the early ninth century produced a defence of images cast in Platonic terms, which debated the nature of likeness and the relation of the image to the archetype. Iconophiles such as the patriarch Nicephorus, author of several iconophile writings in the early ninth century, defended icons from the iconoclast charge that they were in fact worshipped by differentiating them from what they represented:

the notion of 'participation' that had entered the argument about the relation of image to prototype was one of likeness only, a matter of form. Icons were like their subjects, but they were not identical with them, for they were different in nature.[58]

On the face of it, the debate over images divided Byzantium, and indeed some iconophiles, including Theodore, the abbot of the Studite monastery in Constantinople, were sent into imprisonment and exile. As we saw, the *Life* of St Stephen the Younger tells the story of an iconophile martyr persecuted by the tyrant Constantine V. Bishops and churchmen found themselves faced by personal dilemmas of resistance or accommodation to an imperial policy that changed with the changing rulers over a period of more than a century, and when it was officially over in 843 the successful iconophiles set about composing an 'official' iconophile version of the controversy and its protagonists that drove out the version of the iconoclasts. If Byzantine iconoclasm was an attempted reformation it was a reformation without popular support and a reformation that failed. Some historians react by de-emphasising the role played by images and instead stress political factors,[59] and indeed a variety of different factors worked together to make the presenting issues seem so vitally important. Defeat, loss of territory, the collapse of Byzantium's urban structures, a near-fatal Arab siege of Constantinople in 717 and natural disasters all shaped the policies of Leo III and Constantine V. Much also changed during the period of more than a century during which images were debated, and the eventual 'triumph' of images had a great deal to do with the interests of key individuals. But the theological issues that lay behind the attack on religious images led by Leo III and Constantine V had already been developing during the preceding century, which helps to explain the intensity and sophistication of the debate in the eighth and ninth centuries, and this debate extended to the theory of representation, discussion of likeness and 'true image', and even the status of artists, who were accused by the iconoclasts of being no better than deceivers out for personal gain. In response the iconophiles put forward the theory that one can still hear among Orthodox icon-painters today: that it is not the artist who is responsible for the work but God Himself. A council held in 869–70, after the end of the iconoclast controversy as such, prescribed that a maker of religious images must himself be of good standing ecclesiastically:

No one is to paint in the holy churches who has been anathematized by what has been decreed, nor to teach in a similar place, until they have turned back from their deceit. Therefore, if anyone after our declaration

were to allow these in whatever manner to paint holy icons in the church
or to teach, if he is a cleric, he will endanger his rank, if he is a layman he
will be banished and deprived of the divine mysteries.[60]

The resolution of the crisis in favour of religious images had a profound effect in legitimising them to play an even more intimate role within
Byzantine society thereafter. Images were used even more often than
before to convey doctrinal messages.[61] The ending of iconoclasm also gave
them the authority of the establishment, both secular and ecclesiastical,
and meant that visual art was given an even heavier task of significa-
tion. Image did match text in importance, just as the iconophiles had
claimed. A distinct iconographic repertoire according to which saints were
immediately recognisable by their icons, and with characteristic themes
such as the Anastasis (the Resurrection, showing Christ climbing out of
Hades, leading up Adam and Eve and the prophets who had foretold
His coming) or the Hetoimasia (the 'prepared' throne for the Second
Coming of Christ) made visual art in Byzantium a complex system of
representation. Sometimes a text is inscribed on the image, mosaic or
fresco that provides the key to the intended symbolic meaning, but there
was no simple relation between the text and the image. Byzantine religious images were not flat, nor were their viewers passive. A mosaic of
Christ in the narthex of the eleventh-century church of Hosios Loukas
in Greece bears the words 'I am the light of the world: he who follows
me will not walk in darkness but will have the light of life'; the image
draws in the viewer, who is about to enter the church and so, in
the imagery also used in baptism, pass symbolically from spiritual darkness into the light of life offered in the Eucharist. On Holy Saturday,
867, the patriarch Photius delivered a homily in Hagia Sophia at the
formal inauguration of the restored mosaic of the Virgin and Child, still
to be seen high up in the apse (fig. 19). His description of the image
ascribes to it a realism that modern critics have found hard to understand; but he also sets out a theory of vision that conceives of a dynamic
relation between the image and the congregation.[62] This was a highly
intellectual exposition. But the stories that abounded after the ending of
iconoclasm about 'active icons' repelling threats from Saracens and Jews
or flying over water also express this dynamic quality, and in the late
Byzantine urban processional liturgies icons 'greeted' each other as they
passed. Going into the interior of Byzantine churches was a sensory
experience involving smell and hearing as well as vision, and worshippers responded to icons then as now by bowing down in front of them
and kissing them.

Byzantine religious art was not static. Within this field of images types developed over time, and new ones evolved, such as the cycles with scenes from the life of the Virgin, deriving from the Akathistos hymn. Depictions of the Virgin also developed over time, towards a more emotional and maternal style, though still often with a strong doctrinal content. The famous icon known as the Hodegetria ('she who shows the way', or, 'of the monastery "of the Hodegoi", those who show the way'?), was taken round the city in a regular weekly procession on Tuesdays in late Byzantium; both the icon and the processions were copied in other Orthodox milieux such as Serbia, and travellers from Russia and the West, including England, wrote their impressions of the spectacle offered by these processions and the 'usual' miracle at the church of Blachernae, home of the Virgin's garment or *maphorion*, when each Friday evening the veil before the icon of the Virgin in this church miraculously lifted. The church of the Virgin at Blachernae had been rebuilt after a serious fire in 1069, and in 1075 Michael Psellus was asked by the Emperor Michael Doukas to compose a speech commemorating a recent occasion when the unexpected movement of the veil had seemed to settle a difficult dispute. Psellus managed to draw on pagan and Neoplatonic material while praising the power of the Virgin.[63] The lifting of the veil on Fridays was interpreted as a reference to the veil of the Temple at the Crucifixion; but it was not guaranteed to happen and it was not a good omen for Alexius I Comnenus as he left the city on campaign in the difficult early years of his reign that the 'usual miracle' did not occur.[64] There was also development in other features: for example, the iconostasis or *templon*, the now-familiar screen hung with icons between the nave and sanctuary of Orthodox churches, took its form only from the twelfth century. Before that, the sanctuary was usually divided off by a more open arrangement of marble, whereas the developed wooden form of screen also encouraged a conventional arrangement of icons, with an epistyle and a crucifix above.

Byzantine art has been a touchstone for marginality; by the middle of the nineteenth century, it was judged to have succeeded or failed according to how far it could be seen as continuing the classical tradition, identified with ancient Greece. As is well known, Greece and Greek intellectuals in the nineteenth century had difficulties in coming to terms with Byzantium, and this is manifested in the interpretation of Byzantine art, constantly compared with classical art. In the nineteenth century Byzantine art was either condemned for not being like classical, or else praised as somehow exemplifying continuity with the same tradition.[65] There were problems with both these approaches in relation to the role given to Christianity and the fact that the Byzantine artistic tradition grew as much from the 'decadent' Roman Empire as from classical Greece. The case of Byzantine literature is if anything even more acute. Many scholars took as their starting point the Byzantine habit of *mimesis*, imitation of classical literature, and looked for the classical elements, causing a sharp reaction in other quarters.[66] When approached as 'literature', the same Byzantine veneration for classical models and classical writers has contributed, together with the modern privileging of everything 'European' and classical, to the devaluing of Byzantine literature itself and Byzantine culture as a whole. Byzantine literature, as the product of a period in which the 'Greek spirit' was allegedly overcome or even temporarily extinguished, no less than in the Ottoman period,[67] thus shares in a hermeneutic uncertainty that extends also to the literature of modern Greece.

9

Byzantium and Europe

For immediately as the Virgin's garment went round the walls, the barbarians gave up the siege and broke camp, while we were delivered from impending capture and were granted unexpected salvation. For the Lord looked not on our sins but on our repentance, nor did He remember our iniquities, but He looked on the affliction of our hearts, and inclined His ear to the confession of our lips.

> The patriarch Photius attributing the raising of the siege of Constantinople by the Rus' in AD 860 to the protection afforded to the city by the relic of the Virgin's robe, trans. Cyril Mango, *The Homilies of Photius, Patriarch of Constantinople* (Washington, DC, 1958), *Hom.* IV, pp. 102–3

Memories die very hard, especially in south-eastern Europe. The six hundredth anniversary of the famous battle at Kosovo Polje in 1989 raised the emotional level considerably, and memories both of this event and of the Ottoman failure to take Vienna in 1683 have been cited many times in subsequent debates about Europe. In Serbia, Albania, Hungary and no doubt in other countries in central and eastern Europe, hotels and public buildings are apt to carry lurid depictions of the heroic struggle against the Turks; the term 'occupation' is still not infrequently heard in Greece in relation to the Ottoman period. Behind this powerful memory of the Ottoman Empire on the part of its former subjects lies the role played in the formation of Europe by Byzantium. In the 1990s the idea of Europe came again to the fore, as western European countries continued – with varying degrees of enthusiasm – the effort to shape a new European entity, and central and eastern European states formerly subjected to the Eastern successor of Byzantium strove to reinvent themselves as 'European'. Even Turkey could be envisaged, though not without resistance, as joining this expanded Europe, but for the countries that see themselves as having been on the frontier, or that were in some cases for centuries ruled by the Ottomans, a Europe that embraced modern Turkey, albeit the homeland of Byzantium, would require profound mental readjustment. In this narrative, the notion of Catholic Christendom in a (western) Europe has been revived within a wider context in which it is Islam that is defined as 'Europe's primary alter';[1] at the same time a resurgence of ethnic nationalism among the new member states and the would-be member states has led at best to painful adjustments and at worst to conflict. The role, or rather the absence, of Byzantium in this debate badly needs discussion.[2]

The Byzantines knew 'Europe' either as one of the three continents of Europe, Asia and Libya (Africa) identified in classical antiquity, or alternatively as an ecclesiastical and civil province of Thrace, but not as a political idea. After the Arab conquests of the seventh century, 'Libya' fell from view and the three continents shrank to two, Europe and Asia. When the Byzantines encountered the Franks and Normans and other crusaders they regarded them as 'barbarians', or as 'Latins', for they themselves were the 'Romans'. In the meantime the continent of Europe was developing a new identity, that of Christendom, but even when Byzantium was in contest with the papacy, or defending the Adriatic coastal area against the Normans, Dyrrachium and its hinterland were seen not as part of a western Europe distinct from Byzantium but as one of the outposts of the Byzantine, that is the Roman, Empire. In the catalogue of themes in the tenth-century *De thematibus* of Constantine Porphyrogenitus the theme of Dyrrachium is one of the 'European' themes listed after Thrace, which contains 'new Rome (Constantinople), the queen of cities and of the whole world'.[3] When Alexius I became emperor, Dyrrachium was considered so crucial to security that its governors were close relatives of Alexius himself. The Byzantines were certainly conscious of the activities of the Italian city states and the critical question of who controlled Italy, as of the fundamental change in their political world when the western Europeans suddenly started to have designs on the East, but they did not formulate this change as deriving from a new and expansionist Europe of which they themselves were not a part. The position of Byzantium was, nevertheless, ambiguous; it looked in different directions at once. Rome had been the capital of an empire that extended round the entire Mediterranean. In contrast, Constantinople lay on the strait that conventionally divided 'Europe' from 'Asia', with a hinterland on the European side on which it was dependent for water and other necessities; at the same time it had a provincial territory that lay to the east and that, in the first centuries of its existence, included the whole of the coastal areas of the eastern Mediterranean.

When much of this vast area was lost during the Arab conquests Byzantium's sphere of interest turned to the north and north-east, and in the centuries that followed the attention of the emperors was always divided, and often uncomfortably so, between the Balkans, the north and the traditional Byzantine territory in Anatolia. The family of peoples over which Byzantium claimed paternal influence in its tenth-century diplomatic heyday reflected this non-Mediterranean orientation.

Yet Byzantium had been born out of a Mediterranean empire, and saw itself as the continuation of Rome. In 1463 Mehmet II, the conqueror of Constantinople, famously visited Ilium, believed to be the site of Troy, following in the footsteps of Alexander, as well as the Roman emperors Hadrian and Caracalla, and in the words he uttered there claimed Byzantium for Europe and the Ottoman Empire for Asia: 'God has reserved for me the right to avenge this city and its inhabitants . . . for their injustice to us Asiatics.'[4] When Byzantium appears at all in wider modern thinking about Europe, it is as the transmitter of classical manuscripts and classical learning, albeit itself an inferior editor of classical texts, not an instigator but a facilitator of Italian humanism, and, of course, as the parent of Russian and Slav Orthodox culture. In the prevailing narrative of European identity, 'Europe' as an idea took shape only in the late middle ages, when it succeeded the concept of Christendom. Both are Western; indeed, Christendom is often qualified as 'western Christendom'. In this narrative of Europe Byzantium is conspicuously absent.[5] In historiography about the expanding (western) Europe in the centuries after 1000, with its eastward adventures, Byzantium has usually featured as an ambivalence, less an ally than a duplicitous threat. The subtitle of Robert Bartlett's book, *The Making of Europe*, dealing with the period 950–1350, is revealing: *Conquest, Colonization and Cultural Change.*[6] The book begins with 'the expansion of Latin Christendom' and has Catholic Europe and its 'long frontier' as one of its themes. R. I. Moore takes a similar time period in *The First European Revolution, c.970–1215*, which belongs, like Peter Brown's book, in the important series entitled The Making of Europe edited by Jacques le Goff.[7] Here again we encounter Latin Christendom and Latin Europe, but while some brief comparisons are drawn with contemporary Islam, Moore accepts Paul Magdalino's analysis of Byzantium's failure in the twelfth century to develop a class comparable with the 'clerks of Latin Christendom' who, it is suggested, enabled western Europe to rise above the tribalism, dynastic ties and local loyalties that would otherwise have hindered the 'restless dynamism' of the Europeans.[8] The 'growth of the capacity to sustain city life' and the transmission of learning in

'Latin Europe's twelfth-century renaissance' are also staples of the argument. Byzantium is not explicitly linked with Islam, when the latter's divergence from this model is argued, but the implication is there.

Jacques le Goff's own contribution in the series stands in sharp contrast to this emphasis on the energetic driving force of Europe as a new factor in the period after the millennium. Le Goff's argument is that 'it was in the Middle Ages that Europe first appeared and took shape both as a reality and as a representation'.[9] This thesis is not new; as le Goff points out, it goes back to an earlier generation of medievalists, who, moreover, associated the rise of Europe with the end of the ancient world, and even if that 'end' is now interpreted as a slower process, it also recalls a large body of traditional scholarship about the 'founders of the Middle Ages' – familiar figures like Boethius, Cassiodorus, Pope Gregory the Great and Isidore of Seville. My point here is not to enter the argument about when Europe began, but rather to insist on the persistent absence of Byzantium except as an occasional hostile other, here placed on a par in that role in the early Middle Ages with Islam.[10] An essay published in Polish by Bronislaw Geremek in 1983 discusses the references to Europe in Carolingian sources, and lays more stress on the gradual process whereby Byzantium was assigned to the East; in a well-known letter of Pope Leo IV (847–55), 'Europe is made over to Rome, and, presumably, Asia is left to Byzantium'.[11] Of course, religious polemic between Rome and Constantinople is an area in which difference is stressed, and Geremek argues in general for a late dating – not the later Middle Ages but 'the first two centuries of the modern period' (p. 115) – for the permanent introduction of the notion of Europe into intellectual and social consciousness. The fall of Constantinople inspired a more inclusive view of Eastern Christianity, but also required a drawing of boundaries, with Europe in the West. For Anthony Pagden, the 'collapse' of the Byzantine Empire meant that 'Greek culture was submerged for nearly 400 years. European society, despite its continuing indebtedness to Greek science and philosophy, became predominantly a Latin one'.[12]

For Le Goff the crusades were not a colonial enterprise but an aberration. Their effect on Byzantium was certainly negative, and for the West they turned out to be a distraction that led to rivalry and dissension between the crusading states themselves; nevertheless they did widen the gap between the western and eastern, that is, Latin and Greek, Europes, and demonstrate that the future of Christendom lay in Europe, not the Middle East.[13] As for central Europe, Le Goff writes of the Christianisation of western and central Europe around the time of the

millennium, with Hungary, the Croats and the Czechs won for Roman
Catholicism against the efforts of the Byzantines to make them Orthodox. The position of Hungary was particularly critical. It became
progressively Catholic from the reign of Stephen (1000–38), but this
outcome had not been obvious to begin with and the Hungarians were
well acquainted with the Byzantines, both as invaders and potential allies. By its very position Hungary was poised between the West and the
East, and King Bela IV in the thirteenth century saw himself as occupy-
ing a frontier position in the battle between civilisation and barbarism,
represented by the eastern Tatars.[14] In the fourteenth century it was
Byzantium that needed the help of the Hungarians against the Ottomans.
But in Le Goff's narrative Byzantium itself has been not so much consigned to the East as elided, for ever overshadowed by the awareness of
its eventual conquest.

What one might term the 'Eurocentric' narrative of the formation of
Europe dominates one part of the current literature and leaves little room
for Byzantium. What, though, of the other part, in which new national
states are attempting to claim their identity by laying claim to Byzantium? The European narrative is also intertwined with that of nations
and nationalism. Current historiography on the end of classical antiquity has as one of its central themes the 'ethnogenesis' of the various
groups that settled in Europe and were transformed in some cases
into peoples with a distinct political identity. In this complex process
ethnicity, language and culture were all elements in a fluid and shifting
situation and did not necessarily map together; in this sense the backward projections by modern nations of their own history into the
early medieval past are indeed 'myths of nations'.[15] On the other hand
there are similarities between the huge literature on nations and nationalism and the debate about the idea of Europe, for while it is probably
fair to say that most writers on the subject follow the modernist and
constructivist interpretation identified with Ernest Gellner and Eric
Hobsbawm, there is considerable disagreement as to the date when
nations came into being, and indeed about what constitutes a nation,
while some writers, especially Anthony D. Smith in a long stream of
books and articles, argue that at least in some essential elements the
development began much earlier. In 1972 Dimitri Obolensky could write
of the overall prestige of Byzantium as a factor that acted as a restraint
on the 'incipient nationalism' of the emergent east European states in
the medieval period.[16] As with the literature on the development of the
idea of Europe, however, this vast debate is conducted in the main
in relation to western Europe and without reference to Byzantium or

Byzantine history.[17] One recent contribution that gives space to some, though not all, of the Balkan states with which Byzantium came into direct contact is Adrian Hastings in his Wiles lectures of 1996, published as *The Construction of Nationhood*.[18] Hastings, who is also a 'perennialist' rather than a modernist, devotes a chapter to the south Slavs, the inhabitants of Slovenia, Croatia, Herzegovina, Bosnia, Montenegro and Serbia, though not of Bulgaria or Macedonia. He places more weight on religion than many writers, including the Orthodoxy of the Serbs, but the interaction of the inhabitants of these areas with Byzantium is not seen as a major factor in their emergence during the medieval period. Hastings also lays great stress both on the existence of a widely used vernacular literature as a factor in nation-building,[19] and on religion, but here again, in making a contrast between Christianity and Islam, it is Catholicism and Reformation Protestantism, not Orthodoxy, that he has in mind.

My point is not to claim Byzantium as a proto-nation, though it did at various times have several of the elements that various contributors to the nation and nationalism debate have laid down as characteristic: shared memory, defined cultural characteristics, myths of foundation, defined territory (sometimes in theory at any rate), name and religion. The Byzantines certainly possessed self-consciousness, and while most Byzantine literature was an elite literature, one might be able to make a case for the horizontal ties of a felt shared character that Benedict Anderson insists are crucial.[20] Self-definition by reference to an Other, both internal and external, is also one of the salient characteristics of a nation that was shared by the Byzantines. It is, rather, the simple absence of Byzantium from this discussion of emergent medieval peoples that is so striking.

Islam was not the only alternative player in the medieval period. In central and eastern Europe before the arrival of the Ottomans, Catholicism and Orthodoxy were the two poles round which political loyalty revolved. Some of the attempts made by both the popes and the Byzantines to extend their influence had paradoxical results. The Byzantine 'missions to the Slavs' led by the brothers Constantine (later called Cyril) and Methodius in the ninth century coincided with the clash between the papacy and Constantinople over the appointment of Photius as patriarch and Pope Nicholas's declaration in 863 condemning Photius's election (known as the Photian schism). Both the papacy and Byzantium were conscious of the developing Slav princedoms. The Rus' attacked Constantinople in a dangerous siege in 860, in which, as in the siege by the Avars and Persians in 626, the city's survival was attributed to the active intervention of the Virgin. But Byzantium also represented potential protection, and in 862 Ratislav of Moravia asked for Byzantine help to counteract the Frankish missionaries already operating among his people. Through the creation of the first Slavonic alphabet, Glagolitic, and the translation of the Scriptures into Slavonic by Constantine, followed by the establishment of a Slavonic liturgy, Byzantium placed itself perhaps unwittingly on the side of vernacular and 'national' Christianity, in sharp contrast to the demands of the papacy. In Moravia (the modern Czech Republic and Slovakia) the Frankish influence in fact prevailed, despite a short-lived episode of support for Constantine and Methodius from the papacy. A similar situation presented itself in Bulgaria, whose prince Boris (d. 907) also had to consider the rival merits of Byzantium and the West, and in the longer term, Bulgaria can be seen as one of the clearest examples of Orthodox success. The early Bulgarian state used Greek by default for its official dealings, but Boris's Orthodox baptism in c.864, under the sponsorship of the Emperor Michael III, enabled Bulgaria to take advantage of the work of Constantine and Methodius and to develop its own vernacular liturgy using Old Church Slavonic. Boris's conversion to Orthodoxy came as a result of the prompt intervention of Caesar Bardas after Boris had made approaches to the West; it was top-down and highly political, and Boris had to put down protests from his own boyars. He nevertheless continued to look also to the papacy as he considered the organisation of the new Bulgarian church, and, in a surviving letter, the patriarch Photius wrote to him setting out the essentials of orthodoxy and heresy as decreed in the seven ecumenical councils, but also complaining of the activities of papal missionaries in Bulgaria. Boris (now known as Boris-Michael) sent legates to Constantinople in 869 and, despite the representations made by papal representatives, a council in 870 led to Bulgaria's relation with Byzantium being confirmed and Bulgaria being placed under the patriarch of Constantinople. Disciples of Constantine/ Cyril and Methodius were active in Bulgaria in the 880s, and by the 890s Church Slavonic was officially adopted for Bulgarian liturgical use. Relations deteriorated under Boris's successors, even though Symeon (tsar 893–927) had been partly educated in Constantinople. Symeon's ambitions to become emperor of the 'Greeks and Bulgarians' brought him as far as Constantinople in 913, where he was able to force the patriarch to offer him a form of crowning, and to reduce Byzantium in 914 to a willingness to pay tribute. The situation was recovered only with considerable difficulty after a Serbian defeat of the Bulgarians in 926 and the death of Symeon in 927. Like Symeon, Byzantium was drawn into the complexities of having to deal with the ambitions of the Serbs and Croats, and with the Turkic Magyars, who had emerged as a new entrant settled between the Danube and the Dnieper in the early years of Symeon's reign. In the later tenth century Tsar Samuel (d. 1014) also sought independence from Byzantium and defeated Basil II in a rout in which the Bulgarians even seized the Byzantine imperial tent and regalia. It took Basil II until 1014 to reverse this defeat, in the series of campaigns for which he has been remembered in later Byzantine and Greek mythology as the 'Bulgar-slayer'. Despite all this, the reconquest of Bulgaria and its organisation as a Byzantine province from 1018 to 1187 found Orthodoxy well established. Basil II's charters provided for the archdiocese of Ochrid, with the continuation of all the bishoprics that had previously existed under Samuel (though it is important to realise that Byzantine Bulgaria, considered at least in terms of ecclesiastical centres, stretched from Naupaktos in the south to Belgrade in the north, and from Thessalonike and Macedonia in the west to the coast of Albania, where the important route of the Via Egnatia began at Dyrrachium and Avlon). The metropolitans of Dyrrachium, Larissa and Thessalonike evidently protested, and gained ecclesiastical independence from Ochrid.[21] In about 1090, thus in the reign of Alexius I Comnenus, Theophylact Hephaistos, born in Euboea, 'master of the rhetors' in Constantinople and a pupil of Michael Psellus, was appointed to the autocephalous archbishopric of Ochrid and all the Bulgarians, a post that he apparently held until his death after 1126. The feeling of exile and the complaints of rusticity on the part of a Byzantine intellectual sent to the provinces are both personal and literary themes in his many letters, but Theophylact was more sympathetic to Slavic culture than some Bulgarian and other scholars used to maintain, nor was he the crude colonial administrator of other portrayals.[22] For all his yearning for the intellectual world of Constantinople, Theophylact seems to have done his best to respect the Slavic Christian tradition already established in his see, where Old Church Slavonic existed alongside Greek in the liturgy and Greek patristic works were translated into Slavonic. Theophylact himself seems to have been the author of the important Greek *Life* of St Clement of Ochrid, a Slav, the disciple of Constantine/Cyril and Methodius, who taught at Ochrid and preached the Gospel in Slavonic for thirty years in Macedonia.

Theophylact's correspondence includes several letters to the dukes of Dyrrachium and others, including the bishops of Corfu, Belgrade, Skopje, Prisdiana (Prizren) and Kastoria, but neither civil nor ecclesiastical administration was evenly spread or reached to all parts of this vast area. Moreover, when he became emperor in 1081 Alexius I Comnenus faced a very serious military situation on two fronts, both on the Adriatic coast and further inland. Bari had fallen to the Normans in 1071, while Hungarians and Pechenegs overran Thrace and Macedonia, revolts were raised by two duces of Dyrrachium, and Bodin the son of Michael of Duklja was proclaimed emperor of the Bulgarians at Prizren. Anna Comnena describes Alexius's defeat by the Normans at Dyrrachium in 1081 and the divided loyalties of the population in Corfu and the Adriatic towns. Venetian support for Byzantium against the Normans helped Alexius by blockading Robert Guiscard, and Dyrrachium was regained, to become a prestige post for members of the imperial family. Alexius managed to win a victory over the Pechenegs at Lebounion in 1091, but only five years later he had to face Bohemond and the First Crusade. Alexius had to juggle affairs in the west, the north and the east. Despite the oath of loyalty he had taken to Alexius in Constantinople Bohemond had taken Antioch for himself and posed a serious threat. After three years of Muslim captivity and a weakening of the crusaders' position in northern Syria in 1104 he returned to Italy to recruit more men.[23] The city of Dyrrachium, modern Durres (ancient Epidamnus), lay at the head of the Via Egnatia and was thus directly on his route back to the east. This time, however, Alexius had learned that he could not defeat the heavily-armed Norman knights in pitched battle and adopted cleverer tactics. Again he received Venetian support in the form of a naval blockade, and Bohemond sued for peace, which was agreed in the Treaty of Devol (Diabolis) on the Via Egnatia in 1108.[24] Like the Venetians, the Hungarians also needed to be secured as allies, though they themselves were in competition for influence in Dalmatia and Croatia and Byzantine concessions were necessary to both.

Illyricum had a long history of Latin influence: in the late Roman Empire it had been under the ecclesiastical jurisdiction of Rome and was transferred to Constantinople only in the eighth century. From the ninth century onwards Roman influence spread in Croatia, Dalmatia and northern Albania, with a Latin metropolitan see created at Antivari (Bar) in the eleventh century. Another of Theophylact's writings was a treatise *On the errors of the Latins*, addressed, however, not to the Catholics in Bulgaria but to an ex-pupil. The Catholic presence gradually increased alongside the Orthodox see in Dyrrachium, assisted by the settlement of Venetians and other Italians, and the Orthodox bishopric declined in influence. After 1204 much of central and southern Albania came under the influence of the Despots of Epirus, with a consequent degree of restoration of the Orthodox hierarchy, but Dyrrachium in the thirteenth century was contested by the Venetians, the Serbs and Manfred of Sicily and the Catholic presence in the north continued, especially with the arrival of the preaching orders. Dyrrachium was under the control of Venice from 1392 until 1501 when it fell to the Ottomans. In contrast with Orthodox Serbia and Bulgaria, the local leaders in Albania at the time of the Ottoman conquest were divided between Orthodox and Catholic.[25]

The future of the Serbs was also unclear at first. In the 1150s Stefan Nemanja (Desa) had ousted his brother Uroš as Grand Župan of Raška; Uroš had been formally reinstated with some pomp and ceremony by Manuel I Comnenus, but then had been replaced by Desa in 1161. However Desa proved difficult and it took three further campaigns by Manuel to deal with him, at the end of which, in 1172, he was publicly humiliated and forced to prostrate himself before Manuel. According to the Byzantine historian Cinnamus, 'he sought an audience . . . [and] came and approached the tribunal with head uncovered and arms bare to the elbow, his feet unshod; a rope haltered his neck, and a sword was in his hand. He offered himself to the emperor for whatever treatment he desired.'[26] This is nearer to vassalage than to the federal idea of Obolensky's Byzantine commonwealth. After Manuel's death in 1180 Nemanja annexed part of the Dalmatian coast, including Kotor, where the Latin church was well established. He was only defeated by Isaac Angelos in 1190, but now the Serbs were recognised with an imperial marriage between Isaac's niece and Stefan Nemanja's middle son. Stefan's son, the future St Sava, who had been a monk at the monasteries of Pantaleimon and Vatopedi on Mount Athos, returned to Serbia and his father's monastery of Studenica when Latin control was established on Mount Athos after 1204, and with his *Life* of his father established Stefan Nemanja for ever in Serbian historical memory as both monastic and Orthodox. Sava's brother Stefan (1195–27) turned away his imperial first wife, married instead the granddaughter of Enrico Dandolo the Doge of Venice, and had himself crowned king in 1217 by a papal representative. Even so, only two years later Sava was able to consolidate Serbian Orthodoxy by securing the support of the Empire of Nicaea, the rival of the Despotate of Epirus, and himself became the first archbishop of an independent Serbian church, organised with its own network of bishoprics and literature in Slavonic. This was the foundation of the Serbian Orthodox state, which under Stefan Uroš I (1243–76) and Stefan Uroš Milutin (1282–1321), and above all Stefan Uroš IV Dušan (1331–55) under whom a Serbian patriarchate was established at Peć (now in Kosovo), acted independently and sometimes in opposition to Byzantium.

But Serbia had also adopted Byzantine titles, Byzantine ceremonial and Byzantine influences in architecture and religious life. Nemanja became a monk at the Serbian monastery of Hilandar on Mount Athos, and Serbian monasteries were founded in Constantinople and Thessalonike. Stefan Uroš II Milutin, whose wife was Simonis, the daughter of Andronikos II, built the 'King's Church' at Studenica and the church of the Dormition at Gračanica in Kosovo; frescoes showed the king in full Byzantine-style regalia holding a model of his new foundation. At Gračanica, Milutin and Simonis are shown in a scene of imperial investiture, with Simonis described as 'Palaiologina, the daughter of the Emperor Andronikos Palaiologos'. Prizren, also in Kosovo, was already a bishopric and the site of a cathedral in the eleventh century, and in the thirteenth and fourteenth centuries this too was an important Serbian centre, with the monastery of the Archangels nearby and also the church of the Virgin Ljeviška, rebuilt by Milutin in the early fourteenth-century, with royal portraits of Milutin and his father in the narthex. Among the many other foundations which can be attributed to the Serbian kings of this period, the Dečani monastery is one of the most splendid, built with many Romanesque features for Stefan Uroš III Dečanski (1322–31) and Stefan Dušan (1332–55) by a Franciscan from Kotor. The church still houses the tomb of Stefan Dečanski, while as at Gračanica and Peć a fine fresco depicts the Nemanjid family tree.[27]

It is always tempting to project backwards the history of later periods, and particularly so for a period when borders (if they existed at all) were constantly changing, and in which there is so much emotional memory invested. However, the contours of Catholic and Orthodox Europe in the later medieval period were by no means predetermined, nor was Byzantium a passive recipient of Western initiatives or victim of Western ambition. By the tenth century Byzantium's claim to international prestige was manifested not only in diplomacy but also on setpiece occasions such as the marriage of Theophano, niece of John I Tzimiskes, to the German Otto II, which took place in St Peter's in Rome in 972, or the visit of Princess Olga of Rus' to Constantinople in 957, which was followed eventually by the conversion of her grandson Vladimir in 989. Vladimir was granted an imperial marriage to the sister of the Emperor Basil II in return for this very important step, which the Russian Primary Chronicle represents as a careful choice on his part after research about the merits of Islam, Roman Catholicism and the Orthodoxy represented by Byzantium. Diplomacy, visits and gift-giving always accompanied considerations of politics and imperial interest, and Byzantium's aim, set out in Constantine Porphyrogenitus' mid-tenth century treatise on the administration of the empire, was to ensure its stability and prestige as the universal imperial power, an aim in which the idea that Constantinople stood at the head of a family of nations was a powerful ideological tool. How far the rulers of the peoples concerned actually accepted the idea, as Dimitri Obolensky argued in his classic work, *The Byzantine Commonwealth*, is another matter.[28] Obolensky saw the various attacks and invasions of Byzantine territory in south-eastern Europe, including the support given in the twelfth and thirteenth centuries by Serbia and Bulgaria to Frederick Barbarossa and to Charles of Anjou, as transitory incidents in an overall situation in which the prestige of Byzantium was accepted. The two factors that were fundamental to foreign policy in Byzantine eyes, and that were generally accepted by others, were Orthodoxy and the idea of the universal sovereignty of the Byzantine emperor. As Obolensky himself argued, the height of this sense of cohesion was reached around the year 1000, after which there was indeed a great change. We might now feel that his conception of cultural diffusion plays too much to the ideas of the Byzantines themselves and see the manoeuvres of the various players in the twelfth century and later as understandable moves in a highly fluid situation in which the outcome was far from clear. However, the aims set out in the preface to the *De administrando imperio*, namely the provision of advice on the relation of the various foreign peoples to the empire, how to use them, and the nature of the appropriate diplomatic gifts in each case, were never forgotten. As for the claim of universalism, even in the fourteenth and fifteenth centuries, when actual power was weak or non-existent, the patriarchate in Constantinople continued to insist in its dealings with Bulgaria and Russia on the universalism of the Byzantine church and even of the empire. But Byzantium was also capable in other periods of defending its interests by force, as Alexius I Comnenus showed. Byzantium also played a major role in state-formation. The twelfth and especially the thirteenth centuries presented a complex and different series of challenges in the Balkans, in which there was competition not only between Byzantium, the emergent states and pressure from the West, whether from the papacy, the Normans, the Venetians, Manfred of Sicily, or from Anjou, but also between the peoples of central and eastern Europe themselves. Here, therefore, Byzantium was a player in a far more complicated set of rivalries. Between 1204 and 1261 Byzantium itself was fragmented, yet the Laskarid government based at Nicaea still involved itself in south-east Europe, and, despite the rivalry between them, the Despotate of Epirus also kept a strong Byzantine influence alive. The Adriatic coast was critical, and the important outpost of Dyrrachium survived the invasion of the Mongols in 1241, who plundered Dalmatia and some of the towns in northern Albania, only to change hands between Michael II of Epirus, John III Doukas Vatatzes of Nicaea and Manfred of Sicily, and subsequently Charles of Anjou. Manfred was a short-lived though dangerous player in this competition, allied first to Nicaea through the marriage of his sister to John III Vatatzes, then to Epirus through his own marriage to Helena the daughter of Michael II, by which his control of the coastal areas that he had already seized was confirmed; his influence ended, however, when he was killed in 1266 at Benevento in battle against Charles of Anjou. In this difficult period of rivalries and uncertainty, the Byzantine influence was still felt.

Byzantium's role in the formation of medieval Europe is undeniable. For Obolensky, this consisted above all of the Orthodox tradition.[29] The 'post-Byzantine' legacy is clearly visible both in Orthodox countries and in those that had a partial experience of Byzantium in church architecture and religious artefacts, and in the monastic and spiritual influence above all of Mount Athos, which has enjoyed a revival since the 1990s, but also of Meteora in Thessaly and of many monastic centres in the Balkans. Byzantine culture also survives both at 'high' levels and as part of folk-culture. Byzantine influence did not end with the fall of Constantinople. Indeed, 1453 was not the end of the story, since Ottoman control came later in other places while Ottoman architecture also drew on many Byzantine elements; the place given to the Orthodox church under Ottoman rule, and the loss of Byzantine political and civil structures meant that churches and monasteries continued to function and even to flourish as the repositories of Orthodox identity. The sense of unbroken continuity with the past in Orthodox church decoration, with its depictions of the early Church Fathers, was reinforced during the Ottoman period as local churches, for example on the Greek islands, continued to be rebuilt and repainted as the need arose with similar iconographic schemes. For all the complex issues of conversion and Islamicisation, for the Orthodox populations identification with the local church or monastery, whether in villages or in larger centres, was a crucial part of their consciousness. The influence of Byzantium was not limited to religious life or religious architecture, or folk customs, but was also a matter of political structures, which imitated the monarchical pattern of Byzantium but arguably without the various checks and intellectual challenges that were present in Byzantium itself. When the Orthodox states of southeastern Europe were subsumed into the Ottoman Empire the possibility for such a development was closed off, leading to the permanent identification of Byzantium with absolutism on the one hand and Orthodox spirituality on the other. The negativity that surrounds the idea of Byzantium is especially evident in the modern discourse of 'balkanism', and the idea of 'byzantinism', or 'byzantinismus' plays an important part among the negative characteristics that mark out the Balkans from 'Europe' and 'the West'.[30] Byzantium is also associated with the perceived absolutism of the East, especially Russia, and often enough with totalitarianism. This set of ideas lies behind the attempt in the 1980s associated with an essay published in Italian by Milan Kundera in 1984, and a book by the Hungarian scholar J. Szúcs, to claim a Central European identity looking to the West rather than the East.[31] Hungary, which was conquered by the Ottomans as late as 1526 and ruled by them for a century and a half, which had also been part of the history of Byzantium and had been poised for a time between Orthodoxy and Catholicism, thus distanced itself from the East. The East meant both Russia and Byzantium and was seen as backward, centralised, illiberal and autocratic rather than sharing the Western virtues of freedom and civil society. Inserting a third, central element, was a defensive move, which fed off an existing stereotype of Byzantium so deep-rooted that it has been embraced by Byzantinists themselves – not only Byzantinists and others fresh from the Soviet system, such as Alexander Kazhdan or the medievalist Aaron Gurevich,[32] but also the 'Western' scholars who denigrate Byzantium as unoriginal, unenlightened and repressive.

In this discourse, an elision between 'Byzantine' and 'Ottoman' is another important factor, the latter also cast in the role of the 'East' and of 'decline'. Sometimes this comes dangerously close to an identification of Orthodoxy, or even 'Slavic Orthodoxy' with this sense of backwardness, a partaker in the binary opposition between Christianity and Islam. But the alternative narrative of the 'Turkish yoke' presents for Orthodox countries, nowhere more acutely than in Greece, the dilemma of their own relation to the Byzantine past. In their re-invention of themselves as the heirs of Pericles and their desire to purify and Hellenise their most iconic monument the inhabitants of the backward Ottoman village that was early nineteenth-century Athens tore down all the later accretions from the Acropolis and exposed the Parthenon as it had probably never been seen before. Under the Ottomans the Parthenon had housed a mosque, but the return to classical purity also expunged all traces of the church of the Theotokos into which the temple had been transformed in the Byzantine period and which was a place of sanctity and even pilgrimage.[33]

The story of the difficult reception of the Byzantine past in the new Greek state in the nineteenth century has often been told. Against the

Enlightenment ideas with which the idea of Greek independence had been invested Byzantium seemed to belong to a tradition of darkness and medievaldom, and to be dangerously associated, especially through the Church, with Ottoman rule, or the so-called *Tourkokratia* – even though, paradoxically, Mount Athos, of all places, had been home to an Athonite Academy that was part of the Greek Enlightenment. Questions of Greek identity were of burning importance, and Jakob Fallmerayer's notorious challenge to this identity in his emphasis on the extent of Slavic settlement in the early Middle Ages, which seemed to impugn the reputation of Greece in the Byzantine period, provoked an intensely nationalist assertion of ethnic and cultural continuity.[34] The erasure of Byzantium in favour of the classical past, however, left an uncomfortable gap in Greek history, and a different strand in the nineteenth century claimed Byzantium for a conception of the past that was at once nationalist and Orthodox. Just as other Balkan countries had their memories of national struggle against the Ottomans, so the Greeks had 1453. An article written in 1987 described the fall of Constantinople (known in modern Turkey as 'the conquest of Istanbul') as 'a national trauma, a calamity that annihilated Greek culture, prevented Greek participation in the western Renaissance and plunged the country into cultural and economic poverty'.[35] The ignominious failure in the early twentieth century of the 'Great Idea' of regaining Constantinople was a crushing blow that placed further challenges in the way of an objective view of Byzantium. At the same time the emergence of modern Turkey presented acute problems of understanding, especially for a state whose own boundaries were established only as a result of a series of late nineteenth- and twentieth-century conflicts. As a self-consciously European and 'western' state, albeit with its own Muslim minority, and bordered by a number of countries with substantial Muslim populations, and with a future that seemed unpredictable after the removal of federal Yugoslavia, in the late twentieth century the place occupied by Greece in the debates about European identity became a highly sensitive issue. A concomitant revival of Orthodoxy in Greece, the Balkans and Russia does nothing to alleviate these tensions.

Finally, the consideration of Byzantium in relation to Europe raises the question of Orientalism. It is true that the discourse of Orientalism is at heart constructed around a binary opposition of East and West, and crucially between the West and Islam, whereas the Other of south-eastern Europe is also a matter of boundaries within Christianity.[36] In the case of Byzantium, however, we are dealing with an entity that, even if viewed only geographically, was part of the history of the East as well as of Europe. Byzantium thus both partakes in the debates about Europe and is a victim of Orientalist associations with backwardness, exoticism and autocracy. If Byzantine art is seen as belonging in the Orientalist sphere this is also because, in contrast with classicist readings of Byzantine literature, it has not been seen as classical. This takes us back both to the difficult question of how to interpret Byzantine art and to the question of periodisation: when, and why, is it justifiable to start to speak of 'Byzantium' rather than of the later Roman Empire or simply late antiquity? An important part of the explanation for the slow development of Byzantine studies as an academic discipline is the prestigious position held by classical studies in most Western European countries, which was reinforced by the classicism and romantic Hellenism of the eighteenth century. Byzantium might stand for mysterious ruins, but not for civilisation. Only in the last decades of the nineteenth century did Byzantine studies emerge as an academic discipline, and even now it is far less well established than the study of classical antiquity. In academic terms, Byzantium still exists on the margins. As far as the question of Byzantium and Europe is concerned the role of Greece is therefore a paradox at several levels, not least because Greece, precisely because it is seen as the very birthplace of European culture, and thus the seat of the values held most dear, is also the place where the legacy of Byzantium is most contentious.

10

Byzantium and the Mediterranean

> The Mediterranean is both a zone of easy lateral transmission of ideas and a barrier which promotes divisions between cultural systems
> Horden and Purcell, *The Corrupting Sea*

The world of late antiquity, from the late third to the seventh century, was a Mediterranean world. Rome ceased to be the political capital of the empire in the third century when emperors found themselves out on the battlefield and in constant danger of military usurpation. Nevertheless, after some order had been restored by the fourth century, Rome remained the centre of tradition and culture, while the western court settled at Milan or Ravenna. Constantine's refoundation of the classical polis of Byzantion was not, as is often imagined, a drastic move of the empire to the east, and even the so-called division of the empire into two halves in AD 395 did not change the essential unity of Roman culture across the Mediterranean. Constantinople grew steadily in size and influence, but in the sixth century Justinian still thought in terms of a united Mediterranean empire of which Constantinople would truly be the capital. Even the Arab conquests of the seventh century did less than might have been supposed – and less than has often been assumed – to change the Mediterranean culture of the time. Byzantium's sphere over the centuries encompassed both the north–south and the east–west axes,[1] and while in later centuries it looked to the north and to Europe, its relations with the Mediterranean world did not cease.

Especially with the publication of Peregrine Horden and Nicholas Purcell's *The Corrupting Sea*, the concept of Mediterranean history has attracted renewed attention.[2] Their book de-emphasised towns, and stressed the roles of continuities in relation to 'connectivity', ecology and natural history, production and exchange. The purpose of this chapter is to emphasise the ways in which the Byzantines, at different times in their history, also belonged to, and acted in, this Mediterranean sphere. What constitutes 'the Mediterranean world' is one of the issues raised by Horden and Purcell's book: only the coastal strip, or the hinterland on a more generous definition? And what about the Adriatic, centre of much Byzantine attention in the Comnenian and later periods? Whatever view one takes, the Byzantines constitute a presence that must be included in Mediterranean history. Their relations with the Arabs and the Muslim world are an important part of that story, as are their dealings with the crusaders and their religious rivalries with the Latins, and they seem to exemplify the statement at the head of this chapter particularly well. If they fit less well the claim in *The Corrupting Sea* of shared 'Mediterranean' values based on honour and shame, the time and energy spent by the Byzantines on promoting their religious system nevertheless give some credence to Horden and Purcell's idea of Mediterranean connectivity through shared monotheistic systems.[3]

Most of the long-distance trade and carrying of goods across the Mediterranean between Constantinople, North Africa, Egypt and the prosperous eastern provinces of Syria and Palestine that was such a feature of the late antique period came to an end with the cessation of the tax in grain in the early seventh century and the first Arab conquests, particularly once the Arabs built a fleet and were thus able to move further west. They attacked Cyprus in 649, took Egypt in 641, won a crushing naval victory off the coast of Lycia in 655, took Rhodes, Chios and Cyzikos in 654 and 670 and built the new Arab city of Kairouan in North Africa in 662. Their naval victory in 655 led to a treaty with Constans II under which the Byzantines had to pay a large tribute to Mu'awiya. The Arabs also invaded Asia Minor on an annual basis, and their naval success enabled them to mount a dangerous siege of Constantinople in 674 that the Byzantines were only just able to repel. Heraclius's retreat from Syria after the defeat at the River Yarmuk in 636 opened the way for the Arabs in Palestine, Syria, Armenia and western Anatolia. Nevertheless Michael McCormick has shown that travel across the Mediterranean, including pilgrimage to the Holy Land, continued even in the later seventh century,[4] and the important archaeological work done at many sites in Israel, Jordan and Syria often shows, as, for example, at Scythopolis/Bet Shean in northern Israel and Dehès in Syria, that the local economy continued to flourish and that in such centres the Arab conquest as such left little or no archaeological trace. In local terms in this very important swathe of the eastern Mediterranean the mid-eighth century was more important than the early to mid-seventh as a time of fundamental change. It was the fall of the Umayyads and the building of Baghdad in Iraq as the new Abbasid capital that dealt a blow to the infrastructure that the Umayyads had maintained and thereby caused the economic downturn. Much has been made in the past of the disaffection of the non-Chalcedonians in the eastern provinces as a factor that led to the Arab success, and it is true that the separation of the Miaphysites, or Jacobites, also known as the Syrian Orthodox, took place in the sixth and seventh centuries. Heraclius was attempting to settle differences with the Armenians even as he was on campaign against the Persians in the early seventh century, and his own solution to the Christological differences actually alienated the Chalcedonian bishops in Palestine and the East even as the first Arab forces crossed into Syria. These divisions were serious: the Jacobites succeeded in setting up an alternative church with its own hierarchy, liturgy, literature and traditions and a similar division in Egypt on the eve of the Arab invasion had the result that the Coptic church, which continued to exist under Arab rule, was also non-Chalcedonian. But there is no good evidence that the conquests were actually assisted by disaffected Eastern Christians, and contemporaries were more interested in putting the blame, if any, onto the Jews, just as they had blamed the Jews in Palestine for helping the Persians to conquer its cities and sack Jerusalem in 614.

The Byzantine influence continued in the eastern Mediterranean under the Umayyads, both because the latter adopted much of the existing administrative structure and because they continued to use Greek until the end of the seventh century. Anastasius, a Cypriot monk from St Catherine's monastery on Sinai, travelled round Palestine in the later seventh century and observed the building of a mosque on the Temple Mount in Jerusalem and other signs of the new order, but at first the Muslims were a small minority, some of whom lived in new settlements rather than in existing cities, and conversion to Islam in Syria and Palestine was not encouraged. It was the eventual decline of the urban centres, hastened by the eastward move of the Caliphate to Baghdad, that provided the conditions that favoured conversion. We are ill-informed about Byzantine North Africa in the later seventh century, but Carthage did not fall to the Arabs until the very end of the century and recent research has made it clear that Christianity continued even though the conditions for Islamicisation were more favourable than in Syria and Palestine. The continued existence of monasteries such as St Sabas near Jerusalem, St Theodosius in the Judaean desert and St Catherine's on Mount Sinai was an important factor in maintaining Byzantine influence. At the same time, the composition of the monastic body and the languages used at both monasteries became much more mixed. A substantial body of Christian writings in Greek began to be translated into Arabic, and John of Damascus's disciple Theodore Abu Qurra wrote in both languages. The patriarchate of Jerusalem also continued, and still retains its Greek ecclesiastical identity today even though the vast majority of Palestinian Orthodox are Arab. Its patriarchs often lived in Constantinople during the centuries immediately following the Arab conquest, but a Greek–Byzantine church was maintained until a Latin patriarch was appointed in the crusader state. The seventh-century invasions of Palestine also had the effect of spreading Byzantine influence westwards, and Greek-speaking monks and clergy, including Sophronius the later patriarch of Jerusalem, and Maximus Confessor, fled to Egypt, North Africa and Sicily under the pressure of the Persian invasion; this had a lasting impact on the Greek culture of Sicily and south Italy. During the seventh and eighth centuries and into the ninth, when letters in Constantinople were at a low ebb, it was Greek writers from Palestine who kept the tradition alive and in some cases migrated to Constantinople; although the evidence of damaged mosaic floors in churches seems to show that there was a local Christian iconoclast movement in Palestine in the eighth century alongside the iconoclast policies of Caliph Yazid II,[5] not only John of Damascus but also other iconophiles such as Michael Syncellus, George Syncellus and the two brothers known as the Grapti ('written-upon') because they were branded for their devotion to icons, all came from Palestine.

There is surprisingly little evidence that the Byzantines were conscious of Islam as a new religion. The Persian sack of Jerusalem and capture of the True Cross in 614, and their occupation of Syria, Palestine and Egypt, gave rise to apocalyptic hopes of liberation among the Jewish population of the region and to a Greek literature of atrocities in which the Jews were cast as the traitors who had assisted the invaders. Heraclius's successful campaign against the Persians led to the collapse of the Sasanian Empire and a triumphant re-entry into Jerusalem in 630. This extraordinary sequence of events stimulated several examples in Greek and Syriac of literary dialogues between Christians and Jews, the Jews always with the losing role. The so-called *Doctrina Jacobi*, the 'Teaching of Jacob the newly-baptized', is one of the most interesting and most circumstantial of these; it is also the earliest in the sequence, dating from the late 630s, which was not only the time of the first appearance of the Arabs in Syria but also of a harsh Byzantine reaction against Jews that took the form for the first time of an imperial decree that all Jews must be baptised. Jacob, the dialogue's main interlocutor, is a converted Jew who comes from a world of Jewish traders operating between the coastal cities of Palestine, Carthage and Constantinople. Jacob has dimly heard of a new prophet among the Saracens – as had Maximus Confessor in Carthage, from whom we have a surviving letter mentioning the fact. But the focus in this literature, which continues in the seventh and eighth centuries, is on the Jews. In the later seventh century Anastasius of Sinai is the first Greek writer to refer (though very briefly) to the beliefs of the Arabs. A letter supposedly from the Emperor Leo III to the Caliph Umar II (717–20) recorded by an Armenian historian would, if genuine, be the earliest Byzantine refutation of Islam, but is likely to belong to a later date.[6] John of Damascus, writing in the middle of the eighth century, knew Islam in the form of a Christian heresy, a candidate for an additional chapter at the end of his long catalogue of earlier heresies.[7] The chapter seems to show an acquaintance with elements in the Quran as well as with oral ethnographic material, but the knowledge displayed is extremely limited, and the same reference to a pre-Islamic Meccan cult of Aphrodite appears in the work of the patriarch Germanos of Constantinople and in the *De administrando imperio* of Constantine Porphyrogenitus. In the late seventh century, as the reality of Muslim rule began to be realised and the Caliphate adopted a less benign policy towards its Christian population, apocalyptic texts also flourished, prophesying a last emperor who would establish the Christian dispensation at the end of time. Eventually there were Byzantine attempts to defend Orthodoxy and refute the teachings of the Quran by Niketas in the early ninth century and much later, in the thirteenth century, by Bartholomew of Edessa, and later still by the Emperor John Cantacuzene.[8] Islam was still treated on the model of Christian heresies; accordingly there were formulae to be followed in the case of the reception back into the Orthodox faith of those who had converted to Islam. The great theologian and metropolitan of Thessalonike, Gregory Palamas, was a member of a party captured in March 1454 by the Turks near Gallipoli, and after unsuccessful attempts by his captors to extract a large ransom for so important a person he spent a whole year in Turkish captivity. He too was drawn into discussion and disputes about the merits of Christianity versus Islam, but his own account of his experiences reveals something of the interplay of the Ottomans in Bursa and Nicaea with the Christian population that still lived in the area (in Nicaea clustering round the monastery of Hyakinthos with its church in which the apse mosaic of the Virgin had been obliterated during Iconoclasm and subsequently restored).[9] But the Arab conquests and the rise of Islam did not give rise to any serious Byzantine attempts to analyse the new religion.

By the end of the seventh century the Umayyad state began to take a more aggressive line towards the Christian population of Syria. The

Fig. 23 Jerusalem, with the Dome of the Rock in the foreground

Dome of the Rock in Jerusalem, built by Caliph Abd al-Malik in 692, drew heavily on Byzantine precedent and used Byzantine craftsmen, but was deliberately sited on the Temple Mount and carried a mosaic inscription with Quranic verses directed against Christians. Christians were forbidden to display crosses, the existing coinage, which imitated Byzantine models, was replaced and Arabic was substituted for Greek as the language of administration. The Arab presence in the Mediterranean also now reached further west; the term 'pirates' is often used in connection with Arab activity at sea, but this fails to give a broad enough impression. Three Arab sieges of Constantinople, in 669, 674–78 and 717–18 were enough to cause serious alarm to its population. During the eighth and ninth centuries Byzantium was not in a position to mount a serious counter-attack, and in 806 Harun al-Rashid reached as far west as Heracleia. Palermo in Sicily fell to Arabs from Spain in 831 and they invaded southern Italy and took Taranto in 839. When Crete fell in the 820s it became an important Arab naval base and Arabs frequently feature in the Byzantine sources as raiders, especially on the Aegean islands. The *Life* of St Theoktiste of Lesbos tells of a female solitary who was taken prisoner by Arab raiders on Lesbos but managed to escape when the ship made a stop on the island of Paros. The *Life* is told by a certain Niketas Magistros who claims to have met the saint while he himself was en route to Crete in the reign of Leo VI (886–912) on a mission in the company of the Byzantine admiral Himerios to the Arab authorities there. While on Paros Niketas is told that the commander of the Arabs on Crete had tried to take away the ciborium from the church on Paros and use it in a mosque.[10] Another female saint, Theodora of Thessalonike (812–92), found her way to Thessalonike with her husband and father when her brother was killed in an Arab attack on the island of Aegina; according to this *Life* Aegina was deserted as a result of the raids, although this may be an exaggeration, to judge from the *Life* of St Athanasia of Aegina.[11] The grandparents of St Luke of Stiris, the founder of the monastery of Hosios Loukas, had fled Arab raids on Aegina and Phocis and settled at Itea near Delphi, and Arab raids are often mentioned on the Greek coast, the islands and Mount Athos in the ninth and tenth centuries; later, according to his *Life*, Luke himself prophesied that Crete would be recovered from the Arabs, which came to pass in 961.[12] The Arab capture of Crete, and the siege and capture of Amorium, the capital of the Anatolikon theme, on the border of Galatia and Phrygia, in 838 followed an episode when the caliphate gave substantial assistance to a Byzantine rebel, Thomas the Slav, who was for a time successful in gaining control in Asia Minor and even briefly besieging Constantinople in 821. Byzantine officers and officials captured by the Arabs at Amorium were taken to Samarra and eventually put to death; they became known as the 'forty-two martyrs of Amorium' and their hagiographer has them debating the superiority of Christianity over Islam while they were held in prison before finally being executed on the banks of the Euphrates.

The enslavement of prisoners was practised by all parties and this presented many commercial opportunities, with the additional element in the case of Christian prisoners taken by the Arabs of possible issues of conversion.[13] Consciousness of these contemporary realities lies behind many references to the Arabs by Byzantine writers, and as well as references in historical sources to such attacks there were hagiographical accounts of the massacre of monks of St Sabas and of the 'sixty martyrs' of Jerusalem in 724.[14] But there were also more peaceful contacts, for instance the story that the Caliph al-Mamun tried to attract the learned Leo the Mathematician to Baghdad; the future patriarch Photius while still a secular official was also sent on an embassy there, and Constantine/Cyril, who brought Christianity to the Slavs, was an envoy to Samarra in about 850. The correspondence of Photius's nephew, the patriarch Nicholas Mystikos, includes a letter to the caliph in which he mentions a mosque available to Arab prisoners in Constantinople: he complains of false rumours that the 'Saracen house of prayer' had been closed, and assures the caliph that Arab prisoners of the Byzantines are given full freedom of worship and are not required to convert; the caliph should therefore put an end to the bad treatment of Byzantine prisoners by the Arabs.[15] The mosque is attested in both Byzantine and Arabic sources, and was rebuilt or replaced in 1201 and again after being destroyed in 1204. In the context of the Ottoman siege of 1398 Bayezid demanded that a Muslim judge be appointed for Muslim workers in the city. A few Byzantine intellectuals learned Arabic, for instance Symeon Seth from Antioch in the reign of Alexius I, who could translate Arabic stories into Greek, but a different impression is given by the practice of parading Arab prisoners in Constantinople in imperial triumphs and bringing them into imperial banquets at Easter still wearing their chains.[16]

The effects of Arab control in Sicily and the establishment of Arab rule in Egypt, North Africa and Spain moved the focus of attention to the central Mediterranean and the defence of Greece and south Italy from the theme of Cephallonia. Despite the Byzantine losses and Arab sea-raids the Byzantine themes in south Italy were not given up, though, as the Normans were to find, the culture of Sicily was permanently marked by the Arab presence. The Byzantines were lucky that, for whatever reason, there was in fact no Arab attempt at more thorough-going conquest in Italy. In the East the decline of the Abbasid caliphate in the tenth century gave Byzantium the chance of reasserting itself, and the general John Kourkouas achieved the surrender of Melitene in 934. He then had to return to Constantinople to face and defeat the Rus'. Saif ad-Dawla, the Hamdanid emir of Aleppo, was now a problem, but in 944 John took Amida, Dara and Nisibis on the old Persian frontier, besieged Edessa and regained the Mandylion, on which it was believed that Christ's face was imprinted. As noted above, this was received back into Constantinople with great pomp and circumstance.[17] In 961 Crete was finally recovered from the Arabs, and Cyprus in 965; Antioch and Aleppo were taken in 968 by Nikephoros II Phokas (963–9) and northern Syria brought under Byzantine control, while under his murderer and successor John I Tzimiskes (969–76) the Byzantines recovered Damascus, Tiberias and Caesarea and almost reached Jerusalem. Both emperors adopted an aggressive policy towards Muslims in the Holy Land. It was an extraordinary reversal of their losses to the Arabs three centuries before.

Despite the insecurity caused by Arab raids, Mediterranean sea-trade by no means ceased, though its type and its commodities changed. The sea-routes become better known to us with the entry of Venice into the European orbit in the eighth century, and it is clear that Arab shipping, which was very active in the ninth and tenth centuries between Tunisia, Libya, Egypt and Sicily, brought new opportunities for trade, including Eastern imports into Europe and above all the slave trade. If c.700 was the nadir of Mediterranean trade, with the initial Arab invasions and the drastic downturn and reshaping of the Byzantine economy, the volume of trading activity soon began to look up; Byzantines certainly engaged with this trade on an individual basis.[18] Nor was trade only by sea: Eastern trade with Constantinople is attested from Trabzon and Armenia and a tenth-century treaty with Aleppo provided for customs dues on trade through Syria. There were also exchanges between Constantinople and the caliphate of luxury diplomatic gifts, such as horses, slaves and brocades.[19] Constantinople now had to provision itself from its European hinterland and the north instead of with the grain of Egypt and North Africa. But fresh markets also opened up and Byzantium learned to operate within a new type of Mediterranean economy.

Early in the eleventh century the future St Lazaros of Mount Galesion was an eye-witness of the destruction of the church of the Holy Sepulchre in Jerusalem on the orders of the Fatimid caliph al-Hakim, and of the persecution of Christians at the same time; his biographer says that many Christians left the Holy Land for 'Romania', i.e. the rest of the Byzantine world, but he also makes it clear that some, including some monks, converted to Islam.[20] A treaty made between Byzantium and the Fatimids in 1027 and 1036 allowed for the restoration of the church, which was undertaken by Constantine IX Monomachos, allowed the reconversion of these new Muslims, something usually strictly forbidden under Islamic law, and guaranteed the mosque in Constantinople.

As in other periods of Byzantine history the tenth and eleventh centuries were characterised by shifting populations and movements of peoples. The letters, contracts and religious materials in Hebrew, Aramaic and Greek, and often a mixture of languages, from the Geniza archive (a cache of documents covering the period roughly 950–1150 found in an ancient synagogue in Old Cairo) have revealed the lively involvement of that Jewish community in trade across the Mediterranean between Muslim Spain and Egypt and between North Africa and Syria, and at the same time the often surprising personal stories of individuals and families.[21] By the tenth century Jews had also migrated to Constantinople and other cities, and there were Jewish communities in the towns of south Italy under Byzantine rule. In the 1160s Benjamin of Tudela found a large Jewish community in Constantinople, many engaged in leatherworking. In the East, the Byzantine successes of the tenth century caused Muslim populations from Aleppo to flee towards Damascus or Baghdad and their places to be taken by non-Muslims; large numbers of prisoners were taken by Byzantine armies, some of whom were enslaved. Political factors caused the usual prohibitions on conversion to be set aside, and when Muslims returned they were sometimes required to be baptised. Pragmatism dictated policy, and attempts at repopulation required compromise: thus John Kourkouas tried to repopulate Melitene, taken in 934, with non-Chalcedonian Christians on the promise that they would not suffer from Byzantine religious persecution, a policy that Nikephoros Phokas tried unsuccessfully to reverse in 969.[22] But pragmatism also conflicted with other motivations, and the heterodoxy of the Syrian Jacobites was a problem for Constantinople. In 1029 their patriarch and a large number of Jacobite bishops and monks were summoned to Constantinople for trial; their condemnation for heresy was formally confirmed by an act of synod of 1032 with many signatures, from the patriarch of Constantinople and thirty-seven metropolitans to the Chalcedonian patriarch of Antioch,[23] whose see had been a renewed centre of Chalcedonian ecclesiastical organisation since the Byzantine regained the city in 969. Armenians also moved westwards, towards Cappadocia, in the late tenth century, and they too posed a religious problem for the Byzantines, not least because like the Latins they also used unleavened bread in the Eucharist. Armenia was briefly ruled by Byzantium from 1045 as the theme of Iberia, but in the 1040s this led Constantine IX Monomachos to attempt to deal with the heterodox Armenians in the same way as the Jacobites. As a result anti-Armenian and anti-Latin polemic developed together. The movements of peoples were complex, and have more to do with religion than ethnicity. Successful as it was in the East in the tenth century, Byzantium was not ruling an empire with discrete boundaries, but dealing with a fluid zone in which there might at various times be enclaves of influence but where, overall, there was an increasingly mixed population. There were no frontiers as such, only zones of movement and immigration, and this naturally affected both Byzantium's military capability and its political alignments.

It is a paradox that Byzantium's defeat by the Seljuks at Manzikert in 1071 in fact heralded two centuries of renewed involvement in the eastern Mediterranean. Alexius I got more than he expected when his request for mercenary assistance produced an army of 30,000 crusaders,

Fig. 24   Ani, north-east Anatolia, Armenian capital, briefly ruled by
Byzantium in the eleventh century. Photo Daniel L. Schwartz

and his efforts at management and containment drew the Byzantines
into new eastern warfare while they were at the same time engaged with
the Pechenegs from the north and in the defence of south Italy and the
Adriatic coast. Alexius's armies were overstretched, but in addition
Byzantium soon had to deal with the new phenomenon of crusader
states in the East, and with the mounting hostility of the Latins towards
Byzantium. In the end the crusades were a failure, and they brought to
Byzantium the disaster of 1204. Much is still misunderstood about these
events, both because of the bias of the various primary sources and
because of the preconceptions brought to their study by generations of
earlier scholars.[24] The simplified popular view of a series of easily identifiable and definable 'crusades' covers a multitude of motivations and
actual causes, and in the vast and ever-expanding secondary literature
on the crusades Byzantium's role is still refracted through the hostile
accounts in the Western sources. This picture of Byzantine military weakness and political duplicity, as well as the image of Byzantium as a passive
victim, is beginning to be put right as scholarship on Byzantium engages

more fully with the crusader scholarship written from the perspective of western Europe.[25] For two centuries after the launch of the First Crusade in 1098 Byzantium faced the intervention of successive waves of westerners moving by land towards the East, the establishment of quasi-independent 'states' and a new mix of Christian and Muslim culture in the Holy Land. The effect of the crusades was to keep the Seljuks inland in Anatolia, and Turkish sea-power did not become established before the fourteenth century; nevertheless sea-routes to the Holy Land became critical in the twelfth century for pilgrims as well as for the naval expeditions and naval support needed for the military operations. All this required a balancing act in which Byzantium's interests were not necessarily the same as those of the Franks. Byzantium could not avoid becoming involved. At first Alexius thought that the crusaders could be controlled through imposing oaths of fealty and through the sheer prestige of the empire, but as Ralph Lilie has argued, it is not clear, at least at this stage, that the Byzantines appreciated all the dimensions of the crusading venture, or its genuinely religious motivation.[26] Byzantine interests also involved, not least, the need to secure its western interests from any threats from the rear, as well as to weigh up the strengths of the Seljuks and the emirs of Aleppo in the East against the likely actions of the Franks or the security of the crusader states and their likely future. This explains why Byzantium often seemed to be surprisingly uninterested in military ventures. Manuel I followed his spectacular entry to Antioch in 1158 by returning to Constantinople. A joint siege of Damietta in Egypt by Manuel I and Amalric of Jerusalem in 1169 was a failure, but in 1175 Manuel felt impelled to organise a Byzantine crusade in view of the situation in the East after the deaths of both Nureddin and Amalric; Saladin was now a major threat and the advisors of the young leper king of Jerusalem seemed to be looking to Frederick Barbarossa for support. A large Byzantine fleet was dispatched, intended for Egypt, and Manuel led a massive force, which included Serbs and Hungarians, against the Seljuks near Konya (Ikonion). This was a total disaster, and Manuel suffered a crushing defeat at Myriokephalon to the west.[27] After the death of Manuel I in 1180 and the defeat of the crusaders by Saladin at Hattin in 1187, Byzantium's direct involvement in Syria ceased. There had been violence in Constantinople in 1171 when the Venetians attacked the new trading quarter granted by chrysobull to the Genoese,[28] and bloodshed directed against Latins in 1182 in the context of the rise to power of Andronikos II; in the same year the Normans attacked and sacked Thessalonike. The Latin capture of Constantinople in 1204, which predictably gave rise to Byzantine claims of

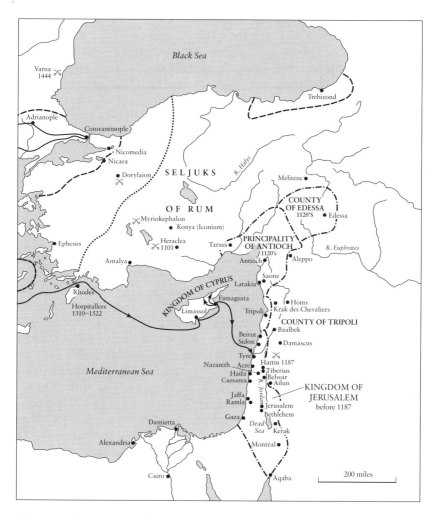

Map 10   The eastern Mediterranean in the time of the crusades. Adapted from Geoffrey Hindley, *The Crusades: A History of Armed Pilgrimage and Holy War* (London, 2003), p. xiii

Latin atrocities as well as Latin plundering, established Latin rule, even if fragmented, not only over the capital but also in Greece and the islands, including Crete. In this Latin Romania acute issues of hybridity and adaptation soon arose, especially in relation to religion, property and marriage. The European provinces of Byzantium maintained some continuity from 1230 as the Despotate of Epirus and Thessaly, but when the Byzantines from Nicaea managed to regain Constantinople in 1261 the world had changed drastically from what it had been before 1204; henceforth the Byzantine state existed in a fragmented world. This world included new states and new powers – Serbia, Hungary, not to mention western Europe and the Italian city-states, the Seljuks and the Ottomans. Byzantium was only one of a plethora of different and shifting powers. In particular the Mediterranean world was now highly complex and entailed new economic relationships and new cultural and religious interactions.

The fracture in Byzantine continuity in 1204 thus came at a time when Mediterranean society was already looking very different. Even though the Latins also failed in their attempt to set up Latin rule in Constantinople and the Byzantines almost miraculously returned, there was no longer space or a future for a hegemonic empire ruled from Constantinople. However, the idea that Byzantium was bound to fail because it did not share in the energy, expansionism and innovation of Europe in the twelfth century, as many people continue to believe, is a colonialist myth. It reminds one of the classic debates about the end of the Roman Empire: did it fall, or was it pushed, or, in the more colourful language of the French historian André Piganiol, was it assassinated?[29] One of the arguments of this book is that the vicissitudes over Byzantium's long existence were dictated at least as much by external factors as by internal ones. Facing up to the pressure of their own past was for the Byzantines one of their greatest challenges, but it is one whose effects modern historians tend to exaggerate.

With the European expansion towards the East, borders again became blurred or non-existent. Crusader historians debate about the extent to which communities were integrated, whether the Latin presence was colonial and whether the crusades should indeed be seen as marking the beginnings of European colonialism and expansionism. Historians of Byzantine art conduct a similar debate about the degree of influence or symbiosis detectable in the visual art and architecture of the crusader states and Latin-ruled areas: did a 'crusader art' represent the imposition of Western ideas, or was there in the artistic production of these areas a much more equal negotiation between the local and the external influences?[30] The question can be posed in several ways, in relation to organisation, motivation, economics and culture. Some 'colonies' were quite deliberate, such as the maritime colonies of the Italian city-states; there were virtually self-contained settlements at Acre, Beirut, Tyre, Tripoli, Laodicea and Antioch, as well as in Constantinople over the Golden Horn at Pera-Galata, on the basis of privileges granted by the Byzantines themselves.[31] As we saw, a contemporary estimate put the number of westerners in Constantinople in the late twelfth century at as many as sixty thousand.[32] But in other cases migration and settlement was much looser. Colonisation as such implies an integral relationship with the mother city or state, but this was lacking during the crusades, which can now be seen less as the onslaught of the West on the East than as a series of shifting coalitions with no clear 'sides' and certainly no lasting alliances. Even if commercial interests were not the driving factor of the crusades, the crusades undoubtedly brought profound changes to Mediterranean trade, movement and shipping. There was indeed a mixing of populations through settlement and population movement, and this had profound repercussions, though they differed greatly from area to area, and in terms of material culture in the East there was in any case little to choose between Byzantines, Armenians, Seljuks and crusaders. Against this background, the treatment of the central opposition in traditional crusader history between 'East' and 'West' can be seen to be deeply ideological;[33] if this is replaced by a model of interaction then there is, among other things, far more space for Byzantium. The eleventh-century rebuilding of the church of the Holy Sepulchre in Jerusalem by Constantine IX Monomachos was followed by further imperial patronage in the twelfth century by Manuel I Comnenus in conjunction with Amalric, the Latin king of Jerusalem; new mosaics bore the names of local artists in Greek, Latin and Syriac, and the iconography blended local, Western and Byzantine elements. Of course the experience was not always benign. Large numbers of new churches were built by the Latins in the Holy Land in the twelfth and thirteenth centuries, and mosques were converted into churches in Jerusalem and elsewhere, at Acre and Caesarea, for example. But even so there was more sharing of worship between Eastern and Western Christians than might have been thought, or has sometimes been argued.[34] In other areas, such as the Morea in southern Greece, Latin rule after 1204 was succeeded in some parts by the return of Byzantine control. The Frankish duchies of Athens and Thebes passed to the Catalans and the Florentines before being conquered by the Ottomans. Cyprus had been the scene of shared Byzantine and Arab rule in the period after the conquests and was subsequently under

Byzantine control until 1192 when it was sold by Richard the Lionheart to the Templars and then handed over to Guy de Lusignan.[35] Crete was also held at different times by Byzantines, Arabs and Venetians. This obviously led to a high level of cultural interaction, if not mixing. In the case of the Morea, Sharon Gerstel has argued that after the return to Byzantine control Orthodox artists still incorporated Latin features such as heraldic devices, and Latin characteristics also manifested themselves in language and social customs.

The sack of Constantinople in 1204 brought fragmentation and the mixing of Latins and Greeks.[36] Life on the Aegean islands, for example, became an unpredictable mosaic of peoples, made more complex by spontaneous movements and deliberate resettlement, but this varied greatly from one place to another and according to the size of the island. In these conditions, and given the reality of Turkish raids, the slave trade flourished mightily. Nowhere were the boundaries more permeable but also more contested than in matters of religion, and here too the situation was both localised and complex. Many stories tell of Latins using Greek churches and clergy and vice versa, or of local populations that were largely unaware of significant distinctions between the Latin and the Orthodox rites. A similar situation prevailed in south Italy and Sicily. A great distance lay between what happened on the ground and the attention given in political and theological circles to the differences between the two churches.

It is now agreed that in terms of what happened on the ground and in actual relations the so-called 'schism' of 1054 made little difference. Psellus was given the task of drawing up the accusation against Michael Cerularius when, after the Emperor Isaac Comnenus (1057–9) had exiled the patriarch for his high-handedness and personal pretensions, the latter still refused to abdicate. Michael died in 1059 before his trial for heresy and treason could take place.[37] He was replaced by Psellus's friend Constantine Leichoudes, but Psellus's document survives and demonstrates that the personal and the political were, as ever, intertwined. While refusing to accept the primacy of the papacy (he called a council in 1057–8 to remove the pope's name from the Orthodox diptychs, though it is probably not the case that he closed Latin churches in Constantinople) Cerularius's behaviour had also appeared to challenge the position of the emperor, both on a personal level and on behalf of the Church's right to be the guardian of Orthodoxy.[38] There was in fact no clear date at which a 'schism' took place between East and West; the divide opened up only gradually and contemporaries did not see 1054 as a crucial moment in the process. Moreover, neither 'the West' nor 'the

East' were monolithic entitities. Byzantine heresiological works detailing Latin 'errors' listed a range of grievances and differences ranging from the Latin use of unleavened bread (*azymes*, 'without yeast') in the Eucharist and the Latin addition of the *filioque* clause in the Creed to the fact that Latin clergy did not wear beards, and a further dimension was added to the mixture by the sack of Constantinople in 1204. From then until the fall of Constantinople in 1453 feelings were split in Constantinople between the pro- and anti-unionists, those who favoured union with the papacy and those who were passionately opposed to it. After 1204 practical issues arose as Latin clergy and Latin settlers moved to areas with Orthodox populations, and the gulf between what actually happened at local level and the policies of the Byzantine elite could be very large. This had already happened before 1204 in the crusader states, and local effects varied considerably; in Jerusalem Orthodox and Latins managed to get on together even though in the late twelfth century Orthodox and Byzantine interests sided with Saladin against the Latins. The Orthodox hierarchy was maintained in theory if not in practice, with patriarchs of Antioch such as the canonist Theodore Balsamon residing in Constantinople and influencing policy there. In southern Italy and Cyprus a *modus vivendi* was found between the Latin and the Orthodox churches and clergy. After 1204 this situation changed when a Latin patriarch was installed in Constantinople, though even now Orthodox clergy and heads of monasteries differed in their willingness to accept Latin bishops.[39] The election of a rival Orthodox patriarch at Nicaea in 1208 signalled the refusal of the Byzantines in exile at Nicaea to accept any rapprochement with the papacy. Treatises attacking the errors of the Latins were in fact written over a long chronological period (from the ninth century onwards) on the pattern of the tracts against Christian heresies that were first being written as early as the second century AD, and they mirrored the similarly long history of Christian answers to Jewish and Muslim 'objections'.[40] But now, after 1204, in the anti-Latin treatise of Constantine Stilbes, the metropolitan of Cyzicus, papal primacy and the claims that Latin bishops had led the attack on Constantinople are themes as prominent as the *filioque* and the use of *azymes* in the Eucharist.[41] After the return to Constantinople in 1261, as we have seen, Michael VIII Palaiologos's many problems made him desperate to make an agreement with the papacy, but he was opposed bitterly by many, and the depth of feeling only deepened later in the period.

By the thirteenth and fourteenth centuries the eastern Mediterranean was as much the place of Italians and Turks as it was of Byzantines. Crete, colonised by 3,500 Venetians, remained under Venetian control until

1669. But the crusader states did not survive the fall of Acre in 1291, and Mongol overlordship of the Seljuks checked the eastward expansionism of the Latins. Instead, there was now a westward migration of peoples from the East into Asia Minor. The Black Death, which had reached Constantinople by the mid-fourteenth century, was a further factor that affected the demographic balance of the Mediterranean. The Ottomans, whose dynasty was traced from Osman (d.1326) were the rulers of one of the Turkic kingdoms that split up Asia Minor between them; their support for John VI Cantacuzene against the young John V Palaiologos drew them, in 1354, across the Bosphorus into the European hinterland of Constantinople, where they were soon able to establish themselves at Adrianople (Edirne) and bring in Turkish settlers from Asia Minor. By the turn of the fourteenth century many Greeks were serving in the Ottoman navy, and Turkish raids had resulted in the depopulation of Aegean islands and coastal regions alike. Christians migrated from areas that were insecure to Turkish territories in Anatolia, thinking that they would be safer there, even while under Turkish rule.[42] In 1371 the Ottomans defeated the Serbs at the Maritsa river. John V Palaiologos sought alliance, but the cost was the payment of tribute and the provision of troops – in fact submission. The Ottomans advanced to Sofia and Niš and fought the battle of Kosovo Polje in 1389, as a result of which both Murad and Prince Lazar of Serbia met their deaths. The advance of the Ottomans into the Balkans left the Byzantines in Constantinople surrounded and exposed; they were required to participate in Ottoman campaigns in Asia Minor and a siege of Constantinople began in 1394; Thessalonike had already fallen in 1387. A new Mongol threat under Tamerlane temporarily distracted the Ottomans by defeating them at Ankara in 1402 and capturing Bayezid. Thessalonike returned to Byzantium and, as before with invaders from the steppe, the victory was not consolidated and the Mongols retreated. Manuel II Palaiologos returned to Constantinople in 1403 after more than three years of travel in the West, and he left his capital again in 1414–16. But the city was again under siege in 1421 and Thessalonike finally fell to the Ottomans in 1430 and Belgrade ten years later. A 'crusade' or coalition of Christian powers nevertheless mustered after union was proclaimed at the Council of Florence in 1439 and moved south from Hungary, but was defeated at Varna in Bulgaria in 1444. Once cities were in Ottoman hands, resettlement was the order of the day, and from the end of the century the new settlers in Thessalonike included Jews who had been expelled from Spain.[43] The geopolitics of the eastern Mediterranean had made it certain that Constantinople would not survive a third time.

Conclusion

The legacy of Byzantium to the Balkans and to the West is well known and undisputed. We have seen the long lasting influence of Byzantium on architecture, religion and society in countries like Bulgaria, Serbia, Russia and Greece, as well as the role that Byzantium played in preserving texts from classical antiquity and transferring manuscripts and knowledge of Greek to the Italian Renaissance. Neither of these important effects can be denied. But the appetite for Greek and for Greek manuscripts on the part of Italian intellectuals had already shown itself well before the end of the fourteenth century and long before the arrival of refugees from Constantinople in Italy after 1453. When Chrysoloras was invited to a teaching post in Greek in Florence in the 1390s Florentines were already keen to acquire Greek books, and a previous generation represented by Boccaccio and Pilato had already stimulated the thirst for translation. There were, after all, also Greek manuscripts in the libraries of the monasteries of Calabria and at Grottaferrata. But a whole industry had developed before 1453; Giovanni Aurispa, for example, brought hundreds of manuscripts back from Greece in the 1420s.[1] Of course the presence of Plethon and Bessarion at the Council of Ferrara-Florence was extremely important, and so was the arrival of intellectuals from Constantinople after 1453. Venice was full of Byzantines by the time that Anna Palaiologina Notaras bequeathed money for a Greek church there in the 1490s, and a Greek confraternity was founded in the city, but the horses from the Hippodrome of Constantinople on the façade of San Marco and the Byzantine enamels on the Pala d'Oro had already been taken there after 1204. The cultural drift from East to West had started long before 1453.

It may be as true that the fall of Constantinople released western Europe to be itself, as that the riches of classical Greek literature had been preserved by Byzantium. The arrival of Greek manuscripts in Italy, particularly in Venice, antedated the first printing press by only a few decades, and the first printed edition of a Greek text was produced in Venice in 1499 under the patronage of a Cretan called Nicholas Vlastos, who was employed by Anna Notaras Palaiologina whose father had been captured by the Turks in the siege of Constantinople.[2] Aldus Manutius in Venice used Greek typesetters to set works in Greek that had come with the exiles from Constantinople. Byzantium missed the printing revolution, but the intellectual culture of the last phase of Byzantium made a huge contribution to the development of humanism in western Europe.

But 'legacy' is a somewhat problematic concept, and in any case it is not the whole story; moreover to judge a society by its after-effects on others is hardly a compliment. This book has tried to show that Byzantium and the Byzantines are worth studying for themselves, not merely in comparison with classical antiquity or as transmitters of classical learning for the benefit of the West. Byzantium has acquired a new relevance in the emerging national histories of contemporary Eastern Europe, and the complex and changing shape and involvement of the Byzantine state in Europe, in the East and in the Mediterranean, can be seen to have gone closely together with the advances and fortunes of Islam from the seventh century onwards. The Ottoman Empire did not merely succeed that of Byzantium; it permitted the continuance of Orthodox culture and thereby preserved the 'legacy' of Byzantium to find expression in a revival of Orthodoxy in the post-communist states of Eastern Europe. Byzantium is worth studying for all these reasons, but above all, Byzantium is interesting and important for itself, as a centralised and complex state capable of extracting tax, fielding an army and maintaining itself over a very long time period, which encompassed at one end the transition from the ancient to the medieval world and at the other the beginnings of the Renaissance and the rise of western Europe.

Chronology

YEAR	EMPERORS	PATRIARCHS OF CONSTANTINOPLE	WEST	EAST
306	Constantine proclaimed at York			
312	Constantine defeats Maxentius		Battle of Milvian Bridge, Rome	
324	Constantine defeats Licinius			Battle of Chrysopolis, near Chalcedon
324–37	Constantine sole emperor			325 Council of Nicaea 330 Inauguration of Constantinople 335 Dedication of Church of Holy Sepulchre, Jerusalem
337–40	Constantine II, Constantius II and Constans			
340–61	Constantius II			
361–3	Julian			Julian dies on Persian campaign

Chronology *(cont'd)*

YEAR	EMPERORS	PATRIARCHS OF CONSTANTINOPLE	WEST	EAST
363–4	Jovian			
364–75	Valentian I, with Valens from 367			
375–8	Valens, Gratian and Valentinian II			
378–95	Theodosius I			381 Second Ecumenical Council, Constantinople
378–83	with Gratian and Valentinian II	379–81 Gregory Nazianzen		
383–92	with Valentinian II and Arcadius			
392–5	with Arcadius and Honorius			
395–408	Arcadius	398–404 John Chrysostom	395–423 Honorius	
408–50	Theodosius II	428–31 Nestorius	423–5 John; 425–55 Valentinian III; 430 Death of St Augustine	431 Council of Ephesus
450–7	Marcian		455 Petronius Maximus; 455–6 Avitus	451 Council of Chalcedon
457–74	Leo I		457–61 Majorian; 461–5 Libius Severus	

Date	Emperor	Patriarch of Constantinople	West / Popes	Councils and events
474	Leo II			
474–91	Zeno		467–72 Anthemius 472 Olybrius 473–4 Glycerius 474–5 Julius Nepos 475–76 6 Romulus Augustulus	
491–518	Anastasius			
518–27	Justin I			
527–65	Justinian I	552–65 Eutychius	534 Belisarius reconquers North Africa	553–4 Fifth Ecumenical Council, Constantinople
565–78	Justin II	565–77 John Scholasticus		
578–82	Tiberius II	577–82 Eutychius		
582–602	Maurice		590–604 Pope Gregory the Great	
602–10	Phocas			
610–41	Heraclius	610–38 Sergius		614 Persians capture Jerusalem 630 Heraclius recovers True Cross 632 death of Muhammad 636 Battle of R. Yarmuk
641–68	Constans II		649 Lateran Synod, Rome	
668–85	Constantine IV			680–1 Sixth Ecumenical Council, Constantinople
685–95	Justinian II			692 Council in Trullo (Quinisext), Constantinople

Chronology (cont'd)

YEAR	EMPERORS	PATRIARCHS OF CONSTANTINOPLE	WEST	EAST
695–8	Leontios			
698–705	Tiberius III		698 Carthage falls to Arabs	
705–11	Justinian II			
711–13	Philippikos			
713–16	Anastasius II			
716–17	Theodosius III	715–30 Germanus		
717–41	Leo III			
			735 Bede dies at Jarrow	
741–75	Constantine V			754 Iconoclast Council of Hieria
775–80	Leo IV			
780–97	Constantine VI	784–806 Tarasius		787 Second Council of Nicaea
797–802	Irene		800 Coronation of Charlemagne	
802–11	Nikephoros I	806–15 Nicephorus		
811	Stavrakios			
811–13	Michael I Rangabe			
813–20	Leo V the Armenian			
820–29	Michael II the Amorian			
829–42	Theophilos			
842–67	Michael III	843–7 Methodius		843 Restoration of icons

Emperors	Patriarchs	Events
		863 Mission of Constantine/Cyril and Methodius to Moravia
MACEDONIAN EMPERORS 867–1025		
867–86 Basil I	847–58 Ignatius	
886–912 Leo VI the Wise	858–67 Photius	
	867–77 Ignatius	
	877–86 Photius	
912–13 Alexander	901–7 Nicholas I Mystikos	
	907–12 Euthymius	
912–59 Constantine VII Porphyrogenitus	912–25 Nicholas I Mystikos	
920–44 Romanos I Lekapenos		
959–63 Romanos II		936, Otto I, crowned emperor 962
963–1025 Basil II		
963 Regency of Theophano (widow of Romanos II)		988 Baptism of Vladimir, Kiev
963–9 Nicephorus II Phocas	996–8 Sisinnios	
969–76 John I Tzimiskes		
1025–8 Constantine VIII		1018 Bulgaria organized as Byzantine province
1028–34 Romanos III Argyros		
1034–41 Michael IV the Paphlagonian		
1041–2 Michael V Kalaphates		

Chronology (cont'd)

YEAR	EMPERORS	PATRIARCHS OF CONSTANTINOPLE	WEST	EAST
1042	Zoe and Theodora	1043–58 Michael Cerularius		
1042–55	Constantine IX Monomachos			
1055–6	Theodora alone			
1056–7	Michael VI Stratiotikos			
1057–9	Isaac I Komnenos (abdicated)			
1059–67	Constantine X Doukas	1059–63 Constantine Leichoudes		
1067–71	Romanos IV Diogenes	1064–75 John Xiphilinus	1071 Bari falls to Normans	1071 Battle of Manzikert
1071–8	Michael VII Doukas		1073–85 Pope Gregory VII; 'Gregorian reforms'	
1078–81	Nicephorus III Botaniates			
COMNENIAN EMPERORS 1081–1185			1095 Urban II launches First Crusade at Clermont	1099 Crusaders capture Jerusalem
1081–1118	Alexius I Comnenus			
1118–43	John II Comnenus			
1143–80	Manuel I Comnenus		1152–90 Frederick Barbarossa	1176 Seljuk victory at Myriokephalon

Date	Ruler/Empire		Date	Events
1180–3	Alexius II		1181/2–1226	St Francis of Assisi
1183–5	Andronikos I		1187	Saladin captures Jerusalem
1185–95	Isaac II Angelos			
1195–1203	Alexius III Angelos			
1203–4	Isaac II and Alexius IV			
1204	Alexius IV			
LATIN EMPIRE 1204–1261	EMPERORS AT NICAEA		1204	Sack of Constantinople by Fourth Crusade Alexius I Comnenus emperor at Trebizond *Latin rule in Constantinople*
1204–22	Theodore I Laskaris		1215	University of Paris confirmed by papal bull
1222–54	John III Doukas Vatatzes		1225–74	St Thomas Aquinas
			1237–41	Mongols invade Europe
1254–8	Theodore II Laskaris	1254–9 Arsenius (at Nicaea)		
1258–61	John IV Laskaris			
PALAIOLOGAN EMPERORS 1259–82	Michael VIII Palaiologos		1261	Byzantines return to Constantinople

Chronology (cont'd)

YEAR	EMPERORS	PATRIARCHS OF CONSTANTINOPLE	WEST	EAST
1261, RECAPTURE OF CONSTANTINOPLE		1261–5 Arsenios (at Constantinople) 1266–5 Joseph 1275–82 John Bekkos	1274 Union of Lyons	
1282–1328	Andronikos II	1282–3 Joseph 1283–9 Gregory II of Cyprus		
1293–1320	Michael IX			
1328–41	Andronikos III			
1341–76	John V			
1341–54	John VI Cantacuzene			
1376–9	Andronikos IV			
1379–91	John V (restored)			
				1387 Thessalonike captured by Ottomans
1390	John VII			
1391–1425	Manuel II			1394 Ottoman siege of Constantinople
1425–48	John VIII		1438–9 Council of Ferrara/Florence	1430 Second fall of Thessalonike to Ottomans
1449–53	Constantine XI Palaiologos	1454 Gennadios Scholarius		1453 Fall of Constantinople
1453, FALL OF CONSTANTINOPLE				

References

Byzantium has become much more accessible to the general reader in recent years. The three-volume *Oxford Dictionary of Byzantium*, edited by the late Alexander Kazhdan (New York, 1990) marked a major step forward in this regard, and there are now several short introductions to Byzantium, which differ considerably from each other: Warren Treadgold, *A Concise History of Byzantium* (Basingstoke, 2001), which is related to, though not an abridgement of, his longer *History of the Byzantine State and Society* (Stanford, 1997); Michael Angold, *Byzantium: The Bridge from Antiquity to the Middle Ages* (London, 2001), John Haldon, *Byzantium: A History* (Stroud, 2001) and Timothy Gregory, *A History of Byzantium* (Oxford, 2005). Jonathan Harris (ed.) *Palgrave Advances in Byzantine History* (Basingstoke, 2005), contains essays by different authors, with a concentration on bibliography in English. The 6 volumes of the New Cambridge Medieval History published between 1995 and 2004 contain authoritative chapters on Byzantium by leading scholars, many of which are fundamental. See also the essays in G. Cavallo (ed.) *The Byzantines* (Chicago, 1997) and Liz James (ed.) *A Companion to Byzantium* (Oxford, 2007).

BACKGROUND TEXTS

Angold, Michael ([1985] 1997). *The Byzantine Empire 1025–1204: A Political History* (London).
Angold, Michael (1995). *Church and Society in Byzantium under the Comneni, 1081–1261* (Cambridge).
Angold, Michael (2001). *Byzantium: The Bridge between Antiquity and the Middle Ages* (London).
Bartlett, Robert (1993). *The Making of Europe: Conquest, Colonization and Cultural Change, 950–1350* (Princeton).
Beck, H.-G. (1959). *Kirche und theologische Literatur im byzantinischen Reich* (Munich).
Beck, H.-G. (1971). *Geschichte der byzantinischen Volksliteratur* (Munich).
Bowersock, Glen, Brown, Peter and Grabar, Oleg (1999). *Late Antiquity: A Guide to the Post-Classical World* (Cambridge, MA).

Cavallo, G. (ed.) (1997). *The Byzantines*, Eng. trans. (Chicago) (originally published as Browning, Robert, Cavallo, Guglielmo, Cesaretti, Paolo (eds) *L'Uomo Bizantino*, Milan, 1992).

Cheynet, J.-C. (2005). *Histoire de Byzance*, Que sais-je? (Paris).

Garnsey, Peter and Humfress, Caroline (2001). *The Evolution of the Late Antique World* (Cambridge).

Gregory, Timothy E. (2005). *A History of Byzantium* (Oxford).

Haldon, John (2001). *Byzantium. A History* (Stroud).

Hamilton, Bernard (2003). *The Christian World of the Middle Ages* (Stroud).

Harris, Jonathan (ed.) (2005). *Palgrave Advances in Byzantine History* (Basingstoke).

Herrin, Judith (1987). *The Formation of Christendom* (Oxford and Princeeton).

Hunger, H. (1978). *Die hochsprachliche profane Literatur der Byzantiner* (Munich).

Kazhdan, Alexander and Constable, Giles (1982). *People and Power in Byzantium: An Introduction to Modern Byzantine Studies* (Washington, DC).

Kazhdan, Alexander and Epstein, Ann (1985). *Change in Byzantine Culture in the Eleventh and Twelfth Centuries* (Berkeley and Los Angeles).

Krumbacher, K. (1897). *Geschichte der byzantinischen Litteratur von Justinian bis zum Ende des oströmischen Reiches, 527–1453* (2nd edn Munich).

Laiou, Angeliki (ed.) (2002). *The Economic History of Byzantium: From the Seventh through the Fifteenth Century* (3 vols, Washington, DC).

Laiou, Angeliki E. and Maguire, Henry (eds) (1992). *Byzantium: A World Civilization* (Washington, DC).

Maas, Michael (ed.) (2005). *The Cambridge Companion to the Age of Justinian* (Cambridge).

Magdalino, Paul (1993). *The Empire of Manuel I Komnenos, 1143–1180* (Cambridge).

Mango, Cyril (1972). *The Art of the Byzantine Empire 312–1453* (Englewood Cliffs, NJ, repr. Toronto, 1986) (translated sources).

Mango, Cyril (1980). *Byzantium: The Empire of New Rome* (London).

Mango, Cyril (ed.) (2002). *The Oxford History of Byzantium* (Oxford).

Nicol, D. M. (1993). *The Last Centuries of Byzantium, 1261–1453* (Cambridge).

Ostrogorsky, George (1968). *History of the Byzantine State*, Eng. trans. (Oxford).

Runciman, Steven (1968). *The Great Church in Captivity* (Cambridge).

Treadgold, Warren (1997). *A History of the Byzantine State and Society* (Stanford).

Treadgold, Warren (2001). *A Concise History of Byzantium* (Basingstoke).

Whittow, Mark (1996). *The Making of Orthodox Byzantium 600–1025* (Basingstoke, Berkeley and Los Angeles).

EXHIBITION CATALOGUES

Buckton, David (ed.) (1994). *Treasures of Byzantine Art and Culture from British Collections* (London).

Evans, Helen C. (ed.) (2004). *Byzantium: Faith and Power (1261–1557)* (New York).

Evans, Helen C. and Wixom, William D. (eds) (1997). *The Glory of Byzantium: Art and Culture of the Middle Byzantine Era, AD 843–1261* (New York).

Weitzmann, K. (ed.) (1979). *The Age of Spirituality: Late Antique and Early Christian Art, Third to Seventh Century.* Catalogue of the Exhibition at the Metropolitan Museum of Art, 19 November 1977 to 12 February 1978 (New York).

REFERENCE

Haldon, John (2005). *The Palgrave Atlas of Byzantine History* (Basingstoke).

Kazhdan, Alexander (ed.) (1990). *The Oxford Dictionary of Byzantium* (3 vols, New York).

McKitterick, Rosamund (ed.) (2004). *Atlas of the Medieval World* (Oxford).

New Cambridge Medieval History (1995–2005). (7 Vols, Cambridge).

PRIMARY SOURCES

Note: where possible translations have been indicated, but many Byzantine works still do not exist in modern editions or translations. Individual works in Greek are also often known by Latin titles, and these have been kept.

Actes de Lavra.	Ed. P. Lemerle et al., (1970–82) (4 vols, Paris).
Agathias. *Histories.*	Ed. R. Keydell (1967). CFHB 2 (Berlin); Eng. trans. D. Frendo (1975) CFHB 2A (Berlin).
Antony. *Life of.*	Ed. G. J. M. Bartelinck (1994). Sources chrétiennes 400 (Paris); trans. R. C. Gregg (1980) *The Life of Antony and the Letter to Marcellinus* (New York).
Book of the Pontiffs (Liber Pontificalis).	Trans. R. Davis (2001) (rev. edn, Liverpool).
Book of the Prefect.	Ed. J. Koder (1991) *Das Eparchenbuch Leons des Weisen*, CFHB 33 (Vienna).
Choniates, Michael. *Letters.*	Ed. F. Kolovou (2001). CFHB 41 (Berlin and New York) and S. P. Lambros (1879–80) (2 vols, Athens).
Choniates, Niketas. *Historia.*	Ed. J.-L. Van Dieten (1975). CFHB 11 (2 vols, Berlin/New York); trans. H. J. Magoulias (1984) *O City of Byzantium: Annals of Niketas Choniates* (Detroit).

Choniates, Niketas. *Orationes et Epistulae.*
Ed. J.-L. Van Dieten (1972). CFHB 3 (Berlin).

Chronicon Paschale.
Eng. trans. Michael Whitby and Mary Whitby (1989) *Chronicon Paschale 284–628 AD* (Liverpool).

Cinnamus, John, *Epitome.*
Ed. A. Meineke (1836). CSHB (Bonn); Eng. trans., C. Brand (1976) *Deeds of John and Manuel Comnenus by John Kinnamos* (New York).

Anna Comnena, *Alexiad.*
Eng. trans. E. R. A. Sewter (1969) *The Alexiad of Anna Comnena* (Harmondsworth).

Constantine VII Porphyrogenitus. *De Administrando Imperio.*
Ed., trans. and comm. G. Moravcsik and R. J. H. Jenkins (1985). CFHB 1 (2 vols, 2nd edn, repr. Washington, DC).

Constantine VII Porphyrogenitus. *De Thematibus.*
Ed. A. Pertusi (1952). Studi e Testi 160 (Vatican).

Constantine VII Porphyrogenitus. *De Cerimoniis (Book of Ceremonies).*
Ed. J. J. Reiske (1829–30). CSHB (Bonn); partial ed. and French trans. A. Vogt (1935–40) *Le Livre des cérémonies* (2 vols, Paris).

Constantine VII Porphyrogenitus. *Three Treatises on Imperial Military Expeditions.*
Ed. and trans. John Haldon (1990). CFHB 28 (Vienna).

Corippus.
Ed. and trans. Averil Cameron (1976). *Corippus, In laudem Iustini minoris libri quattuor* (London).

Ekloga.
Ed. L. Burgmann (1983). *Das Gesetzbuch Leons III und Konstantinos V* (Frankfurt am Main).

Eusebius of Caesarea. *Life of Constantine.*
Trans. with intro. and comm. Averil Cameron and Stuart G. Hall (1999) (Oxford).

Geoffrey de Villehardouin *La Conquête de Constantinople.*
Ed. E. Faral (1973) (5th edn, Paris).

Gregory II of Cyprus, *Autobiography.*
Ed. W. Lameere (1937) *La Tradition manuscrite de la correspondence de Grégoire de Chypre* (Brussels and Paris).

Irene of Chrysobalantos. *Life.*
Ed. J. O. Rosenqvist (1986) (Uppsala).

John Cameniates (alt. Kaminiates) *De expugnatione Thessalonicae.*
Ed. G. Böhlig (1973) (Berlin).

John the Lydian. *De Magistratibus.*
Trans. T. F. Carney (1971) (Lawrenceville, KS).

Lazaros of Mt Galesion, *Life of.*   Trans. R. P. H. Greenfield (2000) *The Life of Lazaros of Mt. Galesion: An Eleventh-Century Pillar Saint* (Washington, DC).

Leontius, Patriarch of Jerusalem. *Life of.*   Ed. and trans. D. Tsougarakis (1993) (Leiden).

Liber Pontificalis see *Book of the Pontiffs*

Liudprand of Cremona. *Antapodosis.*   Ed. J. Becker (1913) (Hanover and Leipzig); Eng. trans. F. A. Wright (1993) *Liudprand of Cremona: The Embassy to Constantinople and Other Writings* (London).

Liudprand of Cremona. *Relatio de legatione Constantinopolitana.*   Ed. and trans. B. Scott (1993) (London).

Malalas, John. *Chronicle.*   Ed. J. Thurn (2000) CFHB 35 (Berlin and New York); Eng. trans. Elizabeth Jeffreys, Michael Jeffreys and Roger Scott, et al. (1986 repr. 2004) *The Chronicle of John Malalas* (Melbourne).

Michael the Syrian, *Chronicle.*   Ed. J.-B. Chabot, *Chronique de Michael le Syrien*, 5 vols. (1899–1924) (Paris).

Nicephorus I, patriarch. *Refutatio et eversio.*   Ed. J. Featherstone (1997) CCSG 33 (Turnhout).

Nicephorus I, patriarch. *Antirrhetici I–III.*   Trans. M.-J. Monzain-Baudinet (1989) *Discours contre les Iconoclastes* (Paris).

Nicephorus Gregoras. *Historiae*   (1829–55) CSHB (3 vols, Bonn).

Nicholas Mesarites.   Trans. G. Downey (1957) 'Description of the Church of the Holy Apostles at Constantinople', *Transactions of the American Philosophical Society* 47 (1957), 855–924

Nicholas of Sion. *Life of.*   Trans. I. Ševčenko and N. Ševčenko (1984) *The Life of Nicholas of Sion* (Brookline, MA).

Pachymeres, George *Relations historiques.*   Ed. A. Failler, with French trans. by V. Laurent (1984–2000) CFHB 24 (5 vols, Paris).

Parastaseis Syntomoi Chronikai.   Eng. trans. and comm. Averil Cameron and Judith Herrin (eds) in conjunction with Alan Cameron, Robin Cormack and Charlotte Roueché (1984) *Constantinople in the Eighth Century* (Leiden).

Philaretos. *Life of.*

Ed. L. Rydén (2002) *The Life of St Philaretos the Merciful Written by his Grandson Niketas: a critical edition with introduction, translation, notes, and indices* (Uppsala).

Photius, *Homilies.*

Trans. Cyril Mango (1958) *The Homilies of Photius, Patriarch of Constantinople* (Cambridge, MA).

Procopius, *Wars* I–VIII, *Secret History, Buildings.*

Trans. H. B. Dewing and G. Downey (1914–28) (Cambridge, MA); trans. G. A. Williamson (1966) *Secret History* (Harmondsworth).

Psellus, Michael. *Chronographia.*

Trans. E. R. A. Sewter (1966) *Fourteen Byzantine Rulers* (Harmondsworth).

Robert of Clari, *The Conquest of Constantinople.*

Trans. E. H. McNeal ([1936] 1964) (New York).

Sozomen. *Ecclesiastical History.*

Trans. ([1891] 1976) in Nicene and Post-Nicene Fathers 2 (reprint, Grand Rapids).

Stephen the Younger. *Life of.*

Ed. M.-F. Auzépy (1997) *Vie d'Étienne le jeune par Étienne le diacre* (Aldershot).

Strategikon.

Trans. George. T. Dennis (1984) *Maurice's Strategikon: Handbook of Byzantine Military Strategy* (Philadelphia).

Theodore of Sykeon. *Life of.*

Ed. and trans. A.-J. Festugière (1970) Subsidia Hagiographica 48 (2 vols, Brussels); partial Eng. trans. in E. Dawes and N. H. Baynes (eds) (1948 repr. 1977), *Three Byzantine Saints* (Crestwood, NY).

Theophanes. *Chronographia.*

Trans. and comm. Cyril Mango and Roger Scott, with the assistance of Geoffrey Greatrex (1997) *The Chronicle of Theophanes Confessor: Byzantine and Near Eastern History* AD *284–813* (Oxford).

Theophanes Continuatus.

Ed. I. Bekker (1838), CSHB (Bonn).

Zonaras. *Epitome historion.*

Ed. M. Pinder and Th. Büttner-Wobst (1841–97), CSHB (3 vols, Bonn).

Zosimus. *New History.*

Trans. and comm. R. Ridley (1982), Byzantina Australiensia 2 (Sydney).

Geanokoplos, D. (1984). *Byzantium: Church, Society and Civilization Seen Through Contemporary Eyes* (Chicago).

Grumel V., Darrouzès, J., Laurent, V. (1932–79). *Les Regestes des actes du patriarcat de Constantinople, I. Les actes des patriarches* (7 vols, Paris); also H. Hunger and O. Kresten (1981–) *Das Register des Patriarchats von Konstantinopel* (Vienna).

Haldon, John F. (1990). *Constantine Porphyrogenitus: Three Treatises on Imperial Military Expeditions*, ed., trans. and comm., CFHB 28 (Vienna).

Oikonomides, N. (ed.) (1972). *Les Listes de préséance byzantines des IXe et Xe siècles* (Paris).

Talbot, Alice-Mary (ed.) (1996). *Holy Women of Byzantium: Ten Saints' Lives in English Translation* (Washington, DC).

Thomas, John and Constantinides Hero, Angela, with the assistance of Giles Constable (eds) (2000). *Byzantine Monastic Foundation Documents: A Complete Translation of the Surviving Founders' Typika and Testaments*, Dumbarton Oaks Studies 35 (5 vols, Washington, DC).

Ward, Benedicta (1987). *Harlots of the Desert: A Study of Repentance in Early Monastic Sources* (Kalamazoo).

GENERAL

Abulafia, David (ed.) (2003). *The Mediterranean in History* (London).

Abulafia, David and Berend, Nora (eds) (2002). *Medieval Frontiers: Concepts and Practices* (Aldershot).

Alcock, Susan (2005). 'Alphabet soup in the Mediterranean basin: the emergence of the Mediterranean serial', in Harris (ed.), *Rethinking the Mediterranean* (Oxford), pp. 314–36.

Alexiou, Margaret (1986). 'Modern Greek studies in the west, between the classics and the orient', *Journal of Modern Greek Studies* 4, 3–15.

Anderson, Benedict (1983). *Imagined Communities: Reflections on the Origin and Spread of Nationalism* (London).

Angold, Michael (1975). *A Byzantine Government in Exile: Government and Society under the Laskarids of Nicaea, 1204–1261* (Oxford).

Angold, Michael (1999). 'Byzantium in exile', in D. Abulafia (ed.), *The New Cambridge Medieval History* (Cambridge) V, c.1198–c.1300, pp. 543–68.

Angold, Michael (2002). 'The Byzantine empire, 1025–1118', in D. Luscombe and J. Riley-Smith (eds), *The New Cambridge Medieval History* (Cambridge), IV, c.1024–c.1198, part 2, pp. 217–53.

Ahrweiler, Hélène and Laiou, Angeliki E. (eds) (1998). *Studies on the Internal Diaspora of the Byzantine Empire* (Washington, DC).

Arbel, Benjamin, Hamilton, Bernard and Jacoby, David (eds) (1989). *Latins and Greeks in the Eastern Mediterranean after 1204* (London).

Asad, Talal (2003). *Formations of the Secular: Christianity, Islam, Modernity* (Stanford).

Ashcroft, Bill, Griffiths, Gareth and Tiffin, Heken (eds) (1995). *The Post-Colonial Studies Reader* (London).

Auzépy, Marie-France (ed.) (2003). *Byzance en Europe* (Saint-Denis).

Avramea, A., 'Land and sea communications, fourth to fifteenth centuries', in Angeliki E. Laiou, (ed.) (2002). *The Economic History of Byzantium* (Washington, DC), 1, pp. 57–90

Barber, Charles (2002). *Figure and Likeness: On the Limits of Representation in Byzantine Iconoclasm* (Princeton).

Barber, Charles (2005). 'Art history', in Jonathan Harris, ed., *Palgrave Advances in Byzantine History* (Basingstoke), pp. 147–56.

Bartlett, Robert (1993). *The Making of Europe: Conquest, Colonisation and Cultural Change 950–1350* (London).

Baumer, Christoph (2006). *The Church of the East: An Illustrated History of Assyrian Christianity* (London).

Beard, Mary (2003). *The Parthenon* (Cambridge, MA).

Beaton, R. (1996). *The Medieval Greek Romance* (rev. edn, London).

Beaucamp, J. (1990, 1992). *Le Statut de la femme à Byzance (4e–7e siècle)* (2 vols, Paris).

Belting, Hans (1994). *Likeness and Presence: A History of the Image before the Era of Art* (Chicago).

Berend, Nora (2001). *At the Gate of Christendom: Jews, Muslims and 'Pagans' in Medieval Hungary, c.1000–c.1300* (Cambridge).

Berger, Albrecht (1988). *Untersuchungen zu Patria Konstantinupoleos*, Poikila Byzantina 8 (Bonn).

Bhabha, Homi K. (1994). *The Location of Culture* (London).

Bois, Guy (1992). *The Transformation of the Year One Thousand: The Village of Lournand from Antiquity to Feudalism* (Eng. trans., Manchester).

Bowden, William (2003). *Epirus Vetus: The Archaeology of a Late Antique Province* (London).

Bowersock, G. W. (1990). *Hellenism in Late Antiquity* (Ann Arbor).

Bowersock, G. W. (2005).'The east–west orientation of Mediterranean studies and the meaning of north and south in antiquity', in W. V. Harris (ed.), *Rethinking the Mediterranean* (Oxford), pp. 167–78.

Brown, Peter (1971). *The World of Late Antiquity* (London).

Brown, Peter (1992). *Power and Persuasion in Late Antiquity: Towards a Christian Empire* (Madison).

Brown, Peter (1995). *Authority and the Sacred: Aspects of the Christianisation of the Roman World* (Cambridge).

Brown, Peter (2003). *The Rise of Western Christendom: Triumph and Diversity, AD 200–1000* (2nd rev. edn, Oxford).

Browning, Robert (1983). *Medieval and Modern Greek* (2nd edn, Cambridge).

Brubaker, Leslie (1999). *Vision and Meaning in Ninth-Century Byzantium: Image and Exegesis in the Homilies of Gregory of Nazianzus* (Cambridge).

Brubaker, Leslie (1999). 'The Chalke gate, the construction of the past, and the Trier ivory', *Byzantine and Modern Greek Studies* 23, 258–85.

Brubaker, Leslie and Haldon, John (2001). *Byzantium in the Iconoclast Era (ca. 680–850): The Sources. An Annotated Survey*, Birmingham Byzantine and Ottoman Monographs 7 (Aldershot).

Bryer, Anthony (1971). 'The first encounter with the west', in P. Whitting (ed.), *Byzantium: An Introduction* (Oxford), pp. 85–110.

Bryer, Anthony (1998). 'Byzantium: the Roman Orthodox world, 1393–1492', in Christopher Allmand (ed.), *New Cambridge Medieval History*, c.1415–c.1500 (Cambridge) VII, pp. 771–95.

Bryer, Anthony and Cunningham, Mary (eds) (1996). *Mount Athos and Byzantine Monasticism* (Aldershot).

Bryer, Anthony and Herrin, Judith (eds) (1977). *Iconoclasm* (Birmingham).

Burton-Christie, D. (1993). *The Word in the Desert: Scripture and the Quest for Holiness in Early Christian Monasticism* (New York).

Bury, J. B. (1889). *History of the Later Roman Empire: From Arcadius to Irene (395 AD to 800 AD)* (London).

Bydén, B. (2003). *Theodore Metochites'* Stoicheiosis astronomike *and the Study of Natural Philosophy and Mathematics in Early Palaiologan Byzantium* (Göteborg).

Cameron, Alan (1976). *Circus Factions* (Oxford).

Cameron, Alan (1993). *The Greek Anthology from Meleager to Planudes* (Oxford).

Cameron, Averil (1987). 'The construction of court ritual: the Byzantine *Book of Ceremonies*', in Cannadine, David and Price, Simon (eds) *Rituals of Royalty: Power and Ceremonial in Traditional Societies* (Cambridge), pp. 106–36.

Cameron, Averil (1991). *Christianity and the Rhetoric of Empire: The Formation of Christian Discourse* (Berkeley and Los Angeles).

Cameron, Averil (1992). *The Use and Abuse of Byzantium*, Inaugural Lecture, King's College London, 1990 (London).

Cameron, Averil (1993). *The Mediterranean World in Late Antiquity*, AD 395–c.600 (London).

Cameron, Averil (ed.) (1995). *The Byzantine and Early Islamic Near East III: States, Resources, Armies*, Studies in Late Antiquity and Early Islam I (Princeton).

Cameron, Averil (2000). 'Bury, Baynes and Toynbee', in Robin Cormack and Elizabeth Jeffreys (eds) *Through the Looking Glass: Byzantium through British Eyes* (Aldershot), pp. 163–76.

Cameron, Averil (2002). 'The long late antiquity: a late twentieth-century model', in T. P. Wiseman (ed.), *Classics in Progress: Essays on Ancient Greece and Rome* (Oxford), pp. 165–91.

Cameron, Averil (2006). 'Byzantium and Europe', in J.-M. Spieser (ed.), *Présence de Byzance* (Lausanne).

Cheynet, Jean-Claude (1990). *Pouvoir et contestations à Byzance (963–1210)* (Paris).

Cheynet, Jean-Claude (2002). 'Les Limites de pouvoir à Byzance: une forme de tolérance?' in K. Nikolaou (ed.), *Toleration and Repression in the Middle Ages: In Memory of Lenos Mavromattis* (Athens), pp. 15–28.

Chuvin, P. (1990). *A Chronicle of the Last Pagans* (Eng. trans., Cambridge, MA).

Čirković, Sima (2005). *The Serbs* (Oxford).

Clucas, Lowell (ed.) (1988). *The Byzantine Legacy in Eastern Europe* (New York).

Connor, Carolyn L. (2004). *Women of Byzantium* (New Haven).

Constantelos, D. J. (1968). *Byzantine Philanthropy and Social Welfare* (New Brunswick).

Constantelos, D. J. (1992). *Poverty, Society, and Philanthropy in the Late Mediaeval Greek World* (New Rochelle).

Constas, N. (1995). 'Weaving the body of God: Proclus of Constantinople, the Theotokos and the loom of the flesh', *Journal of Early Christian Studies* 3.2, 169–94.

Cormack, Robin (1985). *Writing in Gold* (London).

Cormack, Robin (1997). *Painting the Soul* (London).

Cormack, Robin (1997). 'Women and icons and women in icons', in Liz James (ed.), *Women, Men and Eunuchs: Gender in Byzantium* (London), pp. 24–51.

Cormack, Robin and Jeffreys, Elizabeth (eds) (2000). *Through the Looking Glass: Byzantium through British Eyes* (Aldershot).

Cunningham, Mary B. and Allen, Pauline (eds) (1998). *Preacher and Audience: Studies in Early Christian and Byzantine Homiletics* (Leiden).

Curčič, S. and Mouriki, D. (eds) (1991). *The Twilight of Byzantium: Aspects of Cultural and Religious History in the Late Byzantine Empire.* Papers from the colloquium held at Princeton University, 8–9 May 1989 (Princeton).

Curčič, S. (2004). 'Religious settings of the late Byzantine period', in Helen C. Evans (ed.), *Byzantium: Faith and Power (1261–1557)* (New York), pp. 65–77.

Dagron, G. (1984). *Constantinople imaginaire: études sur le receuil des Patria* (Paris).

Dagron, G. (1991). 'Holy images and likeness', *Dumbarton Oaks Papers* 45, 23–33.

Dagron, Gilbert (2003). *Emperor and Priest: The Imperial Office in Byzantium* (Eng. trans., Cambridge).

Dagron, G. (2002). 'The urban economy, seventh-twelfth centuries', in Laiou (ed.), *Economic History of Byzantium* (Washington, DC) Vol. 2, pp. 393–461.

Dagron, G. et al. (2000). 'L'Organisation et le déroulement des courses d'après le *Livre des Cérémonies*', *Travaux et Mémoires* 13: 1–200.

de Lange, Nicholas (2000). 'Hebrews, Greeks or Romans? Jewish culture and identity in Byzantium', in Dion Smythe (ed.), *Strangers to Themselves: The Byzantine Outsider* (Aldershot), pp. 105–18.

de Ste. Croix, Geoffrey (1981). *The Class Struggle in the Ancient Greek World: From the Archaic Age to the Arab Conquests* (London).

Dölger, F. and Wirth, P. (1924–77). *Regesten der Kaiserurkunden des oströmischen Reiches von 565–1453* (Munich and Berlin).

Ducellier, A. (1987). 'Aux frontières de la romanité et de l'orthodoxie au moyen âge: le cas de l'Albanie', in *L'Albanie entre Byzance et Venise, Xe–XVe siècles* (London), XI.

Dvornik, F. (1966). *Early Christian and Byzantine Political Philosophy: Origins and Background* (2 vols, Washington, DC).

Elsner, Jaś (1995). *Art and the Roman Viewer* (Cambridge).

Elsner, Jaś (1998). *Imperial Rome and Christian Triumph: The Art of the Roman Empire, AD 100–450* (Oxford).

Elsner, Jaś (2000). 'From the culture of spolia to the cult of relics: the Arch of Constantine and the genesis of late antique forms', *Papers of the British School at Rome* 68, 149–84.

Fallmerayer, Jakob Phillip (1830, 1836). *Geschichte der Halbinsel Morea wahrend des Mittelalters* (2 vols, Stuttgart and Tubingen).

Ferguson, Niall (2005). *Colossus: The Rise and Fall of the American Empire* (New York).

Fine, J. (1983). *The Early Medieval Balkans: A Critical Survey from the Sixth to the Late Twelfth Century* (Ann Arbor).

Foss, Clive (1975). 'The Persians in Asia Minor and the end of antiquity', *English Historical Review* 90: 721–47.

Foss, Clive (1996). *Nicaea: A Byzantine Capital and its Praises* (Brookline, MA).

Fowden, Garth (1993). *Empire to Commonwealth: Consequences of Monotheism in Late Antiquity* (Princeton).

Franklin, Simon, and Shepard, Jonathan (1996). *The Emergence of Rus', 750–1200* (London).

Frankopan, Peter (2002). 'The imperial governors of Dyrrakhion in the reign of Alexios I Komnenos', *Byzantine and Modern Greek Studies* 26: 65–103.

Frantz, Alison (1988). *The Athenian Agora XXIV. Late Antiquity AD 267–700* (Princeton).

Galatariotou, Catia (1991). *The Making of a Saint: The Life, Times and Sanctification of Neophytos the Recluse* (Cambridge).

Garland, Lynda (1999). *Byzantine Empresses: Women and Power in Byzantium AD 527–1204* (London).

Geary, Patrick (2002). *The Myth of Nations: The Medieval Origins of Europe* (Princeton).

Grabar, André (1936). *L'Empereur dans l'art byzantin: Recherches sur l'art officiel de l'empire d'orient* (Paris).

Gurevich, Aaron (1992). 'Why I am not a Byzantinist', in Homo Byzantinus. Papers in Honor of Alexander Kazhdan, *Dumbarton Oaks Papers* 46, 89–96.

Gurevich, Aaron (1995). *The Origins of European Individualism* (Oxford).

Haldon, John and Kennedy, Hugh (1980). 'The Arab–Byzantine frontier in the eighth and ninth centuries: military organisation and society in the borderlands', *Zbornik Radova Vizantologskij Instituta* 19, 79–116.

Haldon, John (1990). *Byzantium in the Seventh Century: The Transformation of a Culture* (Cambridge).

Haldon, John (1993). 'Military service, military lands and the status of soldiers: current problems and interpretations', *Dumbarton Oaks Papers* 47, 1–67.

Haldon, John (1999). *Warfare, State and Society in the Byzantine World 565–1204* (London).

Haldon, John (2000). 'Theory and practice in tenth-century military administration. Chapters II, 44 and 45 of the *Book of Ceremonies*', *Travaux et Mémoires* 13: 201–352.

Haldon, John (2001). *The Byzantine Wars: Battles and Campaigns of the Byzantine Era* (Stroud).

Harris, Jonathan (2003). *Byzantium and the Crusades* (London).

Harris, W. V. (ed.) (2005). *Rethinking the Mediterranean*.

Harvey, Alan (1990). *Economic Expansion in the Byzantine Empire, 900–1200* (Cambridge).

Harvey, Alan (1996). 'Financial crisis and the rural economy', in Margaret Mullett and Dion Smythe (eds), *Alexios I Komnenos: I Papers* (Belfast), pp. 167–84.

Hastings, Adrian (1997). *The Constructions of Nationhood* (Cambridge).

Hatlie, Peter (1996). 'Redeeming Byzantine epistolography', *Byzantine and Modern Greek Studies* 20, 213–48.

Heather, Peter (1994). 'New men for new Constantines? Creating an imperial elite in the eastern Mediterranean', in Paul Magdalino (ed.), *New Constantines: The Rhythm of Imperial Renewal in Byzantium, 4th–13th Centuries* (Aldershot), pp. 11–33.

Heather, Peter (2005). *The Fall of the Roman Empire* (Basingstoke and Oxford).

Hendy, Michael (1985). *Studies in the Byzantine Monetary Economy c.300–1450* (Cambridge).

Herrin, Judith (1987). *The Formation of Christendom* (Oxford and Princeton).

Herrin, Judith (2001). *Women in Purple: Rulers of Medieval Byzantium* (London).

Herrin, Judith (2002). 'Toleration and repression within the Byzantine family', in K. Nikolaou (ed.), *Toleration and Repression in the Middle Ages: In Memory of Lenos Mavromattis* (Athens), pp. 173–88.

Hill, Barbara (1999). *Imperial Women in Byzantium 1025–1204: Power, Patronage and Ideology* (London).

Hirschfeld, Y. (1992). *The Judaean Desert Monasteries in the Byzantine Period* (New Haven).

Holmes, Catherine (2005). *Basil II and the Governance of Empire* (Oxford).

Horden, Peregrine, and Nicholas Purcell (2000). *The Corrupting Sea: A Study of Mediterranean History* (Oxford).

Howard-Johnston, James (1995). 'The two great powers in late antiquity: a comparison', in Averil Cameron (ed.), *The Byzantine and Early Islamic Near East III: States, Resources, Armies* (Princeton), pp. 157–226.

Hoyland, R. G. (1997). *Seeing Islam as Others Saw It: A Survey and Evaluation of Christian, Jewish, and Zoroastrian Writings on Early Islam* (Princeton).

Hunger, H. (1969–70). 'On the imitation (mimesis) of antiquity in Byzantine literature', *Dumbarton Oaks Papers* 23–4: 17–38.

Ierodiakonou, K. (ed.) (2002). *Byzantine Philosophy and its Ancient Sources* (Oxford).

Imber, Colin (2002). *The Ottoman Empire* (Basingstoke).

Jackson, Peter (2005). *The Mongols and the West 1221–1410* (Harlow).

James, Liz (2001). *Empresses and Power in Early Byzantium* (Leicester).

Jeffreys, Elizabeth (ed.) (2003). *Rhetoric in Byzantium* (Aldershot).

Jeffreys, Elizabeth, and Jeffreys, Michael (1986). *Popular Literature in Late Byzantium* (Aldershot).

Johnson, Scott (ed.) (2006). *Greek Literature in Late Antiquity: Dynamism, Didacticism, Classicism* (Aldershot).

Jones, A. H. M. (1964). *The Later Roman Empire, 284–602: A Social, Economic and Administrative Survey* (2 vols, Oxford).

Jones, Lynn and Maguire, Henry (2002). 'A description of the jousts of Manuel I Komnenos', *Byzantine and Modern Greek Studies* 26: 104–48.

Jusdanis, Gregory (1987). 'East is east – west is west: it's a matter of Greek literary history', *Journal of Modern Greek Studies* 5: 1–14.

Kaegi, Walter E. (1992). *Byzantium and the Early Islamic Conquests* (Cambridge).

Kaldellis, Anthony (1999). *The Argument of Psellos'* Chronographia (Leiden).

Kalavrezou, I. (ed.) with Angeliki E. Laiou, Alicia Walker, Elizabeth A. Gittings, Molly Fulghum Heintz and Bissera V. Pentcheva (2003). *Byzantine Women and their World* (New Haven).

Kaplan, Michel (1992). *Les Hommes et la terre à Byzance du VIe au XIe siècle: Propriété et exploitation du sol*, Byzantina Sorbonensia 10 (Paris).

Kaster, Robert (1988). *Guardians of Language: The Grammarian and Society in Late Antiquity* (Berkeley and Los Angeles).

Kazhdan, Alexander (1999). *History of Byzantine Literature* I *(650–850)* ed. Lee F. Sherry and Christine Angelidi (Athens).

Kazhdan, Alexander (2001). 'Latins and Franks in Byzantine perception and reality from the eleventh to the twelfth century', in Angeliki E. Laiou and Roy Mottahadeh (eds), *The Crusades from the Perspective of Byzantium and the Muslim World* (Washington, DC), pp. 84–100.

Kazhdan, Alexander P., in collaboration with Franklin, Simon (1984). *Studies on Byzantine Literature of the Eleventh and Twelfth Centuries* (Cambridge).

Kazhdan, Alexander P. and McCormick, Michael (1997). 'The social world of the Byzantine court', in Henry Maguire (ed.), *Byzantine Court Culture from 829 to 1204* (Washington, DC), pp. 167–97.

Kelly, Christopher (2004). *Ruling the Later Roman Empire* (Cambridge, MA).

Kennedy, Hugh (1986). *The Prophet and the Age of the Caliphates* (London).

Kennedy, Hugh (2004). *The Court of the Caliphs: The Rise and Fall of Islam's Greatest Dynasty* (London).

Khoury, A. T. (1972). *Polémique byzantine contre l'Islam* (Leiden).

Kingsley, Sean A. (2004). *Shipwreck Archaeology of the Holy Land: Processes and Parameters* (London).

Kitzinger, Ernst (1977). *Byzantine Art in the Making: Main Lines of Stylistic Development in Medieval Art, 3rd–7th Century* (Cambridge, MA).

Kolbaba, Tia M. (2000). *The Byzantine Lists: The Errors of the Latins* (Urbana, IL).

Kolbaba, Tia M. (2001). 'Byzantine perceptions of Latin religious "errors"', in Laiou and Mottahadeh (eds), *The Crusades from the Perspective of Byzantium and the Muslim World* (Washington, DC), pp. 117–43.

Krueger, Derek (1996). *Symeon the Holy Fool: Leontios's Life and the Late Antique City* (Berkeley and Los Angeles).

Laiou, Angeliki E. (1992). *Mariage, amour et parenté à Byzance aux XIe–XIIIe siècles* (Paris).

Laiou, Angeliki (1993). 'Sex, consent and coercion in Byzantium', in Angeliki E. Laiou, (ed.), *Consent and Coercion to Sex and Marriage in Ancient and Medieval Societies* (Washington, DC) pp. 109–221.

Laiou, Angeliki E. (2002). *Economic History of Byzantium* (3 vols, Washington, DC).

Laiou, Angeliki E. (2002). 'The agrarian economy, thirteenth-fifteenth centuries', in Laiou (ed.), *Economic History of Byzantium* (Washington, DC), 1, pp. 311–75.

Laiou, Angeliki E. (2002). 'The Byzantine economy: an overview', in Angeliki E. Laiou (ed.), *Economic History of Byzantium* (Washington, DC), 3, pp. 1145–64.

Laiou, Angeliki E. (1994). 'Law, justice and the Byzantine historians', in Angeliki E. Laiou and Dieter Simon (eds) *Law and Society in Byzantium, Ninth–Twelfth Centuries* (Washington, DC) pp. 151–85.

Laiou, Angeliki E. and Mottahedeh, Roy P. (2001). *The Crusades from the Perspective of Byzantium and the Muslim World* (Washington, DC).

Laiou, Angeliki E., and Simon, Dieter (eds) (1994). *Law and Society in Byzantium, Ninth–Twelfth Centuries* (Washington, DC).

Laiou-Thomadakis, Angeliki E. (1977). *Peasant Society in the Late Byzantine Empire: A Social and Demographic Study* (Princeton).

Lauxtermann, Marc (1994). *The Byzantine Epigram in the Ninth and Tenth Centuries* (Amsterdam).

Lavan, L., et al. (eds) (2001). *Recent Research in Late-Antique Urbanism* (Portsmouth, RI).

Lavan, L. and Bowden, W. (eds) (2003). *Theory and Practice in Late Antique Archaeology* (Leiden).

Le Goff, Jacques (2005). *The Birth of Europe* (Oxford).

Lemerle, Paul (1986). *Byzantine Humanism, The First Phase: Notes and Remarks on Education and Culture in Byzantium from its Origins to the Tenth Century*. Eng. trans. by Helen Lindsay and Ann Moffatt, Byzantina Australiensia 3 (Canberra).

Lendon, J. E. (1997). *Empire of Honour: The Art of Government in the Roman World* (Oxford).

Liebeschuetz, J. H. W. G. (2001). *The Decline and Fall of the Roman City* (Oxford).

Lieu, Samuel N. C. and Montserrat, Dominic (eds) (1998). *Constantine: History, Historiography, Legend* (London).

Lilie, R.-J. (1993). *Byzantium and the Crusader States, 1096–1204* (Oxford) (Eng. trans. of (1981) *Byzanz und die Kreuzfahrerstaaten*, Munich).

Littlewood, A. R. (ed.) (1995). *Originality in Byzantine Literature, Art and Music* (Oxford).

Littlewood, Antony (2005). 'Literature', in Jonathan Harris (ed.), *Palgrave Advances in Byzantine History* (Basingstoke), pp. 133–46.

Lokin, J. H. A. (1994). 'The significance of law and legislation in the law books of the ninth to eleventh centuries', in Angeliki E. Laiou and Dieter Simon (eds), *Law and Society in Byzantium*, pp. 71–91.

Lowden, John (1997). *Early Christian and Byzantine Art* (London).

Maas, Michael (1992). *John Lydus and the Roman Past: Antiquarianism and Politics in the Age of Justinian* (London).

McClanan, Anne (2002). *Representations of Early Byzantine Empresses: Image and Empire* (London).

McCormick, Michael (1986). *Eternal Victory: Triumphal Rulership in Late Antiquity, Byzantium and the Mediaeval West* (Cambridge).

McCormick, Michael (2001). *The Origins of the European Economy: Communications and Commerce, AD 300–900* (Cambridge).

McKitterick, Rosamond (1990). *The Uses of Literacy in Early Mediaeval Europe* (Cambridge).

Magdalino, Paul (1984). 'The Byzantine aristocratic *oikos*', in M. Angold (ed.), *The Byzantine Aristocracy IX–XIII Centuries* (Oxford), pp. 92–111.

Magdalino, Paul (1989). 'Between Romaniae: Thessaly and Epirus in the Later Middle Ages', in Benjamin Arbel, Bernard Hamilton and David Jacoby (eds), *Latins and Greeks in the Eastern Mediterranean after 1204* (London), pp. 87–110.

Magdalino, Paul (1993). *The Empire of Manuel I Komnenos, 1143–1180* (Cambridge).

Magdalino, Paul (1994). 'Justice and finance in the Byzantine state, ninth to twelfth centuries', in A. E. Laiou and D. Simon (eds), *Law and Society in Byzantium, Ninth–Twelfth Centuries* (Washington, DC), pp. 93–115.

Magdalino, Paul (ed.) (1994). *New Constantines: The Rhythm of Imperial Renewal in Byzantium, 4th–13th Centuries* (Aldershot).

Magdalino, Paul (1995). 'The grain supply of Constantinople, ninth–twelfth centuries', in Cyril Mango and Gilbert Dagron (eds), *Constantinople and its Hinterland* (Aldershot).

Magdalino, Paul (1996). *Constantinople médiévale: études sur l'évolution des structures urbaines* (Paris).

Magdalino, Paul (1997). 'The Byzantine army and the land: from *stratiotikon ktema* to military *pronoia*', in *Byzantium at War (9th–12th c.)* (Athens), pp. 15–36.

Magdalino, Paul (2002). 'The medieval empire (780–1204)', in Cyril Mango (ed.), *Oxford History of Byzantium* (Oxford), pp. 169–213.

Magdalino, Paul (2002). 'The Byzantine empire, 1118–1204', in David Luscombe and Jonathan Riley-Smith (eds), *New Cambridge Medieval History* (Cambridge) IV.2, pp. 611–43.

Magdalino, Paul (ed.) (2003). *Byzantium in the Year 1000* (Leiden).

Maguire, Henry (1997). 'Images of the court', in Helen Evans and William D. Wixom (eds), *The Glory of Byzantium: Art and Culture of the Middle Byzantine Era, AD 843–1261* (New York), pp. 182–91.

Maguire, Henry (ed.) (1997). *Byzantine Court Culture from 829 to 1204* (Washington, DC).

Maguire, Henry (1999). 'The profane aesthetic in Byzantine art and literature', *Dumbarton Oaks Papers* 53, 189–205.

Majcherek, Grzegorz (2004). 'Kom el-Dikka, Excavations and Preservation Work, 2002/2003', in *Polish Archaeology in the Mediterranean* 15 (Warsaw), 25–38.

Mango, Cyril (1971). 'The availability of books in the Byzantine empire, AD 750–850', in *Byzantine Books and Bookmen* (Washington, DC), pp. 29–45.

Mango, Cyril (1972). *The Art of the Byzantine Empire, AD 312–1453* (Englewood Cliffs, NJ).

Mango, Cyril (1975). *Byzantine Literature as a Distorting Mirror*, Inaugural lecture, University of Oxford (Oxford).

Mango, Cyril (1976). *Byzantine Architecture* (New York).

Mango, Cyril (1981). 'Discontinuity with the past in Byzantine literature', in M. Mullett and R. Scott (eds), *Byzantium and the Classical Tradition* (Birmingham), pp. 48–57.

Mango, Cyril (1990). *Le Développement urbain de Constantinople: IV–VII siècles* (2nd edn, Paris).

Mango, Cyril and Dagron, Gilbert (eds) with the assistance of Geoffrey Greatrex (1995). *Constantinople and its Hinterland* (Aldershot).

Markopoulos, A. (ed.) (1987). *Byzantium and Europe: First International Byzantine Conference, Delphi, 20–24 July, 1985* (Athens).

Mathews, Thomas F. (1998). *The Art of Byzantium: Between Antiquity and the Renaissance* (London).

Mathisen, Ralph W. and Sivan, Hagith S. (eds) (1996). *Shifting Frontiers in Late Antiquity* (Aldershot).

Matschke, Klaus-Peter (2002). 'The late Byzantine urban economy, thirteenth–fifteenth centuries', in Angeliki E. Laiou (ed.), *Economic History of Byzantium* (Washington, DC), 2, pp. 454–86.

Matschke, Klaus-Peter (2002). 'Commerce, trade, markets and money, thirteenth–fifteenth centuries', in Angeliki E. Laiou (ed.), *Economic History of Byzantium* (Washington, DC), 2, pp. 755–90.

Mazower, Mark (2000). *The Balkans* (London).

Merrills, A. H. (ed.) (2004). *Vandals, Romans and Berbers: New Perspectives on Late Antique North Africa* (Aldershot).

Millar, Fergus (2006). *A Greek Roman Empire: Power and Belief under Theodosius II (408–450)* (Berkeley and Los Angeles).

Miller, T. S. (1985). *The Birth of the Hospital in the Byzantine Empire* (Baltimore).

Mitchell, Stephen (1993). *Anatolia: Land, Men, and Gods in Asia Minor* (2 vols, Oxford).

Mitchell, Stephen and Greatrex, Geoffrey (eds) (2000). *Ethnicity and Culture in Late Antiquity* (London).

Moore, R. I. (2000). *The First European Revolution, c. 970–1215* (Oxford).

Moore, R. I. (2003). 'The eleventh century in Eurasian history: a comparative approach to the convergence and divergence of medieval civilizations', *Journal of Medieval and Early Modern Studies* 33.1, 1–21.

Morris, Rosemary (1995). *Monks and Laymen in Byzantium, 843–1118* (Cambridge).

Morrisson, Cécile (1976). 'La Dévaluation de la monnaie byzantine au XIe siècle: essai d'interprétation', *Travaux et Mémoires* 6: 3–48.

Morrisson, Cécile (2002). 'Byzantine money: its production and circulation', in Angeliki E. Laiou (ed.), *Economic History of Byzantium* (Washington, DC), 3, pp. 909–66.

Mullett, Margaret (1988). 'Byzantium: a friendly society?' *Past and Present* 118: 3–25.

Mullett, Margaret (1990). 'Writing in early medieval Byzantium', in R. McKitterick, *The Uses of Literacy in Early Mediaeval Europe* (Cambridge), pp. 156–85.

Mullett, Margaret (1997). *Theophylact of Ochrid: Reading the Letters of a Byzantine Archbishop* (Aldershot).

Mullett, Margaret and Scott, Roger (eds) (1981). *Byzantium and the Classical Tradition* (Birmingham).

Mullett, Margaret and Kirby, Anthony (eds) (1994). *The Theotokos Evergetis and Eleventh-Century Monasticism*, Belfast Byzantine Texts and Translations 6.1 (Belfast).

Mullett, Margaret and Kirby, Anthony (eds) (1997). *Work and Worship at the Theotokos Evergetis*, Belfast Byzantine Texts and Translations 6.2.

Mullett, Margaret and Smythe, Dion (eds) (1996). *Alexios I Komnenos I: Papers*, Belfast Byzantine Texts and Translations 4.1 (Belfast).

Nadel, S. F. ([1941] 1961). *A Black Byzantium: The Kingdom of Nupe in Nigeria* (Oxford).

Nelson, R. S. (1989). 'The discourse of icons, then and now', *Art History* 12.2: 144–57.

Nelson, Robert S. (2000). *Visuality before and beyond the Renaissance: Seeing As Others Saw* (Cambridge).

Nelson, Robert S. (2000). 'To say and to see: ekphrasis and vision in Byzantium', in Nelson (ed.), *Visuality Before and Beyond the Renaissance: Seeing As Others Saw* (Cambridge), pp. 143–68.

Neville, Leonora (2004). *Authority in Byzantine Provincial Society, 950–1100* (Cambridge).

Nicol, D. M. (1957). *The Despotate of Epiros* (Oxford).

Nicol, D. M. (1984). *The Despotate of Epiros, 1267–1479* (Cambridge).

Nicol, D. M. (1988). *Byzantium and Venice: A Study in Diplomatic and Cultural Relations* (Cambridge).

Nicol, D. M. (1992). *The Immortal Emperor* (Cambridge).

Nicol, D. M. (1994). *The Byzantine Lady: Ten Portraits 1250–1500* (Cambridge).

Nicol, D. M. (1996). *The Reluctant Emperor: A Biography of John Cantacuzene, Byzantine Emperor and Monk, c.1295–1383* (Cambridge).

Nilsson, Ingela (2005). 'Meutre à Byzance: Byzantine murders in modern literature', *Greek, Roman and Byzantine Studies* 29: 235–38.

Obolensky, Dimitri (1971). *The Byzantine Commonwealth: Eastern Europe 500–1453* (Oxford).

Obolensky, Dimitri (1972). 'Nationalism in Eastern Europe in the Middle Ages', *Transactions of the Royal Historical Society*, 5th ser., 22: 1–16, repr. in D. Obolensky (1982) *The Byzantine Inheritance in Eastern Europe* (London) ch. XV.

Obolensky, Dimitri (1982). *The Byzantine Inheritance in Eastern Europe* (London).

Odorico, P. and Agapitos, P. A. (eds) (2002). *Pour une 'nouvelle' histoire de la littérature byzantine: problèmes, méthodes, approches, propositions*, Actes du Colloque international philologique, Nicosie, Chypre, 25–8 mai 2000 (Paris).

Oikonomides, N. (1972). *Les Listes de préséance byzantines des IX et X siècles* (Paris).

Oikonomides, N. (1979). 'L'Épopée de Digenis et la frontière orientale de Byzance aux Xe et XIe siècles', *Travaux et Mémoires* 7: 375–97.

Oikonomides, N. (1986). 'Silk trade and production in Byzantium from the sixth to the ninth century: the seals of kommerkiarioi', *Dumbarton Oaks Papers* 40: 33–53.

Oikonomides, N. (1988). 'Mount Athos: levels of literacy', *Dumbarton Oaks Papers* 42: 167–78.

Oikonomides, N. (2002). 'The role of the Byzantine state in the economy', in Angeliki E. Laiou (ed.), *The Economic History of Byzantium* (Washington, DC), 3, pp. 973–1058.

Olster, David, 'From periphery to center: the transformation of late Roman self-definition in the seventh century', in Ralph W. Mathisen and Hagis S. Sivan (eds), *Shifting Frontiers in Late Antiquity* (Aldershot), pp. 93–101.

Pagden, Anthony (2001). *Peoples and Empires: Europeans and the Rest of the World, from Antiquity to the Present* (London).

Papadakis, A. (1997). *Crisis in Byzantium: The Filioque Controversy in the Patriarchate of Gregory II of Cyprus (1283–1289)* (rev. edn, Crestwood, NY).

Papamastorakis, T. (2003). 'Tampering with history: from Michael III to Michael VIII', *Byzantinische Zeitschrift* 96: 193–209.

Parry, Ken, et al., (eds) (1999). *The Blackwell Dictionary of Eastern Churches* (Oxford).

Patlagean, E. (2000). 'Les États d'Europe centrale et Byzance, ou l'oscillation des confins', *Revue historique* 302.4: 827–68.

Patrich, J. (1995). *Sabas, Leader of Palestinian Monasticism: A Comparative Study in Eastern Monasticism, Fourth to Seventh Centuries* (Washington, DC).

Pentcheva, Bissera V. (2002). 'The supernatural protector of Constantinople: The Virgin and her icons in the tradition of the Avar siege', *Byzantine and Modern Greek Studies* 26: 2–41.

Philippidis-Braat, A. (1979). 'La Captivité de Palamas chez les Turcs: dossier et commentaire', *Travaux et Mémoires* 7: 109–221.

Piganiol, André, 1947. *L'Empire chrétien (325–395)* (Paris).

Pohl, W. and Reimitz, H. (eds) (1998). *Strategies of Distinction: The Construction of Ethnic Communities, 300–800* (Leiden).

Purcell, Nicholas (2005). 'Four years of corruption', in W. V. Harris (ed.), *Rethinking the Mediterranean* (Oxford), pp. 348–75.

Rapp, Claudia (1994). 'Hagiography and monastic literature between Greek East and Latin West in late antiquity', in *Cristianità d'Occidente e Cristianità d'Oriente (secoli VI–XI)*, Settimane di Studio 51 (Spoleto), pp. 1221–80.

Rapp, Claudia (2005). *Holy Bishops in Late Antiquity: The Nature of Christian Leadership in an Age of Transition* (Berkeley and Los Angeles).

Reinert, Stephen W. (2002). 'Fragmentation (1204–1453)', in Cyril Mango (ed.), *The Oxford History of Byzantium* (Oxford), pp. 248–83.

Ringrose, Kathryn M. (2003). *The Perfect Servant: Eunuchs and the Social Construction of Gender in Byzantium* (Chicago).

Rotman, Youval (2004). *Les Esclaves et l'esclavage de la Méditerranée antique à la Méditerranée médiévale VIe–XIe siècles* (Paris).

Runciman, Steven (1951). *A History of the Crusades* (3 vols, Cambridge).

Runciman, Steven (1958). *The Sicilian Vespers: A History of the Mediterranean World in the Later Thirteenth Century* (Cambridge).

Runciman, Steven (1965). *The Fall of Constantinople 1453* (Cambridge).

Runciman, Steven (1967). 'The place of Byzantium in the medieval world', in J. M. Hussey (ed.), *Cambridge Medieval History* (Cambridge) IV.2, pp. 354–75.

Runciman. Steven (1971). *The Eastern Schism: A Study of the Papacy and the Eastern Churches during the XIth and XIIth Centuries* (Oxford).

Runciman, Steven (1977). *The Byzantine Theocracy* (Cambridge).

Ševčenko, Ihor (1984). 'The Palaeologan renaissance', in Warren Treadgold (ed.) *Renaissances before the Renaissance* (Stanford), pp. 144–71.

Ševčenko, Ihor (1995). 'Was there totalitarianism in Byzantium? Constantinople's control over its Asiatic hinterland in the early ninth century', in Cyril Mango and Gilbert Dagron (eds), *Constantinople and its Hinterland* (Aldershot), pp. 91–105.

Ševčenko, Ihor (2002). 'Palaiologan learning', in Cyril Mango (ed.), *Oxford History of Byzantium* (Oxford), pp. 284–93.

Shepard, Jonathan (1988). 'When Greek meets Greek: Alexius I Comnenus and Bohemond in 1097–98', *Byzantine and Modern Greek Studies* 12: 185–277.

Shepard, Jonathan (1992). 'Byzantine diplomacy AD 800–1204: means and ends', in Jonathon Shepard and Simon Franklin (eds), *Byzantine Diplomacy* (Aldershot), pp. 41–71

Shepard, Jonathan (1999). 'Byzantium in equilibrium, 886–944', 'Bulgaria: the other Balkan "empire"', 'Byzantium expanding, 944–1025', 'Byzantium and the west', in T. Reuter (ed.) *New Cambridge Medieval History* c.900–c.1024 (Cambridge) III, pp. 553–66, 567–85, 586–604, 605–23.

Shepard, Jonathan (2002). 'Emperors and expansionism: from Rome to Middle Byzantium', in David Abulafia and Nora Berend (eds), *Medieval Frontiers: Concepts and Practices* (Aldershot), pp. 55–82.

Shepard, Jonathan, and Franklin, Simon (eds) (1992). *Byzantine Diplomacy* (Aldershot).

Speck, P. (1998). 'Byzantium: cultural suicide?' in L. Brubaker (ed.), *Byzantium in the Ninth Century* (Aldershot), pp. 73–84.

Spieser, J.-M. (1991). 'Hellénisme et connaissance de l'art byzantin au XIXe siècle', in Saïd, S. (ed.), *Hellenismos: Jalons pour une histoire de l'identité grecque*, Actes du Colloque de Strasbourg, 25–7 octobre 1989 (Leiden), pp. 338–62.

Smith, Anthony D. (1983). *Theories of Nationalism* (2nd edn, London).

Smith, Julia M. H. (2005). *Europe after Rome: A New Cultural History 500–1000* (Oxford).

Soulis, George C. (1984). *The Serbs and Byzantium during the Reign of Tsar Stephen Dušan (1331–1355) and his Successors* (Washington, DC).

Stephenson, Paul (1999–2000). 'Byzantium's Balkan frontier, 900–1204: a political overview', in *Byzantium and the North: Acta Byzantina Fennica* 10: 153–67.

Stephenson, Paul (2000). *Byzantium's Balkan Frontier: A Political Study of the Northern Balkans, 900–1204* (Cambridge).

Stephenson, Paul (2000). 'The legend of Basil the Bulgar-slayer', *Byzantine and Modern Greek Studies* 24: 102–32.

Stephenson, Paul (2001). 'Images of the Bulgar-slayer: three art-historical notes', *Byzantine and Modern Greek Studies* 25: 44–68.

Stephenson, Paul (2003). *The Legend of Basil the Bulgar-slayer* (Cambridge).

Stoyanov, Yuri (2000). *The Other God: Dualist Religions from Antiquity to the Cathar Heresy* (New Haven).

Swain, Simon (1996). *Hellenism and Empire: Language, Classicism, and Power in the Greek World, AD 50–250* (Oxford).

Szúcs, J. (1985). *Les trois Europes* (French trans., Paris).

Talbot, Alice-Mary (2005). 'Monasticism', in Jonathan Harris (ed.), *Palgrave Advances in Byzantine History* (Basingstoke), pp. 119–32.

Todorova, Maria (1997). *Imagining the Balkans* (Oxford).

Tougher, Shaun F. (1997). 'Byzantine eunuchs: an overview, with special reference to their creation and origin', in Liz James (ed.), *Women, Men and Eunuchs: Gender in Byzantium* (London), pp. 168–84.

Tougher, Shaun F. (ed.) (2002). *Eunuchs in Antiquity and Beyond* (London).

Toynbee, Arnold (1971). *Constantine Porphyrogenitus and his World* (London).

Treadgold, Warren (ed.) (1984). *Renaissances before the Renaissance* (Stanford).

Treadgold, Warren (1988). *The Byzantine Revival 780–842* (Stanford).

Treadgold, Warren (1995). *Byzantium and its Army 284–1081* (Stanford).

Underwood, Paul A. (ed.) (1966, 1975). *The Kariye Djami* (4 vols, New York) 1–3 (Princeton).

van Rompay, Lucas (2005). 'Society and community in the Christian east', in Michael Maas (ed.), *The Cambridge Companion to the Age of Justinian* (Cambridge), pp. 239–66.

Vassilaki, Maria (ed.) (2000). *Mother of God: Representations of the Virgin in Byzantine Art* (Milan).

Vryonis Jr., Speros (1957). 'The will of a provincial magnate, Eustathius Boilas (1059)', *Dumbarton Oaks Papers* 11: 263–77.

Vryonis, Speros, Jr. (1967). *Byzantium and Europe* (London).

Vryonis, Speros Jr. (1971). *The Decline of Medieval Hellenism in Asia Minor and the Process of Islamization from the Eleventh through the Fifteenth Century* (Berkeley and Los Angeles).

Walter, Christopher (2000). *Pictures as Language: How the Byzantines Exploited Them* (London).

Ward-Perkins, Bryan (2005). *The Fall of Rome and the End of Civilization* (Oxford).

Webb, Ruth (1999). 'The aesthetics of sacred space: narrative, metaphor and motion in "Ekphraseis" of church buildings', *Dumbarton Oaks Papers* 53: 59–74.

Whitby, Mary (ed.) (2006). *Byzantium and the Crusades: The Non-Greek Sources* (Oxford).

Whitby, Michael (1995). 'Recruitment in the Roman armies from Justinian to Heraclius (ca. 565–615)', in Averil Cameron (ed.), *The Byzantine and Early Islamic Near East III: States, Resources, Armies*, Studies in Late Antiquity and Early Islam I (Princeton), pp. 61–124.

Whittow, Mark (1990). 'Ruling the late Roman and early Byzantine city', *Past and Present* 103: 3–36.

Whittow, Mark (1996). 'How the east was lost', in Margaret Mullett and Dion Smythe (eds), *Alexios I Komnenos: I Papers*, Belfast Byzantine Texts and Translations 4.1 (Belfast) 55–67.

Wickham, Chris (2005). *Framing the Early Middle Ages: Europe and the Mediterranean 400–800* (Oxford).

Wilken, Robert L. (1992). *The Land Called Holy: Palestine in Christian History and Thought* (New Haven).

Williams, Patrick and Chrisman, Laura (eds) (1993). *Colonial Discourse and Post-Colonial Theory* (London).

Wilson, N. G. (1983). *Scholars of Byzantium* (London).

Wilson, N. G. (1992). *From Byzantium to Italy: Greek Studies in the Italian Renaissance* (London).

Winkelmann, F. (1985). *Byzantinische Rang- und Ämterstruktur im 8. und 9. Jahrhundert*, Berliner byzantinische Arbeiten 53 (Berlin).

Winkelmann, F. (1987). *Quellenstudien zur herrschenden Klasse von Byzanz im 8. Und 9. Jahrhundert* (Berlin).

Zakythinos, D. (1975). *Le Despotat grecque de Morée*, rev. Chryssa Maltezou (2 vols, 2nd rev. edn, London).

Notes

The spelling of Greek names always presents problems, especially in a book whose chronological span runs from late antiquity to the fifteenth century. Here I have preferred simplicity and familiarity to total consistency. Thus familiar forms such as Constantine are kept, instead of Konstantinos, especially in the earlier period, but when writing of Middle and Late Byzantium, Greek forms predominate, with the *Oxford Dictionary of Byzantium* as the main model. Consonant with the aims of the series, I have cited primary sources in English translation where possible, and the references concentrate on publications in English.

PREFACE

1 Anthony Kenny, *Medieval Philosophy: A New History of Western Philosophy* 2 (Oxford, 2005), p. 28.
2 Anthony D. Smith, *The Antiquity of Nations* (Cambridge, 2004).
3 Following Steven Grosby, *Biblical Ideas of Nationality: Ancient and Modern* (Winona Lake, IN, 2002).
4 Peter Heather, *The Fall of the Roman Empire* (Basingstoke and Oxford, 2005); Bryan Ward-Perkins, *The Fall of Rome and the End of Civilization* (Oxford, 2005).
5 R. I. Moore, 'The eleventh century in Eurasian history: a comparative approach to the convergence and divergence of medieval civilizations', *Journal of Medieval and Early Modern Studies* 33.1 (2003): 1–21.
6 A. Gurevich, *The Origins of European Individualism* (Oxford, 1995), chapter 1.
7 W. V. Harris, ed., *Rethinking the Mediterranean* (Oxford, 2005), responding to Peregrine Horden and Nicholas Purcell, *The Corrupting Sea: A Study of Mediterranean History* (Oxford, 2000).
8 See Judith Herrin, *The Formation of Christendom* (Oxford and Princeton, 1987); Peter Brown, *The Rise of Western Christendom: Triumph and Diversity, AD 200–1000*, 2nd edn (Oxford, 2003).
9 See Patrick Geary, *The Myth of Nations: The Medieval Origins of Europe* (Princeton, 2002) and the publications arising from the European Science

Foundation Project in the 1990s on *The Transformation of the Roman World*, AD 400–900, for instance Walter Pohl and Helmut Reimitz, eds, *Strategies of Distinction: The Construction of the Ethnic Communities, 300–800* (Leiden, 1998).

10   For example Robert Bartlett, *The Making of Europe: Conquest, Colonisation and Cultural Change 950–1350* (London, 1993); see Chapter 9 below.

11   Chris Wickham's important book, *Framing the Early Middle Ages: Europe and the Mediterranean, 400–800* (Oxford, 2005), published as this book went to press, adopts a comparative approach across western Europe and the Mediterranean world, including Byzantium, in order to understand shared or contrasting characteristics of the form and financing of the state, aristocracies, the peasantry and the structures of local rural society, urban society and economy, and networks of exchange (p. 6).

12   For the period c.680–850, Leslie Brubaker and John Haldon, *Byzantium in the Iconoclast Era (ca.680–850): The Sources. An Annotated Survey* (Aldershot, 2001) have informative sections on architecture (pp. 3–36), archaeology (pp. 146–58), coins and numismatics (pp. 116–28) and sigillography (seals) (pp. 129–37), including reference to current work and bibliography; the survey by Ken Dark, 'Archaeology', in Jonathan Harris, ed., *Palgrave Advances in Byzantine History* (Basingstoke, 2005), pp. 166–84, also clearly indicates how far work done to date has concentrated on ecclesiastical remains.

1 WHAT WAS BYZANTIUM?

1   S. F. Nadel, *A Black Byzantium: The Kingdom of Nupe in Nigeria* (Oxford, 1941, rev. 1961).

2   A typical title is R. Guerdan, *Vie, grandeurs et misères de Byzance* (Paris, 1954).

3   As illustrations of this tendency, in S. Vryonis's book *Byzantium and Europe* (London, 1967) the last two of the four chapters are headed 'Decline' (from the eleventh century) and 'Prostration and collapse'; in Donald Nicol, *The Last Centuries or Byzantium, 1261–1453* (Cambridge, 1993) one chapter is entitled 'Symptoms and causes of decline', and Part 3 of the book is headed 'The mortal illness of Byzantium'.

4   See the classic study by Steven Runciman, *The Fall of Constantinople 1453* (Cambridge, 1965) and the moving account in D. M. Nicol, *The Immortal Emperor* (Cambridge, 1992).

5   Alexander Kazhdan, the editor of the *Oxford Dictionary of Byzantium*, is a case in point. His early publications were written in this context, until he arrived in the West in the 1970s and settled at Dumbarton Oaks in Washington where he had a considerable impact on younger North American Byzantinists.

6 See Robin Cormack and Elizabeth Jeffreys, eds, *Through the Looking Glass: Byzantium through British Eyes* (Aldershot, 2000).

7 See e.g. Angeliki Laiou and Henry Maguire, eds, *Byzantium: A World Civilisation* (Washington, DC, 1992).

8 See the essays in Robin Cormack and Elizabeth Jeffreys, eds, *Through the Looking Glass: Byzantium through British Eyes* (Aldershot, 2000).

9 See especially Peter Brown, *The World of Late Antiquity* (London, 1971), with Glen Bowersock, Peter Brown and Oleg Grabar, eds, *Late Antiquity: A Guide to the Post-Classical World* (Cambridge, MA, 1999); cf. Averil Cameron, 'The long late antiquity: a late twentieth-century model', in T. P. Wiseman, ed., *Classics in Progress: Essays on Ancient Greece and Rome* (Oxford, 2002), pp. 165–91.

10 Cyril Mango, *Le Développement urbain de Constantinople, IV–VII siècles* (Paris, 1985), emphasising the secular and traditional nature of Constantine's foundation and the slowness with which it acquired a Christian identity.

11 Peter Garnsey and Caroline Humfress in *The Evolution of the Late Antique World* (Cambridge, 2001) address the structural issues surrounding these changes.

12 Julia M. H. Smith, *Europe after Rome: A New Cultural History 500–1000* (Oxford, 2005), p. 23.

13 R. Beaton, *The Medieval Greek Romance*, rev. edn, (London, 1996), p. 73.

14 For Justinian's legal work see Tony Honoré, *Tribonian* (London, 1978).

15 Robert Browning, *Medieval and Modern Greek* (London, 1969, 2nd edn Cambridge, 1983).

16 See Chapter 8.

17 See Speros Vryonis, in Laiou and Maguire, eds, *Byzantium: A World Civilization*, 19–31, and Hélène Ahrweiler and Angeliki E. Laiou, eds, *Studies on the Internal Diaspora of the Byzantine Empire* (Washington, DC, 1998).

18 See Dion Smythe, ed., *Strangers to Themselves: The Byzantine Outsider* (Aldershot, 2000).

19 For Anatolia in late antiquity see Stephen Mitchell, *Anatolia: Land, Men, and Gods in Asia Minor*, 2 vols. (Oxford, 1993).

20 But issues of identity and ethnicity, not least in Anatolia, are the subject of much current debate: see e.g. Stephen Mitchell and Geoffrey Greatrex, eds, *Ethnicity and Culture in Late Antiquity* (London, 2000), and for the 'ethnogenesis' of barbarian peoples, W. Pohl and H. Reimitz, eds, *Strategies of Distinction: The Construction of Ethnic Communities, 300–800* (Leiden, 1998); P. Geary, *The Myth of Nations: The Medieval Origins of Europe* (Princeton, 2002).

21 See John Haldon, *The Palgrave Atlas of Byzantine History* (Basingstoke, 2005), pp. 76–7; G. Dagron, 'Minorités ethniques et religieuses dans l'orient byzantin à la fin du Xe et au XIe siècle: l'immigration syrienne', *Travaux et mémoires* 6 (1972), pp. 177–216; D. Zakythinos, *Le Despotat grecque de Morée*, 2 vols., 2nd edn rev. Chryssa Maltezou (London, 1975).

22   For these issues see David Abulafia and Nora Berend, eds, *Medieval Frontiers: Concepts and Practices* (Aldershot, 2002) and D. Power and N. Standen, eds, *Frontiers in Question: Eurasian Borderlands, 700–1700* (London, 1999). The multi-volume *Tabula Imperii Byzantini* (*TIB*) published in Vienna is the most authoritative historical atlas of Byzantium for the areas that it covers; allowing for the caveats expressed above, Haldon, *The Palgrave Atlas of Byzantine History* provides a very large number of clear and well thought-out maps covering the whole period, together with a narrative text.

23   See John Haldon, *Warfare, State and Society in the Byzantine World 565–1204* (London, 1999) and *The Byzantine Wars: Battles and Campaigns of the Byzantine Era* (Stroud, 2001).

24   Benjamin Isaac, *The Limits of Empire: The Roman Army in the East*, rev. edn (Oxford, 1992), S. T. Parker, *Romans and Saracens: A History of the Arabian Frontier* (Philadelphia, 2001).

25   See N. Oikonomides, 'L'Épopée de Digenes et la frontière orientale de Byzance aux Xe et XIe siècles', *Travaux et Mémoires* 7 (1979), pp. 375–97 and Chapters 8 and 10 below.

26   Dimitri Obolensky, *The Byzantine Commonwealth: Eastern Europe 500–1453* (London, 1971), on which see Chapter 9 below; for the change from the linear borders of the Roman Empire (however imperfectly achieved in practice) to the looser Byzantine system see Jonathan Shepard, 'Emperors and expansionism: from Rome to middle Byzantium', in Abulafia and Berend, eds, *Medieval Frontiers*, pp. 55–82, who argues that Byzantium was no less expansionist than Rome, but not 'territorial'; cf. Catherine Holmes, 'Byzantium's eastern frontier in the tenth and eleventh centuries', ibid., pp. 83–104.

27   So the author of the anti-Jewish treatise known as the *Trophies of Damascus* (660s), and 'Methodius', author of a late-seventh century apocalypse: see David Olster, 'From periphery to center: the transformation of late Roman self-definition in the seventh century', in Ralph W. Mathisen and Hagith S. Sivan, eds, *Shifting Frontiers in Late Antiquity* (Aldershot, 1996), pp. 93–101. It was even possible to claim that this idealised empire stretched as far as Britain.

28   N. Oikonomides, 'Byzantine diplomacy AD 1204–1453: means and ends', in Shepard and Franklin, eds, *Byzantine Diplomacy*, pp. 73–88, at p. 88.

29   See Ruth Macrides, 'Dynastic marriages and political kinship', ibid., pp. 263–80.

30   See J. H. W. G. Liebeschuetz, *The Decline and Fall of the Roman City* (Oxford, 2001); Claudia Rapp, *Holy Bishops in Late Antiquity: The Nature of Christian Leadership in an Age of Transition* (Berkeley and Los Angeles, 2005).

31   Obolensky, in Laiou and Maguire, eds, *Byzantium: A World Civilization*, pp. 37–40.

32 Just as there was a remarkable Greek Archbishop of Canterbury in the seventh century, Theodore of Tarsus, who established a centre of Greek learning at Canterbury.

33 See Lowell Clucas, ed., *The Byzantine Legacy in Eastern Europe* (New York, 1988) and below, Chapter 9.

34 See Cyril Mango, *Byzantium: The Empire of New Rome* (London, 1980), a brilliantly astringent survey that deconstructs views of Byzantium based on romantic notions of Orthodoxy; see e.g. p. 104: 'the real villain of the story is, of course, State Orthodoxy', which for Mango directly led to bigotry and narrowness inimical to any idealised idea of hellenism: the Byzantines were firmly medieval, and therefore superstitious: see p. 151: 'To the Byzantine man, as indeed to all men of the Middle Ages, the supernatural existed in a very real and familiar sense.'

35 Vryonis, in Laiou and Maguire, eds, p. 21; for Vryonis's positive emphasis on Orthodoxy see ibid., 31. The 'duality' in Byzantine civilisation was also a theme of Arnold Toynbee and Norman Baynes; see Averil Cameron, 'Bury, Baynes and Toynbee', in Cormack and Jeffreys, eds, *Through the Looking Glass*, pp. 163–76.

36 For Byzantium, the Balkans and Balkanism see Chapter 9, and for an incisive short analysis debating the many pitfalls in the concept of 'Balkan identity' and the usual reasons given for the rise of Balkan nationalism see Mark Mazower, *The Balkans* (London, 2000).

37 Mitchell and Greatrex, eds, *Ethnicity and Culture in Late Antiquity* (London, 2000), pp. xi–xii.

38 *Byzantium: The Empire of New Rome*, p. 26.

39 Ibid., p. 27f.

40 Steven Runciman, 'The place of Byzantium in the medieval world', in J. M. Hussey, ed., *Cambridge Medieval History* IV.2 (Cambridge, 1967), pp. 354–75, at p. 375.

41 Landholding and the development of great estates have been traditional topics of research in Byzantine studies, especially in relation to supposed Byzantine 'feudalism', but the Byzantine village is a relatively new topic: see, however, M. Kaplan, *Les Hommes et la terre à Byzance du VIe au XIe siècle. Propriété et exploitation du sol* (Paris, 1992). Villages are an important theme in Chris Wickham, *Framing the Early Middle Ages: Europe and the Mediterranean 400–800* (Oxford, 2005), e.g. pp. 442–518.

42 The classic work is Homi K. Bhabha, *The Location of Culture* (London, 1994).

43 Bhabha, *The Location of Culture*, p. 235.

44 Ahrweiler and Laiou, eds, *Studies on the Internal Diaspora*, pp. vii–viii.

45 Ibid., pp. 161–81.

46 Even if taken as gender-inclusive, attempts to define 'Byzantine man', such as that in Alexander Kazhdan and Giles Constable, *People and Power in Byzantium: An Introduction to Modern Byzantine Studies* (Washington, DC, 1982) invite some hesitation. The original Italian title of Cavallo, ed., *The*

Byzantines, was *L'Uomo Bizantino* (ed. Robert Browning, Guglielmo Cavallo, Paolo Cesaretti, Milan, 1992).

47 Runciman, 'The place of Byzantium in the medieval world', p. 374.

48 See the memorable account by Steven Runciman, *The Great Church in Captivity* (Cambridge, 1968), chapter 7, with Peter Doll, ed., *Anglicanism and Orthodoxy 300 years after the 'Greek College' in Oxford* (Oxford, 2005).

49 J. B. Bury, *History of the Later Roman Empire: From Arcadius to Irene (395 AD to 800 AD)* (London, 1889), p. v.

50 A. J. Toynbee, *Constantine Porphyrogenitus and His World* (Oxford, 1971), pp. 541–52; cf. p. 543, referring to 'the antithesis between the Byzantine spirit and the Hellenic spirit'.

51 See in particular PBE (*Prosopography of the Byzantine Empire, I. AD 641–867*, ed. J. Martindale (Aldershot, 2001, CD-rom). The editor of the continuation of this prosopography into the Comnenian period renamed it *Prosopography of the Byzantine World* and concluded that it needed to incorporate extensive use of non-Greek sources, especially Arabic.

52 See Cyril Mango, 'Introduction', in Cyril Mango and Gilbert Dagron, eds, with the assistance of Geoffrey Greatrex, *Constantinople and its Hinterland* (Aldershot, 1995), pp. 3–6.

2 THE CHANGING SHAPE OF BYZANTIUM: FROM LATE ANTIQUITY TO 1025

1 The comparative strength of urbanism in East and West has been the subject of much archaeological research: see J. H. W. G. Liebeschuetz, *The Decline and Fall of the Roman City* (Oxford, 2002); L. Lavan et al., eds, *Recent Research in Late-Antique Urbanism* (Portsmouth, RI, 2001); L. Lavan and W. Bowden, eds, *Theory and Practice in Late Antique Archaeology* (Leiden, 2003).

2 Peter Brown, *Power and Persuasion in Late Antiquity: Towards a Christian Empire* (Madison, 1992); *Authority and the Sacred: Aspects of the Christianisation of the Roman World* (Cambridge, 1995).

3 G. W. Bowersock, *Hellenism in Late Antiquity* (Ann Arbor, 1990); P. Chuvin, *A Chronicle of the Last Pagans*, English trans. (Cambridge, MA., 1990); K. Weitzmann, ed., *Age of Spirituality: Late Antique and Early Christian Art, Third to Seventh Century* (New York, 1977).

4 Peter Heather, *The Fall of the Roman Empire* (Basingstoke and Oxford, 2005); Bryan Ward-Perkins, *The Fall of Rome and the End of Civilization* (Oxford, 2005).

5 See Fergus Millar, *A Greek Roman Empire: Power and Belief under Theodosius II (408–450)* (Berkeley and Los Angeles, 2006); the complete record of the Council of Chalcedon is now for the first time available in English translation with historical commentary by Richard Price and Michael Gaddis, *The Acts of the Council of Chalcedon*, 3 vols. (Liverpool, 2005).

6 See Christoph Baumer, *The Church of the East: An Illustrated History of Assyrian Christianity* (London, 2006), and for reference on the Eastern Churches, Ken Parry et al., eds, *The Blackwell Dictionary of Eastern Churches* (Oxford, 1999).

7 For a recent overview see Lucas van Rompay, 'Society and community in the Christian east', in Michael Maas, ed., *The Cambridge Companion to the Age of Justinian* (Cambridge, 2005), pp. 239–66.

8 Sozomen, *Ecclesiastical History* IX.1, 3.

9 A. H. M. Jones, *The Later Roman Empire, 284–602: A Social, Economic and Administrative Survey*, 2 vols. (Oxford, 1964); G. E. M. de Ste. Croix, *The Class Struggle in the Ancient Greek World: From the Archaic Age to the Arab Conquests* (London, 1981); Liebeschuetz, *The Decline and Fall of the Roman City.*

10 *De Mag.* III. 55.4.

11 *Secret History* 18.

12 Though the effects of the plague are difficult to assess: three contemporary accounts depict a catastrophic event, but little or no trace can be found in archaeological sources.

13 On Procopius and other writers of the period see Averil Cameron, *Procopius and the Sixth Century* (London, 1985); for the reign of Justinian generally see Michael Maas, ed., *The Cambridge Companion to the Age of Justinian* (Cambridge, 2005); on the administrative history of the period from Diocletian to c.600 A. H. M. Jones, *The Later Roman Empire, 284–602: A Social, Economic and Administrative Survey*, 2 vols. (Oxford, 1964), is still basic, but see also Averil Cameron, Brian Ward-Perkins, Michael Whitby, eds, *Late Antiquity. Empire and Successors*, AD 425–600 (Cambridge, 2000).

14 Garth Fowden, *Empire to Commonwealth: Consequences of Monotheism in Late Antiquity* (Princeton, 1993).

15 Some of these issues are discussed in the essays in A. H. Merrills, ed., *Vandals, Romans and Berbers: New Perspectives on Late Antique North Africa* (Aldershot, 2004).

16 For the military history of Byzantium up to 1204 and the many changes that took place in the army system see the differing accounts by John Haldon *Warfare, State and Society in the Byzantine World 565–1204* (London, 1999) and Warren Treadgold, *Byzantium and its Army 284–1081* (Stanford, 1995).

17 For Jerusalem and the Christian reactions to the Persian invasion see Robert Wilken, *The Land Called Holy: Palestine in Christian History and Thought* (New Haven, 1992); also on this period Gerrit J. Reinink and Bernard H. Stolte, eds, *The Reign of Heraclius (610–641): Crisis and Confrontation* (Leuven, 2002).

18 W. E. Kaegi, *Byzantium and the Early Islamic Conquests* (Cambridge, 1992); for Heraclius also id., *Heraclius: Emperor of Byzantium* (Cambridge, 2003).

19 Michael Whitby, 'Recruitment in the Roman armies from Justinian to Heraclius (c.565–615)', in Averil Cameron, ed., *The Byzantine and Early*

Islamic Near East III. States, Resources, Armies, Studies in Late Antiquity and Early Islam I (Princeton, 1995), pp. 61–124; J. Howard-Johnston, 'The two great powers in late antiquity: a comparison', ibid., pp. 157–226; W. Treadgold, *Byzantium and its Army 284–108*, p. 64.

20   For signs of decline by this date even in the prosperous cities of the eastern provinces see Liebeschuetz, *The Decline and Fall of the Roman City*, against e.g. M. Whittow, 'Ruling the late Roman and early Byzantine city', *Past and Present* 103 (1990), pp. 3–36. The effects of the Persian invasion have been argued particularly by Clive Foss, cf. 'The Persians in Asia Minor and the end of antiquity', *English Historical Review* 90 (1975), 721–47.

21   Agathias, *Histories* V.13, a situation the historian attributes to the negligence of Justinian and his officials. Agathias is describing the panic that set in at the danger posed to Constantinople in AD 559 when a force of Cotrigur Huns appeared within the crumbling Long Walls; all the treasures from churches on the European side of the Bosphorus across the Golden Horn were brought in for safety and the aged Belisarius had to be called out of retirement to lead the counter-attack.

22   Constantine: Zosimus, *Hist.* II.32; Malalas, pp. 322–3; end of the import of grain from Egypt in 618: *Chron. Pasch.* s.a. 618.

23   J. Durliat, 'L'Approvisionnement de Constantinople', in Cyril Mango and Gilbert Dagron, eds, *Constantinople and its Hinterland* (Aldershot, 1995), pp. 19–33; *Book of the Prefect*, 18; Paul Magdalino, 'The grain supply of Constantinople, ninth–twelfth centuries', ibid., pp. 35–47.

24   Geoffroy de Villehardouin, *La Conquête de Constantinople*, ed. E. Faral, 5th edn (Paris, 1973), II.251.

25   Magdalino, 'Grain supply', p. 35.

26   Sean A. Kingsley, *Shipwreck Archaeology of the Holy Land: Processes and Parameters* (London, 2004); for the numbers of shipwrecks see p. 32.

27   Michael McCormick, *The Origins of the European Economy: Communications and Commerce, AD 300–900* (Cambridge, 2001); Kingsley, *Shipwreck Archaeology*, pp. 115–16.

28   See Chris Wickham, *Framing the Early Middle Ages* (Oxford, 2005), chapter 11, on exchange; Michael Hendy, *Studies in the Byzantine Monetary Economy c.300–1450* (Cambridge, 1985), pp. 619–67, on the fiscal crisis.

29   His visit to Rome had more than a touch about it of authority and rapacity: *Book of the Pontiffs* 78.1 (Vitalian), trans. R. Davis, pp. 73–4.

30   Theoph., AM 6254 (AD 761/2), p. 599 Mango and Scott; cf. 6235 (AD 742/3), ibid., p. 581.

31   See G. Dagron, *Constantinople imaginaire: Études sur le receuil des Patria* (Paris, 1984); for the *Parastaseis*, which reflects eighth-century concerns, see the English translation and commentary by Averil Cameron and Judith Herrin et al., *Constantinople in the Eighth Century* (Leiden, 1984).

32   W. Treadgold, *The Byzantine Revival 780–842* (Stanford, 1988), pp. 337, 360–4, 380–4.

33 For the background see Judith Herrin, *The Formation of Christendom* (Oxford and Princeton, 1987).

34 See Chapter 8 below.

35 *Hom.* 3 and 4, trans. Mango.

36 Simon Franklin and Jonathan Shepard, *The Emergence of Rus', 750–1200* (London, 1996).

37 The classic study is Dimitri Obolensky, *The Byzantine Commonwealth: Eastern Europe 500–1453* (London, 1971).

38 Ed. and trans. Gy. Moravcsik and R. J. H. Jenkins, *Constantine Porphyrogenitus, De Administrando Imperio*, 2 vols. (Washington, DC, repr. 1985).

39 Military treatises: John Haldon, *Constantine Porphyrogenitus: Three Treatises on Imperial Military Expeditions*, CFHB 28 (Vienna, 1990); id., 'Theory and practice in tenth-century military administration. Chapters II, 44 and 45 of the *Book of Ceremonies'*, *Travaux et Mémoires* 13 (2000), pp. 201–352; cf. *Maurice's Strategikon: Handbook of Byzantine Military Strategy*, trans. George. T. Dennis (Philadelphia, 1984) (late sixth century) and the *Taktika* of Constantine VII's father, Leo VI.

40 Haldon, *Three Treatises*, p. 107.

41 Haldon, ibid., p. 151; Michael McCormick, *Eternal Victory: Triumphal Rulership in Late Antiquity, Byzantium and the Early Mediaeval West* (Cambridge, 1986).

42 *De Caer.* I.78.

43 *Ant.* VI.5; for the court, see Henry Maguire, ed., *Byzantine Court Culture from 829 to 1204* (Washington, DC, 1997).

44 Alan Harvey, *Economic Expansion in the Byzantine Empire, 900–1200* (Cambridge, 1990).

45 Paul Stephenson *Byzantium's Balkan Frontier: A Political Study of the Northern Balkans, 900–1204* (Cambridge, 2000); cf. id., 'Images of the Bulgar-slayer: three art-historical notes', *Byzantine and Modern Greek Studies* 25 (2001): 44–68 for Basil's presentation in visual art. As Stephenson shows, the legend has been recreated for ideological purposes in the twentieth century.

46 See Catherine Holmes, *Basil II and the Governance of Empire* (Oxford, 2005).

47 The conversion was publicised by the building of the Tithe church and elaborate palace complex at Kiev: Simon Franklin and Jonathan Shepard, *The Emergence of Rus' 750–1200*, pp. 158–69.

3 THE CHANGING SHAPE OF BYZANTIUM: FROM 1025 TO 1453

1 For a succinct summary of the discussion see Michael Angold, 'The Byzantine empire, 1025–1118', in D. Luscombe and J. Riley-Smith, eds, *New Cambridge Medieval History*, Vol. 4 c.1024–c.1198 (Cambridge, 2002), part 2, pp. 217–53, at pp. 219–22.

2   So S. Vryonis Jr., *The Decline of Medieval Hellenism in Asia Minor and the Process of Islamization from the Eleventh through the Fifteenth Century* (Berkeley and Los Angeles, 1971).

3   Alexander Kazhdan and Ann Epstein, *Change in Byzantine Culture in the Eleventh and Twelfth Centuries* (Berkeley and Los Angeles, 1985), pp. 24–73; see also Paul Magdalino, 'The Byzantine empire, 1118–1204', *New Cambridge Medieval History*, Vol. 4, pp. 611–43, at pp. 628–9. Most Byzantinists would now agree that the term 'feudalism' is best avoided in relation to Byzantium.

4   Robert Bartlett, *The Making of Europe: Conquest, Colonisation and Cultural Change* pp. 950–1350 (London, 1993); G. Dagron, 'The urban economy, seventh–twelfth centuries', in Angeliki E. Laiou, ed., *The Economic History of Byzantium*, Vol. 2. 3 vols. (Washington, DC, 2002), pp. 393–461, at pp. 401–3, who also situates these developments in a Mediterranean context.

5   Described by Anna Comnena, *Alexiad* III, 1–2.

6   Michael Angold, *The Byzantine Empire 1025–1204: A Political History*, rev. edn (London, 1997), pp. 15–23.

7   On the reign of Alexius see Margaret Mullett and Dion Smythe, eds, *Alexios I Komnenos: I Papers*, Belfast Byzantine Texts and Translations 4.1 (Belfast, 1996).

8   Angold, *The Byzantine Empire, 1025–1204*, pp. 48–55; see below, Chapter 10.

9   Peter Frankopan, 'The imperial governors of Dyrrakhion in the reign of Alexios I Komnenos', *Byzantine and Modern Greek Studies* 26 (2002): 65–103.

10   Anna Comnena, *Alexiad* X.6.

11   *Alexiad* X.9; on the Crusades from the point of view of Byzantium: R.-J. Lilie, *Byzantium and the Crusader States, 1096–1204*, Eng. trans. (Oxford, 1993); Angeliki E. Laiou and Roy Mottahadeh, eds, *The Crusades from the Perspective of Byzantium and the Muslim World* (Washington, DC, 2001); Mary Whitby, ed., *Byzantium and the Crusades: The Non-Greek Sources* (Oxford, 2006). For more discussion see Chapter 10.

12   C. Foss, *Nicaea: A Byzantine Capital and its Praises* (Brookline, MA, 1996), pp. 45–9.

13   Further, Chapter 10 below.

14   Cinnamus, *Hist.* pp. 108–9; William of Tyre, *Hist.* p. 280.

15   Paul Magdalino, *The Empire of Manuel I Komnenos, 1143–1180* (Cambridge, 1993), pp. 122–3.

16   See Chapter 8.

17   Magdalino, *The Empire of Manuel I Komnenos*, pp. 392–412.

18   Niketas Choniates, *Hist.* I, pp. 203–5, ed. Van Dieten.

19   This was Leontius, who had been abbot of the monastery of St John on Patmos; his stay in Jerusalem and the difficulties he faced there are described in his *Life*.

20 Cinnamus, *Ep.*, p. 167 Brand.

21 Choniates, *Hist.* p. 538, ed. Van Dieten.

22 Robert of Clari, *Conquest*, p. 94 trans. McNeal; Geoffrey de Villehardouin, *Conquest*, pp. 65–6.

23 Choniates, *Hist.* pp. 647–51, ed. Van Dieten.

24 For the court and government in exile under the Lascarids see Michael Angold, *A Byzantine Government in Exile: Government and Society under the Laskarids of Nicaea 1204–1261* (Oxford, 1975) and *Church and Society in Byzantium under the Comneni 1081–1261* (Cambridge, 1995), pp. 505–65, also C. Foss, *Nicaea: A Byzantine Capital and its Praises* (Brookline, MA, 1996).

25 Translated in Foss, *A Byzantine Capital*.

26 Paul Magdalino, 'Between Romaniae: Thessaly and Epirus in the Later Middle Ages', in Benjamin Arbel, Bernard Hamilton and David Jacoby, eds, *Latins and Greeks in the Eastern Mediterranean after 1204* (London, 1989), pp. 87–110; Donald Nicol, *The Despotate of Epiros, 1267–1479* (Cambridge, 1984).

27 Michael Angold, *A Byzantine Government in Exile: Government and Society under the Laskarids of Nicaea, 1204–1261* (Oxford, 1975); id., 'Byzantium in exile', in D. Abulafia, ed., *The New Cambridge Medieval History* Vol. 5, c.1198–c.1300 (Cambridge, 1999), pp. 543–68; Foss, *A Byzantine Capital*.

28 Jonathan Harris, *Byzantium and the Crusades* (London, 2003), pp. 169–73.

29 George Pachymeres, *Relations historiques* II, pp. 29, 31.

30 Nicephorus Gregoras, *Hist.*, Bonn ed. I, pp. 87–8; see also Pachymeres, heading to Chapter 6 below.

31 See especially Donald Nicol, *The Immortal Emperor* (Cambridge, 1992); Steven Runciman, *The Fall of Constantinople 1453* (Cambridge, 1965).

32 For the Mongols see Peter Jackson, *The Mongols and the West 1221–1410* (Harlow, 2005).

33 Steven Runciman, *The Sicilian Vespers: A History of the Mediterranean World in the Later Thirteenth Century* (Cambridge, 1958); on the ecclesiastical issues see A. Papadakis, *Crisis in Byzantium: The Filioque Controversy in the Patriarchate of Gregory II of Cyprus (1283–1289)*, rev. edn (Crestwood, NY, 1997) and see further Chapter 10.

34 Donald Nicol, *The Last Centuries of Byzantium, 1261–1453* (Cambridge) 1993), pp. 351–61, 377, 386.

35 Stephen W. Reinert, 'Fragmentation (1204–1453)', in Cyril Mango, ed., *The Oxford History of Byzantium* (Oxford, 2002), pp. 248–83, cf. p. 248 'the once magnificent Byzantine empire seemingly devolves into little more than caricature, a disordered and dysfunctional polity'; cf. also the title of S. Curčić and D. Mouriki, eds, *The Twilight of Byzantium: Aspects of Cultural and Religious History in the Late Byzantine Empire.* (Princeton, 1991).

36 Ihor Ševčenko, 'Palaeologan learning', in Mango, ed., *The Oxford History of Byzantium*, pp. 284–93, at p. 285.
37 See the examples in Donald Nicol, *The Byzantine Lady: Ten Portraits 1250–1500* (Cambridge, 1994).
38 See Chapter 8 below.
39 Cyril Mango, *Byzantine Architecture* (New York, 1976), pp. 259–95; Thomas F. Mathews, *The Art of Byzantium: Between Antiquity and the Renaissance* (London, 1998), p. 155; below, Chapter 9.
40 Paul Underwood, ed., *The Kariye Djami*, pp. 1–3 (New York, 1966), 4 (Princeton, 1975; John Lowden, *Early Christian and Byzantine Art* (London, 1997), pp. 408–17.
41 Klaus-Peter Matschke, 'The late Byzantine urban economy, thirteenth–fifteenth centuries', in Laiou, ed., *Economic History of Byzantium*, Vol. 2, pp. 454–86.
42 This is treated in E. Patlagean, 'Les États d'Europe centrale et Byzance, ou l'oscillation des confins', *Revue historique* 302.4 (2000): 827–68, with maps.
43 Donald Nicol, *The Reluctant Emperor: A Biography of John Cantacuzene, Byzantine Emperor and Monk, c.1295–1383* (Cambridge, 1996).
44 Warren Treadgold, *A Concise History of Byzantium* (Basingstoke, 2001), pp. 219–33.
45 Colin Imber, *The Ottoman Empire* (Basingstoke, 2002), p. 8.
46 On whom see Chapter 8 below.
47 Donald Nicol, *The Immortal Emperor* (Cambridge, 1992); id., *The Last Centuries of Byzantium*, pp. 376–90.
48 The numbers vary in the sources: Nicol, *The Last Centuries of Byzantium*, p. 380.
49 Nicol, *The Immortal Emperor*, pp. 74–108.
50 Nicol, *The Last Centuries of Byzantium*, pp. 107–11.

4 THE BYZANTINE MIRAGE

1 See Averil Cameron, 'Byzantium and Europe', in J.-M. Spieser, ed., *Présence de Byzance* (Lausanne, 2006).
2 Alexander Kazhdan and Giles Constable, *People and Power in Byzantium: An Introduction to Modern Byzantine Studies* (Washington, DC, 1982); Alexander Kazhdan and Ann Epstein, *Change in Byzantine Culture in the Eleventh and Twelfth Centuries* (Berkeley and Los Angeles, 1985).
3 The same picture is found in Cyril Mango, *Byzantium: The Empire of New Rome* (London, 1980), pp. 60–73 and John Haldon, *Byzantium in the Seventh Century: The Transformation of a Culture* (Cambridge, 1990), pp. 92–124.
4 Cyril Mango, *Byzantium: The Empire of New Rome*; see R. Beaton, *The Medieval Greek Romance*, rev. edn, (London, 1996), p. 16.
5 For the latter see F. Winkelmann, *Quellenstudien zur herrschenden Klasse von Byzanz im 8. und 9. Jahrhundert* (Berlin, 1987); the changes can be

seen quite clearly reflected in the biographies available in *PBE* I and the volumes of *PmbZ*. See further Chapter 5.

6 *Life of Constantine* III.48.

7 R. M. Harrison, *A Temple for Byzantium: The Discovery and Excavation of Anicia Juliana's Palace-Church in Istanbul* (London, 1989); on the development of the city, Cyril Mango, *Le Développement urbain de Constantinople: IV–VII siècles*, 2nd edn (Paris, 1990); Paul Magdalino, *Constantinople médiévale: études sur l'évolution des structures urbaines* (Paris, 1996).

8 Bissera V. Pentcheva, 'The supernatural protector of Constantinople: The Virgin and her icons in the tradition of the Avar siege', *Byzantine and Modern Greek Studies* 26 (2002): 2–41.

9 D. Obolensky, *The Byzantine Commonwealth: Eastern Europe 500–1453* (London, 1971).

10 N. Oikonomides, *Les Listes de préséance byzantines des IX et X siècles* (Paris, 1972); see Chapter 5.

11 Byzantine political theory: F. Dvornik, *Early Christian and Byzantine Political Philosophy: Origins and Background*, 2 vols. (Washington, DC, 1966).

12 Judith Herrin, *Women in Purple: Rulers of Medieval Byzantium* (London, 2001), pp. 92–9.

13 Anna Comnena, *Alexiad* II.1–III.5.

14 See, for example, the argument of Aaron Gurevich, 'Why I am not a Byzantinist', *Dumbarton Oaks Papers* 46 (1992), 89–96; for this reaction see G. Dagron, *Emperor and Priest: The Imperial Office in Byzantium*, Eng. trans. (Cambridge, 2003), pp. 286–8. Kazhdan's view of 'Byzantine man' also locates him in a strongly autocratic context; however, both the intention and the practicality are questioned by I. Ševčenko, 'Was there totalitarianism in Byzantium? Constantinople\s control over its Asiatic hinterland in the early ninth century', in Cyril Mango and Gilbert Dagron, eds, with the assistance of Geoffrey Greatrex, *Constantinople and its Hinterland* (Aldershot, 1995), pp. 91–105.

15 T. Papamastorakis, 'Tampering with history: from Michael III to Michael VIII', *Byzantinische Zeitschrift* 96 (2003): 193–209.

16 Steven Runciman, *The Byzantine Theocracy* (Cambridge, 1977).

17 Dagron, *Emperor and Priest*.

18 Henry Maguire, ed., *Byzantine Court Culture from 829 to 1204* (Washington, DC, 1997).

19 The *Kleterologion* ('Invitation-list') of Philotheos, of 899, sets out exactly who is to be invited to imperial banquets on specific occasions with their order of precedence.

20 *Book of Ceremonies* II.70 (61)–72 (63).

21 Important work is being done on the *Book of Ceremonies* by Gilbert Dagron and others, and the study by Dagron and others of the symbolic meaning of the Hippodrome rituals is a major contribution: G. Dagron et al.,

'L'Organisation et le déroulement des courses d'après le *Livre des Cérémonies*', *Travaux et Mémoires* 13 (2000): 1–200.

22   *De administrando imperio*, proem; for diplomacy see Jonathan Shepard and Simon Franklin, eds, *Byzantine Diplomacy* (Aldershot, 1992).

23   Shepard, 'Byzantine diplomacy AD 800–1204', in Shepard and Franklin, eds, *Byzantine Diplomacy*, p. 47.

24   Ibid., pp. 41–71.

25   Ed. and trans. Averil Cameron, *Corippus, in laudem Iustini minoris libri quattuor* (London, 1976).

26   The classic treatment is André Grabar, *L'Empereur dans l'art byzantin. Recherches sur l'art officiel de l'empire d'orient* (Paris, 1936).

27   See Henry Maguire, 'Images of the court', in Helen C. Evans and William D. Wixom, eds, *The Glory of Byzantium. Art and Culture of the Middle Byzantine Era, AD 843–1261* (New York, 1997), 182–91, at p. 186.

28   Alexius's innovations and the new titles are noted by Anna Comnena, *Alexiad* III.4, pp. 111–12 Sewter's Eng. trans.

29   The title is taken up by Osbert Lancaster, *Sailing to Byzantium: An Architectural Companion* (London, 1972).

30   Evans and Wixom, eds, *The Glory of Byzantium*; cf. also Helen C. Evans, ed., *Byzantium: Faith and Power (1261–1557)* (New York, 2004).

31   For examples of the textual evidence for Byzantine art see Cyril Mango, *The Art of the Byzantine Empire, AD 312–1453* (Englewood Cliffs, NJ, 1972).

32   Theophanes Continuatus, p. 447f. Bonn.

33   Ingela Nilsson, 'Meutre à Byzance: Byzantine murders in modern literature', *Greek, Roman and Byzantine Studies* 29 (2005): 235–8, at 236.

34   Averil Cameron, *The Use and Abuse of Byzantium*, Inaugural Lecture, King's College London, 1990 (London, 1992).

35   *Secret History* 9, 15.

36   C. Diehl, *Figures byzantines* (Paris, 1906) and in later works; see the papers in M. F. Auzépy, ed., *Byzance en Europe* (Saint-Denis, 2003); A. McClanan, *Representations of Early Byzantine Empresses: Image and Empire* (London, 2002).

5 RULING THE BYZANTINE STATE

1   A. Avramea, 'Land and sea communications, fourth to fifteenth centuries', in Angeliki E. Laiou, ed., *The Economic History of Byzantium*, Vol. 1 (Washington, DC, 2002), pp. 57–90.

2   Michael Maas, *John Lydus and the Roman Past: Antiquarianism and Politics in the Age of Justinian* (London, 1992); Christopher Kelly, *Ruling the Later Roman Empire* (Cambridge, MA, 2004).

3   See Chapter 8.

4   For the Roman and late Roman bureaucracy see J. E. Lendon, *Empire of Honour: The Art of Government in the Roman World* (Oxford, 1997) and Christopher Kelly, *Ruling the Later Roman Empire*.

5   Chris Wickham, *Framing the Early Middle Ages: Europe and the Mediter-ranean 400–800* (Oxford, 2005), pp. 232–40, 596–602.

6   For the seventh to the ninth centuries we now have two such compendia, *PBE* I, in English on CD-rom, and PmbZ, in German and in book form.

7   Alexander P. Kazhdan and Michael McCormick, 'The social world of the Byzantine court', in Henry Maguire, ed., *Byzantine Court Culture from 829 to 1204* (Washington, DC, 1997), pp. 168–72; cf. M. Angold, ed., *The Byzantine Aristocracy, IX–XIII Centuries* (Oxford, 1984).

8   J.-C. Cheynet, *Pouvoir et contestations à Byzance (963–1210)* (Paris, 1990).

9   Mark Whittow, 'How the east was lost', in Margaret Mullett and Dion Smythe, eds, *Alexios I Komnenos: I Papers* (Belfast, 1996), pp. 55–67.

10 See Nicholas Oikonomides, 'Titles and income at the Byzantine court', in Henry Maguire, ed., *Byzantine Court Culture from 829 to 1204* (Washing-ton, DC, 1997), pp. 199–215.

11 John Thomas and Angela Constantinides Hero, eds, with the assistance of Giles Constable, *Byzantine Monastic Foundation Documents: A Complete Translation of the Surviving Founders' Typika and Testaments*, Dumbar-ton Oaks Studies 35 (Washington, DC, 2000), 5 vols.

12 For eunuchs see also Chapter 7.

13 Psellus, *Chronographia* I.3, p. 28 Sewter.

14 Y. Rotman, *Les Esclaves et l'esclavage de la Méditerranée antique à la Méditerranée médiévale VIe–XIe siècles* (Paris, 2004). The Byzantines were importers of slaves and the slave trade flourished, especially in conditions of Arab–Byzantine warfare: see Michael McCormick, *Origins of the Euro-pean Economy: Communications and Commerce, AD 300–900* (Cambridge, 2001), pp. 741–77.

15 The late Roman senatorial order: P. Heather, 'New men for new Constantines? Creating an imperial elite in the eastern Mediterranean', in Paul Magdalino, ed., *New Constantines: The Rhythm of Imperial Renewal in Byzantium, 4th–13th Centuries* (Aldershot, 1994), 11–33.

16 Alan Cameron, *Circus Factions* (Oxford, 1976); G. Dagron et al., 'L'Organisation et le déroulement des courses d'après le *Livre des Cérémonies*', *Travaux et Mémoires* 13 (2000): 1–200.

17 Kazhdan and McCormick, 'The social world of the Byzantine court', 182–5.

18 Wickham, *Framing the Early Middle Ages*, pp. 124–9.

19 Agathias, *Hist.* V.13; see Warren Treadgold, *Byzantium and its Army 284–1081* (Stanford, 1995), pp. 59–64.

20 Eng. trans. G. T. Dennis, *Maurice's Strategikon: Handbook of Byzantine Military Strategy* (Philadelphia, 1984).

21 J. F. Haldon, *Byzantium in the Seventh Century: The Transformation of a Culture* (Cambridge, 1990), pp. 208–20; id., 'Military service, military lands and the status of soldiers: current problems and interpretations', *Dumbar-ton Oaks Papers* 47 (1993): 1–67 and see Mark Whittow, *The Making of Orthodox Byzantium 600–1025* (Berkeley and Los Angeles, 1996), pp. 113–

21; against the supposed Slav context of the Farmers' Law: Wickham, *Framing the Early Middle Ages*, p. 463.

22   For Constans II (641–68) as the instigator see Treadgold, *Byzantium and its Army*, pp. 21–5, 171–3.

23   See *Byzantium in the Seventh Century*, chapters 5 and 6; N. Oikonomides, 'Silk trade and production in Byzantium from the sixth to the ninth century: the seals of kommerkiarioi', *Dumbarton Oaks Papers* 40 (1986): 33–53, argued that the *kommerkarioi* were largely concerned with the silk trade: see, however, Haldon, *Byzantium in the Seventh Century*, pp. 235–8; Treadgold, *Byzantium and its Army*, pp. 181–6.

24   For the *Parastaseis* see Averil Cameron and Judith Herrin, et al., eds, *Constantinople in the Eighth Century* (Leiden, 1984).

25   Wickham, *Framing the Early Middle Ages*, p. 790.

26   N. Oikonomides, 'The role of the Byzantine state in the economy', in Angeliki E. Laiou, ed., *The Economic History of Byzantium*, Vol. 3 (Washington, DC, 2002), pp. 973–1058, at pp. 990–1019.

27   Leonora Neville, *Authority in Byzantine Provincial Society, 950–1100* (Cambridge, 2004), pp. 58–9, 62.

28   Several contributions to Cyril Mango and Gilbert Dagron, eds, *Constantinople and its Hinterland* (Aldershot, 1995) deal with the organisation of the food supply of Constantinople, especially the supply of grain, vegetables and fish.

29   See Paul Stephenson, *The Legend of Basil the Bulgar-slayer* (Cambridge, 2003).

30   On the armies of this period see John Haldon, *Warfare, State and Society in the Byzantine World 565–1204* (London, 1999), pp. 115–20, 123–28; *The Byzantine Wars: Battles and Campaigns of the Byzantine Era* (Stroud, 2001), pp. 109–37; Warren Treadgold, *Byzantium and its Army 284–1081* (Stanford, 1995), pp. 214–19.

31   See Oikonomides, 'The role of the state', pp. 1019–26; Alan Harvey, 'Financial crisis and the rural economy', in Margaret Mullett and Dion Smythe, eds, *Alexios I Komnenos: I Papers* (Belfast, 1996), pp. 167–84.

32   Alan Harvey, *Economic Expansion in the Byzantine Empire 900–1200* (Cambridge, 1990).

33   Zonaras, XVIII.25.19, cf. 29.24 on Alexius's favours to his own family.

34   Paul Magdalino, 'The Byzantine army and the land: from *stratiotikon ktema* to military *pronoia*', in *Byzantium at War (9th–12th c.)* (Athens, 1997), pp. 15–36.

35   For dependent *paroikoi* the surviving documents are largely from southern Macedonia in the fourteenth century and for once permit detailed study: Angeliki E. Laiou-Thomadakis, *Peasant Society in the Late Byzantine Empire: A Social and Demographic Study* (Princeton, 1977); 'The agrarian economy, thirteenth–fifteenth centuries', in Laiou, ed., *Economic History of Byzantium*, Vol. 1, pp. 311–75.

36 Wickham, *Framing the Early Middle Ages*, pp. 60–1; on the term in rela-
    tion to Byzantium see also Alan Harvey, *Economic Expansion in the
    Byzantine Empire, 900–1200* (Cambridge, 1990), Introduction.
37 Oikonomides, 'The role of the Byzantine state', pp. 1050–5.
38 Angeliki E. Laiou, 'The Byzantine economy: an overview', in Laiou, ed.,
    Economic History of Byzantium, Vol. 3, pp. 1147–56.
39 Klaus-Peter Matschke, 'The late Byzantine urban economy, thirteenth-
    fifteenth centuries', in Laiou, ed., *Economic History of Byzantium*, Vol. 2,
    pp. 474–6.
40 Magdalino, 'Grain supply', pp. 36–7.
41 Money: Cécile Morrisson, 'Byzantine money: its production and circulation',
    in Laiou, ed., *Economic History of Byzantium*, Vol. 3, pp. 909–66; for
    markets and against the model of self-sufficiency of large *oikoi* see
    Magdalino, 'Grain supply', pp. 38–47.
42 Laiou, 'The agrarian economy', p. 349.
43 *Actes de Lavra* I, nos. 67–8.
44 Dating: J. H. A. Lokin, 'The significance of law and legislation in the law
    books of the ninth to eleventh centuries', in Angeliki E. Laiou and Dieter
    Simon, eds, *Law and Society in Byzantium, Ninth–Twelfth Centuries* (Wash-
    ington, DC, 1994), pp. 71–91, at p. 71.
45 Paul Magdalino, 'Justice and finance in the Byzantine state, ninth to twelfth
    centuries', ibid., pp. 93–115.
46 Angeliki E. Laiou, 'Law, justice and the Byzantine historians', ibid., pp. 151–
    85.

6 AN ORTHODOX SOCIETY?

 1 Trans. George Dennis, in John Thomas and Angela Constantinides Hero,
    eds, *Byzantine Monastic Foundation Documents: A Complete Translation
    of the Surviving Founders' Typika and Testaments* (Washington, DC, 2000),
    Vol. 1, p. 253.
 2 See Donald M. Nicol, *The Reluctant Emperor: A Biography of John Cant-
    acuzene, Byzantine Emperor and Monk, c.1295–1383* (Cambridge, 1996).
 3 F. Dvornik, *Early Christian and Byzantine Political Philosophy: Origins and
    Background*, 2 vols. (Washington, DC, 1966).
 4 P. Magdalino, 'The medieval empire (780–1204)', in Cyril Mango, ed.,
    Oxford History of Byzantium (Oxford, 2002), pp. 169–213, at p. 206; see
    also G. Dagron, *Emperor and Priest: The Imperial Office in Byzantium*, Eng.
    trans. (Cambridge, 2003), pp. 282–3.
 5 Paul Magdalino, *The Empire of Manuel I Komnenos 1143–1180* (Cam-
    bridge, 1993), p. 287.
 6 Leonora Neville, *Authority in Byzantine Provincial Society, 950–1100* (Cam-
    bridge, 2004), p. 126.
 7 See the discussion by Angeliki E. Laiou, *Mariage, amour et parenté à Byzance
    aux XIe–XIIIe siècles* (Paris, 1992), pp. 21–58.

8   There has been a great deal of writing in recent years on this issue, much of it emphasising the tendentiousness and bias of the contemporary sources, but the collection of essays edited by Anthony Bryer and Judith Herrin, *Iconoclasm* (Birmingham, 1977) remains a good introduction.

9   Charles Barber, *Figure and Likeness: On the Limits of Representation in Byzantine Iconoclasm* (Princeton, 2002).

10 For this alleged incident and for the Triumph of Orthodoxy icon see Robin Cormack, 'Women and icons and women in icons', in Liz James, ed., *Women, Men and Eunuchs: Gender in Byzantium* (London, 1997), pp. 24–51.

11 Theophanes, AM 6267, trans. and comm. Cyril Mango and Roger Scott, p. 619; Theophanes ascribes a similarly unpleasant death to Anastasius, iconoclast patriarch under Constantine V, ibid., p. 591.

12 Cyril Mango, 'The availability of books in the Byzantine empire, AD 750–850', in *Byzantine Books and Bookmen: A Dumbarton Oaks Colloquium* (Washington, DC, 1971), pp. 29–45.

13 On the expansion of monasticism after 843 see Rosemary Morris, *Monks and Laymen in Byzantium, 843–1118* (Cambridge, 1995), pp. 14–30; a succinct account of Byzantine monasticism is given by Alice-Mary Talbot in Jonathan Harris, ed., *Palgrave Advances in Byzantine History* (Basingstoke, 2005), pp. 119–32.

14 See Margaret Mullett and Anthony Kirby, eds, *The Theotokos Evergetis and Eleventh-Century Monasticism*, Belfast Byzantine texts and Translations 6.1 (Belfast, 1994), the first in a series of volumes making available the entire substantial dossier of texts surviving from this monastery.

15 Y. Hirschfeld, *The Judaean Desert Monasteries in the Byzantine Period* (New Haven, 1992) and J. Patrich, *Sabas, Leader of Palestinian Monasticism: A Comparative Study in Eastern Monasticism, Fourth to Seventh Centuries* (Washington, DC, 1995).

16 R. P. H. Greenfield, *The Life of Lazaros of Mt. Galesion: An Eleventh-Century Pillar Saint* (Washington, DC, 2000), pp. 102–4.

17 Tia M. Kolbaba, *The Byzantine Lists: The Errors of the Latins* (Urbana, IL, 2000).

18 Trans. R. C. Gregg, *The Life of Antony and the Letter to Marcellinus* (New York, 1980).

19 Aug., *Conf.* VIII.6.15, 11.29.

20 Benedicta Ward, *Harlots of the Desert: A Study of Repentance in Early Monastic Sources* (Kalamazoo, 1987).

21 Cf. John Tavener's oratorio *Mary of Egypt*. There are deep gender issues in such stories; both women are described by male narrators (the love of the monk Zossima for Mary is one of the themes of the story) and both were fleeing from their earlier sexual lives.

22 Ed. M.-F. Auzépy, *Vie d'Étienne le jeune par Étienne le diacre* (Aldershot, 1997).

23 R. P. C. Hanson, *The Search for the Christian Doctrine of God: The Arian Controversy 318–81* (Edinburgh, 1988), pp. xviii–xx.

24 See Chapter 10.

25 See Bart D. Ehrman, *Lost Christianities: The Battles for Scripture and the Faiths We Never Knew* (Oxford, 2003).

26 Anna Comnena, *Alexiad* XV.8–10, emphasising the lengths to which her father went to get heretics to recant.

27 Yuri Stoyanov, *The Other God: Dualist Religions from Antiquity to the Cathar Heresy* (New Haven, 2000); see the excellent collection of translated texts in Janet Hamilton and Bernard Hamilton, eds, *Christian Dualist Heresies in the Byzantine World c.650–c.1405* (Manchester, 1998).

28 For the limitations on state action see J.-C. Cheynet, 'Les Limites de pouvoir à Byzance: une forme de tolérance?', in K. Nikolaou, ed., *Toleration and Repression in the Middle Ages: In Memory of Lenos Macromattis* (Athens 2002), pp. 15–28.

29 On Jews in the empire: Nicholas de Lange, 'Hebrews, Greeks or Romans? Jewish culture and identity in Byzantium', in Dion Smythe, ed., *Strangers to Themselves: The Byzantine Outsider* (Aldershot, 2000), pp. 105–18; see also Chapter 10.

30 G. Fowden, *Empire to Commonwealth: Consequences of Monotheism in Late Antiquity* (Princeton, 1993).

31 See Chapter 9.

32 P. Allen and C. T. R. Hayward, *Severus of Antioch* (London, 2004).

7 HOW PEOPLE LIVED

1 Chapter 4.

2 M.-F. Auzépy, *Vie d'Étienne le jeune par Étienne le diacre* (Aldershot, 1997).

3 Ed. L. Rydén, *The Life of St Philaretos the Merciful Written by his Grandson Niketas* (Uppsala, 2002); there is a fine discussion of Byzantine rural life by Alexander Kazhdan in G. Cavallo, ed., *The Byzantines*, Eng. trans. Chicago, 1997), pp. 43–73.

4 Ihor Ševčenko and Nancy Ševčenko, *The Life of Nicholas of Sion* (Brookline, MA, 1984). The so-called Sion treasure, some 71 silver and other objects, 30 of them dated to AD 550–65, seems to have been presented by the bishop Eutychianos and others to Nicholas's church.

5 Derek Krueger, *Symeon the Holy Fool: Leontios's Life and the Late Antique City* (Berkeley and Los Angeles, 1996).

6 E. Dawes and N. H. Baynes partial translation of Theodore of Skyeon's *Life* (para 3) in *Three Byzantine Saints*.

7 As now by Chris Wickham, *Framing the Early Middle Ages: Europe and the Mediterranean 400–800* (Oxford, 2005), pp. 406–11, in the context of a discussion of peasants and local societies; the *Life* contains an exceptionally large amount of topographical detail.

8 Ibid., pp. 120, 128; Robin Cormack, *Writing in Gold* (London, 1985), p. 44.

9 Carolyn L. Connor, *Women of Byzantium* (New Haven, 2004), pp. 147–58; women's lives: see also Iole Kalavrezou, ed., with Angeliki E. Laiou,

Alicia Walker, Elizabeth A. Gittings, Molly Fulghum Heintz and Bissera V. Pentcheva, *Byzantine Women and their World* (New Haven, 2003).

10 Trans. Lee Francis Sherry, in Alice-Mary Talbot, ed., *Holy Women of Byzantium: Ten Saints' Lives in English Translation* (Washington, DC, 1996), pp. 143–4; this is one of the first references to the Athinganoi, a rather mysterious Jewish sect.

11 Lynda Garland, *Byzantine Empresses: Women and Power in Byzantium AD 527–1204* (London, 1999); Liz James, *Empresses and Power in Early Byzantium* (Leicester, 2001); Judith Herrin, *Women in Purple: Rulers of Medieval Byzantium* (London, 2001); Barbara Hill, *Imperial Women in Byzantium 1025–1204: Power, Patronage and Ideology* (London, 1999).

12 Psellus, *Chronographia* 6. 20, p. 165, Sewter.

13 Ibid., 6.50–61, pp. 180–5.

14 Ibid., 6A.2, p. 261.

15 The oath is published and the story told by N. Oikonomides, 'Le Serment de l'impératrice Eudocie (1067)', *Revue des Études Byzantines* 21 (1963): 101–28.

16 Judith Herrin, 'Toleration and repression within the Byzantine family', in K. Nikolaou, ed., *Toleration and Repression in the Middle Ages: In Memory of Lenos Mavromattis* (Athens, 2002), pp. 173–88, at p. 187; Angeliki E. Laiou, 'Women in the history of Byzantium', in Kalavrezou, ed., *Byzantine Women and their World*, pp. 23–32, at p. 23; see, however, Angeliki E. Laiou, 'Sex, consent and coercion in Byzantium', in Laiou, ed., *Consent and Coercion to Sex and Marriage in Ancient and Medieval Societies* (Washington, DC, 1993), pp. 109–221.

17 Laiou 'Sex, consent and coercion', p. 196.

18 Joelle Beaucamp, *Le Statut de la femme à Byzance (4e–7e siècle)*, 2 vols. (Paris, 1990, 1992).

19 See Cyril Mango, 'Saints', in Guglielmo Cavallo, ed., *The Byzantines*, Eng. trans. (Chicago, 1997), pp. 255–80, at pp. 266–9.

20 Angeliki E. Laiou, *Mariage, amour et parenté à Byzance aux XIe–XIIIe siècles* (Paris, 1992).

21 Nicholas Constas, 'Weaving the body of God: Proclus of Constantinople, the Theotokos and the loom of the flesh', *Journal of Early Christian Studies* 3.2 (1995): 169–94.

22 See Laiou, *Mariage, amour et parenté à Byzance*, pp. 13–15.

23 See the excellent discussion by Laiou, ibid., pp. 21–58.

24 Anna Comnena, *Alexiad* III.1–2.

25 Paul Magdalino, *Empire of Manuel I Komnenos, 1143–1180* (Cambridge, 1993), pp. 209–17.

26 Theophanes Continuatus pp. 226–8 (Life of Basil); on the Byzantine *oikos* see Paul Magdalino, 'The Byzantine aristocratic *oikos*', in M. Angold, ed., *The Byzantine Aristocracy IX–XIII Centuries* (Oxford, 1984), pp. 92–111.

27 S. Vryonis Jr., 'The will of a provincial magnate, Eustathius Boilas (1059), *Dumbarton Oaks Papers* 11 (1957), 263–77, at 271.

28 Y. Rotman, *Les Esclaves et l'esclavage de la Méditerranée antique à la Méditerranée médiévale VIe–XIe siècles* (Paris, 2004), pp. 182, 154–6.

29 N. Oikonomides, *Les Listes de préséance byzantines des IX et X siècles* (Paris, 1972), pp. 125–34.

30 Kathryn M. Ringrose, *The Perfect Servant: Eunuchs and the Social Construction of Gender in Byzantium* (Chicago, 2003), p. 118.

31 The Holy Bible, Revised Standard Version.

32 Ed. P. Gautier, *Théophylacte d'Achrida, Discours, Traités, Poèmes* (Thessaloniki, 1980), pp. 281–331.

33 B. Ward-Perkins, *The Fall of Rome and the End of Civilization* (Oxford, 2005), pp. 87–120, cf. 'Why the demise of comfort?' ibid., pp. 123–37.

34 Procopius, *Buildings* IV.1.17–27.

35 See Archibald Dunn, 'The transition from *polis* to *kastron* in the Balkans (III–VIIcc.): general and regional perspectives', *Byzantine and Modern Greek Studies* 18 (1994): 60–80, and for Epirus Vetus (southern Albania and northern Greece), William Bowden, *Epirus Vetus: The Archaeology of a Late Antique Province* (London, 2003), pp. 190–3.

36 See, for example, G. P. Brogiolo and B. Ward-Perkins, eds, *The Idea and Ideal of the Town between Late Antiquity and the Early Middle Ages* (Leiden, 1999).

37 M. Kaplan, *Les Hommes et la terre à Byzance du Vie au XIe siècle: Propriété et exploitation du sol*, Byzantina Sorbonensia 10 (Paris, 1992); villages and rural settlement are one of the key themes in Wickham, *Framing the Early Middle Ages*, especially pp. 442–518. Among areas where villages have received a large amount of archaeological attention is the limestone massif of northern Syria in late antiquity where some 700 remains of large villages have been identified: Wickham, pp. 443–50.

38 Ed. A.-J. Festugière, L. Rydén, *Léontios de Néapolis, Vie de Syméon le Fou et Vie de Jean de Chypre* (Paris, 1974), pp. 257–637; partial translation in E. Dawes and N. Baynes, eds, *Three Byzantine Saints* (Crestwood, NJ, 1977) pp. 195–262.

39 D. J. Constantelos, *Byzantine Philanthropy and Social Welfare* (New Brunswick, 1968); *Poverty, Society, and Philanthropy in the Late Mediaeval Greek World* (New Rochelle, 1992); T. S. Miller, *The Birth of the Hospital in the Byzantine Empire* (Baltimore, 1985).

40 Alexander Kazhdan and Giles Constable, *People and Power in Byzantium: An Introduction to Modern Byzantine Studies* (Washington, DC, 1982).

41 Cyril Mango, *Byzantium: The Empire of New Rome* (London, 1980), pp. 229, 254.

42 Norman H. Baynes, 'The thought-world of East Rome', repr. in his *Byzantine Studies and Other Essays* (London, 1974), pp. 24–46.

8 EDUCATION AND CULTURE

1   See A. P. Kazhdan in collaboration with S. Franklin, *Studies on Byzantine Literature of the Eleventh and Twelfth Centuries* (Cambridge, 1984), pp. 1–22.

2   A useful survey of current approaches with bibliography is given by Antony Littlewood, 'Literature', in Jonathan Harris, ed., *Palgrave Advances in Byzantine History* (Basingstoke, 2005), pp. 133–46.

3   Paul Magdalino, *The Empire of Manuel I Komnenos, 1143–1180* (Cambridge, 1993), p. 336; see Elizabeth Jeffreys, ed., *Rhetoric in Byzantium* (Aldershot, 2003).

4   H. Hunger, 'On the imitation (mimesis) of antiquity in Byzantine literature', *Dumbarton Oaks Papers* 23–4 (1969–70): 17–38; cf. A. Kazhdan, ed., *The Oxford Dictionary of Byzantium*, Preface, p. viii, referring to 'the very complex problem of whether Byzantium was a living, developing organism or only a guardian of ancient and patristic traditions'.

5   Mary B. Cunningham and Pauline Allen, eds, *Preacher and Audience: Studies in Early Christian and Byzantine Homiletics* (Leiden, 1998).

6   See H. Belting, *Likeness and Presence: A History of the Image before the Era of Art*, Eng. trans. (Chicago, 1994).

7   Mary Whitby, 'The occasion of Paul the Silentiary's *Ekphrasis* of St Sophia', *Classical Quarterly* 35 (1985): 215–28; R. Macrides and P. Magdalino, 'The architecture of Ekphrasis; construction and context of Paul the Silentiary's poem on Hagia Sophia', *Byzantine and Modern Greek Studies* 12 (1988): 47–82. Many such shorter pieces are translated in Cyril Mango, *The Art of the Byzantine Empire 312–1453* (Englewood Cliffs, NJ, 1972). For the literary features of such descriptions see Ruth Webb, 'The aesthetics of sacred space: narrative, metaphor and motion in "Ekphraseis" of church buildings', *Dumbarton Oaks Papers* 53 (1999): 59–74.

8   Gilbert Dagron, 'Holy images and likeness', *Dumbarton Oaks Papers* 45 (1991): 30–1; *Life* of Irene, ed. Rosenqvist, 56.9–13.

9   See Peter Hatlie, 'Redeeming Byzantine epistolography', *Byzantine and Modern Greek Studies* 20 (1996): 213–48; Margaret Mullett, 'Byzantium: a friendly society?' *Past and Present* 118 (1988): 3–25.

10 Cyril Mango, 'The availability of books in the Byzantine empire, AD 750–850', in *Byzantine Books and Bookmen: A Dumbarton Oaks Colloquium* (Washington, DC, 1971), pp. 29–45.

11 N. G. Wilson, *Scholars of Byzantium* (London, 1983), pp. 120–35.

12 *Letters*, ed. S. P. Lambros (Athens, 1879–80), e.g. *Epp.* 117, 146.

13 N. G. Wilson, *From Byzantium to Italy: Greek Studies in the Italian Renaissance* (London, 1992).

14 Marc Lauxtermann, *The Byzantine Epigram in the Ninth and Tenth Centuries* (Amsterdam, 1994), pp. 217–55; on iconoclast epigrams, ibid., pp. 201–6; Alan Cameron, *The Greek Anthology from Meleager to Planudes* (Oxford, 1993).

15 Margaret Mullett, 'Writing in early medieval Byzantium', in R. McKitterick, *The Uses of Literacy in Early Mediaeval Europe* (Cambridge, 1990), pp. 156–8.

16 R. Kaster, *Guardians of Language: The Grammarian and Society in Late Antiquity* (Berkeley and Los Angeles, 1988).

17 N. Oikonomides, 'Mount Athos: levels of literacy', *Dumbarton Oaks Papers* 42 (1988): 167–78; on Neophytos, see C. Galatariotou, *The Making of a Saint: The Life, Times and Sanctification of Neophytos the Recluse* (Cambridge, 1991) and R. Cormack, *Writing in Gold* (London, 1985), pp. 215–51.

18 Ed. W. Lameere, *La Tradition manuscrite de la correspondance de Grégoire de Chypre* (Brussels and Paris, 1937), p. 189.

19 Grzegorz Majcherek, 'Kom el-Dikka, Excavations and Preservation Work, 2002/2003', in *Polish Archaeology in the Mediterranean* 15 (Warsaw, 2004), 25–38.

20 Agathias, *Hist.* II.30–1; for Athens see Alison Frantz, *The Athenian Agora: Late Antiquity, AD 267–700* (Princeton, 1988), Vol. 24, pp. 86–8.

21 On this period see Scott Johnson, ed., *Greek Literature in Late Antiquity: Dynamism, Didacticism, Classicism* (Aldershot, 2006).

22 P. Lemerle, *Byzantine Humanism, The First Phase: Notes and Remarks on Education and Culture in Byzantium from its Origin to the Tenth Century.* Eng. trans. (Canberra, 1996), pp. 173–7.

23 Ibid., pp. 171–204.

24 Wilson, *Scholars of Byzantium*, p. 149 (K. N. Sathas, *Mesaionike Bibliotheke* V (Paris, 1876), pp. 142–67, esp. pp. 143, 148). An elegant epigram by John Mavropous, in which he asks that Plato and Plutarch be excepted from divine judgement, is translated into French by C. Astruc in *Travaux et Mémoires* 6 (1971): 216.

25 *Chronographia* 7.66, pp. 316–17 Sewter.

26 Magdalino, *The Empire of Manuel I Komnenos*, pp. 325–30.

27 N. G. Wilson, *From Byzantium to Italy*, pp. 54–5.

28 He was not alone: the patriarch Gregory II became titular Latin patriarch, an office in which he was succeeded by Isidore of Kiev, also by now a cardinal, and then in 1463 by Bessarion himself.

29 Wilson, *From Byzantium to Italy*, pp. 57–67.

30 Surviving *typika*, foundation documents for specific monasteries, have been translated into English and are available online. They are an enormously rich source for the basic principles of Byzantine monasticism: see John Thomas and Angela Constantinides Hero, eds, with Giles Constable, *Byzantine Monastic Foundation Documents: A Complete Translation of the Surviving Founder's Typika and Testaments*, 5 vols. (Washington, DC, 2000); see http://www.doaks.org/typ000.html.

31 See Margaret Mullett and Anthony Kirby, eds, *The Theotokos Evergetis and Eleventh-Century Monasticism* (Belfast, 1994); *Work and Worship at the Theotokos Evergetis* (1997).

32   D. Burton-Christie, *The Word in the Desert: Scripture and the Quest for Holiness in Early Christian Monasticism* (New York, 1993).

33   Claudia Rapp, 'Hagiography and monastic literature between Greek East and Latin West in late antiquity', in *Cristianità d'Occidente e Cristianità d'Oriente (secoli VI–XI)*, Settimane di Studio 51 (Spoleto, 1994), pp. 1221–80, at pp. 1248–66.

34   Peter Brown, *Power and Persuasion in Late Antiquity: Towards a Christian Empire* (Madison, WI, 1992); also Averil Cameron, *Christianity and the Rhetoric of Empire: The Formation of Christian Discourse* (Berkeley and Los Angeles, 1991).

35   A. Louth, *St. John Damascene: Tradition and Originality in Byzantine Theology* (Oxford, 2002).

36   K. Ierodiakonou, ed., *Byzantine Philosophy and its Ancient Sources* (Oxford, 2002).

37   B. Bydén, *Theodore Metochites' Stoicheiosis astronomike and the Study of Natural Philosophy and Mathematics in Early Palaiologan Byzantium* (Göteborg, 2003).

38   *Chronographia* 6.38, p. 174 Sewter; A. Kaldellis, *The Argument of Psellos' Chronographia* (Leiden, 1999), p. 186. Kaldellis reads the *Chronographia* as an application of Psellus's Platonising beliefs to contemporary Byzantine society.

39   Kaldellis, *The Argument of Psellos'* Chronographia, p. 118; P. Speck, 'Byzantium: cultural suicide?' in L. Brubaker, ed., *Byzantium in the Ninth Century* (Aldershot, 1998), pp. 73–84.

40   Samuel N. C. Lieu and Dominic Montserrat, eds, *Constantine: History, Historiography, Legend* (London, 1998); G. Dagron, *Constantinople imaginaire: Études sur le receuil des* Patria (Paris, 1984); the late eighth century *Parastaseis syntomoi chronikai* shows both the breakdown of literary education and the scholarly aspirations of the administrative class: Eng. trans. Averil Cameron and Judith Herrin et al., *Constantinople in the Eighth Century* (Leiden, 1984); dated to c.800 by A. Berger, *Untersuchungen zu Patria Konstantinupoleos*, Poikila Byzantina 8 (Bonn, 1988).

41   Nicholas Kataphloron, cited by Magdalino, *Empire of Manuel I Komnenos*, p. 336.

42   For the latter, Angeliki E. Laiou, *Mariage, amour et parenté à Byzance aux XIe–XIIIe siècles* (Paris, 1992).

43   The Second Sophistic has been much studied recently: see Simon Swain, *Hellenism and Empire: Language, Classicism, and Power in the Greek World, AD 50–250* (Oxford, 1996).

44   R. Beaton, *The Medieval Greek Romance*, rev. edn (London, 1996), pp. 30–51.

45   Ibid., pp. 47–8, 214–16. Beaton's Afterword, pp. 207–27 in the revised edition, sums up and discusses the scholarship since his book first appeared in 1989.

46   Ibid., p. 186.

47 Hugh Kennedy, *The Court of the Caliphs: The Rise and Fall of Islam's Greatest Dynasty* (London, 2004).

48 See P. Odorico and P. A. Agapitos, eds, *Pour une 'nouvelle' histoire de la littérature byzantine: problèmes, méthodes, approches, propositions*, Actes du Colloque international philologique, Nicosie, Chypre, 25–'8 mai 2000 (Paris, 2002).

49 I. Ševčenko, 'Palaiologan learning', in Cyril Mango, ed., *Oxford History of Byzantium* (Oxford, 2002), pp. 284–93.

50 Paul Magdalino, *The Empire of Manuel I Komnenos*, pp. 406–9.

51 Cyril Mango, *Byzantium: Empire of New Rome*.

52 There is a helpful survey of recent work by Charles Barber, 'Art history', in Harris, ed., *Palgrave Advances in Byzantine History*, pp. 147–56; there are also many recent introductions to Byzantine art, for example Robin Cormack, *Byzantine Art* (Oxford, 2000); John Lowden, *Early Christian and Byzantine Art* (London, 1997); T. F. Mathews, *The Art of Byzantium: Between Antiquity and the Renaissance* (London, 1998).

53 See e.g. Henry Maguire, 'The profane aesthetic in Byzantine art and literature', *Dumbarton Oaks Papers* 53 (1999): 189–205.

54 Recent survey of datings: Anne McClanan, *Representations of Early Byzantine Empresses: Image and Empire* (London, 2002), pp. 24–6, inclining towards the fifth century and the identification of the empress portrayed with Pulcheria, but for the ninth century and the issues involved see Leslie Brubaker, 'The Chalke gate, the construction of the past, and the Trier ivory', *Byzantine and Modern Greek Studies* 23 (1999): 258–85, at pp. 270–7.

55 McClanan, *Representations of Early Byzantine Empresses*, pp. 135–6.

56 E. Kitzinger, *Byzantine Art in the Making: Main Lines of Stylistic Development in Medieval Art, 3rd–7th Century* (Cambridge, MA, 1977); K. Weitzmann, ed., *The Age of Spirituality: Late Antique and Early Christian Art, Third to Seventh Century*. Catalogue of the Exhibition at the Metropolitan Museum of Art, from 19 November 1977 to 12 February 12 1978 (New York, 1979); against: J. Elsner, *Art and the Roman Viewer* (Cambridge, 1995).

57 J. Elsner, 'From the culture of spolia to the cult of relics: the Arch of Constantine and the genesis of late antique forms', *Papers of the British School at Rome* 68 (2000): 149–84.

58 Nicephorus, *Refutatio*, pp. 109–10.

59 Leslie Brubaker and John Haldon, *Byzantium in the Iconoclast Era (ca.680–850): The Sources: An Annotated Survey*, Birmingham Byzantine and Ottoman Monographs 7 (Aldershot, 2001).

60 Charles Barber, *Figure and Likeness: On the Limits of Representation in Byzantine Iconoclasm* (Princeton, 2002), pp. 114–15.

61 This is particularly clear in the illustrations in a series of manuscripts dating from the ninth century and later: see Leslie Brubaker, *Vision and Meaning in Ninth-Century Byzantium: Image and Exegesis in the Homilies of Gregory*

of Nazianzus in Paris (Cambridge, 1999); cf. also Christopher Walter, *Pictures as Language: How the Byzantines Exploited Them* (London, 2000).

62 R. S. Nelson, 'The discourse of icons, then and now', *Art History* 12.2 (1989): 144–57, at p. 147; id., 'To say and to see: ekphrasis and vision in Byzantium', in R. S. Nelson, ed., *Visuality Before and Beyond the Renaissance: Seeing as Others Saw* (Cambridge, 2000), pp. 143–68; Cyril Mango, ed., *The Homilies of Photius, Patriarch of Constantinople* (Cambridge, MA, 1958), no. 17.

63 *Logos about the usual miracle at Blachernae*, ed. J. Bidez, *Catalogue des manuscrits alchimiques grecs* VI (Brussels, 1928), 187–210.

64 Icons of the Virgin: Maria Vassilaki, ed., *Mother of God: Representations of the Virgin in Byzantine Art* (Milan, 2000).

65 J.-M. Spieser, 'Hellénisme et connaissance de l'art byzantin au XIXe siècle', in S. Saïd, ed., *Hellenismos: Jalons pour une histoire de l'identité grecque*, Actes du Colloque de Strasbourg, 25–7 octobre 1989 (Leiden, 1991), pp. 338–62.

66 Cyril Mango, 'Discontinuity with the classical past in Byzantium', in Margaret Mullett and Roger Scott, eds, *Byzantium and the Classical Tradition* (Birmingham, 1981), pp. 48–57.

67 K. Dieterich, *Geschichte der byzantinischen und neugriechischen Literatur*, 2nd edn (Leipzig, 1909), pp. 10, 20; M. Alexiou, 'Modern Greek studies in the west, between the classics and the orient', *Journal of Modern Greek Studies* 4 (1986): 3–15.

9 BYZANTIUM AND EUROPE

1 Talal Asad, *Formations of the Secular: Christianity, Islam, Modernity* (Stanford, 2003), p. 169.

2 Some have noticed this; but though, for instance, Niall Ferguson, *Colossus: The Rise and Fall of the American Empire* (New York, 2005) contains a chapter on 'Europe between Brussels and Byzantium' Byzantium appears only in its familiar guise as foil to 'European' development.

3 *De them.* 44–6.

4 Critoboulos, *History of Mehmed the Conqueror*, trans. C. T. Riggs Vol. 4 (72) (Princeton, 1954), pp. 181–2.

5 This is not the case in Peter Brown's fine book, *The Rise of Western Christendom: Triumph and Diversity, AD 200–1000*, 2nd edn (Oxford, 2003), which integrates Byzantium into the broader narrative, which in a sense takes the story of late antiquity up to the year 1000. Judith Herrin, *The Formation of Christendom* (Oxford and Princeton, 1987), also covers both western Europe and Byzantium, but ends earlier, at AD 800.

6 Robert Bartlett, *The Making of Europe: Conquest, Colonization and Cultural Change, 950–1350* (Princeton, 1993).

7 R. I. Moore, *The First European Revolution, c.970–1215* (Oxford, 2000); Guy Bois, *The Transformation of the Year One Thousand: The Village of*

Lournand from Antiquity to Feudalism, Eng. trans. (Manchester, 1992) makes AD 1000 critical, and claims that the 'ancient model' persisted until then. From the Byzantine side see Paul Magdalino, ed., *Byzantium in the Year 1000* (Leiden, 2003).

8   Moore, *First European Revolution*, pp. 196–7.

9   Jacques Le Goff, *The Birth of Europe* (Oxford, 2005), p. 1.

10   Ibid., pp. 25–6.

11   MGH *Epistolae* V, p. 607; Bronislav Geremek, 'The common bond and the feeling of community in medieval Europe', in B. Geremek, *The Common Roots of Europe*, Eng. trans. (London, 1996), pp. 70–131, 79.

12   Geremek, pp. 105–8; Anthony Pagden, *Peoples and Empires: Europeans and the Rest of the World, from Antiquity to the Present* (London, 2001), p. 50.

13   Le Goff, pp. 96–8.

14   Le Goff, pp. 44–5, 149.

15   P. Geary, *The Myth of Nations: The Medieval Origins of Europe* (Princeton, 2002).

16   'Nationalism in Eastern Europe in the Middle Ages', XV in D. Obolensky, *The Byzantine Inheritance in Eastern Europe* (London, 1982).

17   See Anthony D. Smith, *Theories of Nationalism*, 2nd edn (London, 1983); contra, E. Gellner, *Nations and Nationalism* (1983).

18   Adrian Hastings, *The Constructions of Nationhood* (Cambridge, 1997).

19   And on the Bible and Christianity, as shaping the process, or even as making it possible at all.

20   Benedict Anderson, *Imagined Communities: Reflections on the Origin and Spread of Nationalism* (London, 1983), p. 7.

21   Margaret Mullett, *Theophylact of Ochrid: Reading the Letters of a Byzantine Archbishop* (Aldershot, 1997), pp. 64–9.

22   See Mullett, *Theophylact*, pp. 266–9; he did not for example impose the Greek-language liturgy, as maintained by J. Fine, *The Early Medieval Balkans: A Critical Survey from the Sixth to the Late Twelfth Century* (Ann Arbor, 1983), p. 220.

23   R.-J. Lilie, *Byzantium and the Crusader States, 1096–1204*, Eng. trans. (Oxford, 1993), p. 73.

24   Anna Comnena, XIII.1–12; Lilie, ibid., pp. 75–81.

25   Albanian Catholics were also found as émigrés in Ragusa (Dubrovnik) and Venice: A. Ducellier, 'Aux frontières de la romanité et de l'orthodoxie au moyen âge: le cas de l'Albanie', XI in his *L'Albanie entre Byzance et Venise, Xe–XVe siècles* (London, 1987).

26   Cinnamus, p. 287, trans Brand, p. 215; Magdalino, *Empire of Manuel I. Komnenos*, p. 79.

27   S. Curčič, 'Religious settings of the late Byzantine period', in Helen C. Evans, ed., *Byzantium: Faith and Power (1261–1557)* (New York, 2004), pp. 65–77; also on the Serbs, George C. Soulis, *The Serbs and Byzantium during*

the Reign of Tsar Stephen Dušan (1331–1355) and his Successors (Washington, DC, 1984); Sima Čirković, *The Serbs* (Oxford, 2005), pp. 20–33.

28 Dimitri Obolensky, *The Byzantine Commonwealth: Eastern Europe, 500–1453* (London, 1971), especially chapters 7, 'The bonds of the commonwealth', and 9, 'Factors in cultural diffusion'.

29 Ibid., 367–70; he also points to continuity under Ottoman rule in the fiscal system, the role of the patriarchate and the Greek millet, the place of the Phanariots and the Rumanian principalities of Wallachia and Moldavia with their capitals at Bucharest and Iasi, immortalised as *Byzance après Byzance* by the Rumanian scholar N. Iorga (Bucharest, 1935).

30 Maria Todorova, *Imagining the Balkans* (Oxford, 1997), pp. 162, 188.

31 J. Szúcs, *Les trois Europes*, French trans. (Paris, 1985); Nora Berend, *At the Gate of Christendom: Jews, Muslims and 'Pagans' in Medieval Hungary, c.1000–c.1300* (Cambridge, 2001).

32 Aaron Gurevich, 'Why I am not a Byzantinist', in Homo Byzantinus. Papers in Honor of Alexander Kazhdan, *Dumbarton Oaks Papers* 46 (1992): 89–96.

33 Mary Beard, *The Parthenon* (Cambridge, MA, 2003).

34 Jakob Phillip Fallmerayer, *Geschichte der Halbinsel Morea wahrend des Mittelalters*, 2 vols. (Stuttgart and Tubingen, 1830, 1836).

35 Gregory Jusdanis, 'East is east – west is west: it's a matter of Greek literary history', *Journal of Modern Greek Studies* 5 (1987): 1–14, at 1.

36 Todorova, *Imagining the Balkans*, p. 16.

10 BYZANTIUM AND THE MEDITERRANEAN

1 For the geographical axes see G. W. Bowersock, 'The east–west orientation of Mediterranean studies and the meaning of north and south in antiquity', in W. V. Harris, ed., *Rethinking the Mediterranean* (Oxford, 2005), pp. 167–78.

2 Averil Cameron, *The Mediterranean World in Late Antiquity, AD 395–c.600* (London, 1993); Peregrine Horden and Nicholas Purcell, *The Corrupting Sea: A Study of Mediterranean History* (Oxford, 2000), with Nicholas Purcell, 'Four years of corruption: an answer to reviewers', in Harris, ed., *Rethinking the Mediterranean*, pp. 348–75; the timespan of Horden and Purcell is long, roughly 3500 BC to AD 1000. See also David Abulafia, ed., *The Mediterranean in History* (London, 2003). Susan Alcock, 'Alphabet soup in the Mediterranean basin: the emergence of the Mediterranean serial', in Harris, ed., *Rethinking the Mediterranean*, pp. 314–36, traces the striking proliferation of journals dealing with the Mediterranean world since the late 1980s.

3 Horden and Purcell, *The Corrupting Sea*, pp. 403–60, 485–523.

4 Michael McCormick, *Origins of the European Economy: Communications and Commerce, AD 300–900* (Cambridge, 2001).

5   Examples and discussion: Leslie Brubaker and John Haldon, *Byzantium in the Iconoclast Era (ca. 680–850): The Sources. An Annotated Survey* (Aldershot, 2001), pp. 30–6.
6   A. Jeffrey, 'Ghevond's text of the correspondence between Umar II and Leo III', *Harvard Theological Review* 37 (1944), 269–332.
7   Ed. R. Le Coz, *Jean Damascène: Écrits sur l'Islam* (Paris, 1992); for the early Islamic state see Hugh Kennedy, *The Prophet and the Age of the Caliphates* (London, 1986).
8   Bartholomew of Edessa: PG 104.1384–447, 1448–58; A. T. Khoury, *Polémique byzantine contre l'Islam* (Leiden, 1972).
9   Texts ed. by A. Philippidis-Braat, 'La Captivité de Palamas chez les Turcs: dossier et commentaire', *Travaux et Mémoires* 7 (1979): 109–221.
10 *Life of S. Theoktiste of Lesbos*, trans. Angela C. Hero, in Alice-Mary Talbot, ed., *Holy Women of Byzantium: Ten Saints' Lives in English Translation* (Washington, DC, 1996), pp. 95–116.
11 *Life of St. Theodora of Thessalonike*, trans. Alice-Mary Talbot, ibid., pp. 159–237; cf. para. 3 and note ad loc.
12 *PG* 111.441–80, para. 60.
13 On the slave trade in the Mediterranean in the eighth and ninth centuries see McCormick, *Origins of the European Economy*, pp. 733–77; 22,000 Christian prisoners were allegedly taken to Crete after the Arab sack of Thessalonike in 904: John Cameniates, *De expugnatione Thessalonicae*, p. 487f.
14 For the relevant texts see the excellent survey by R. G. Hoyland, *Seeing Islam as Others Saw It: A Survey and Evaluation of Christian, Jewish, and Zoroastrian Writings on Early Islam* (Princeton, 1997).
15 *Ep.* 102, PG 111.310–20.
16 Banquets: *Book of Ceremonies* II.52.
17 Chapter 2, p. 38.
18 McCormick, *Origins of the European Economy*, against the accepted idea of the 'rise' of the European economy in the eleventh and twelfth centuries, as well as the Pirenne view that the Arabs controlled the Mediterranean completely, on which see also F. Gabrieli, 'Greeks and Arabs in the central Mediterranean area', *Dumbarton Oaks Papers* 18 (1964): 57–65, at 60–1.
19 M. Canard, 'Les Relations politiques et sociales entre Byzance et les arabes', ibid., 33–56; for Byzantine-Arab relations see also the articles by J. Meyendorff and George C. Miles in the same volume.
20 *Life* of Lazaros of Mt Galesion, trans. Greenfield, paras. 19–20.
21 See S. D. Goitein, *A Mediterranean Society: The Jewish Communities of the Arab World as Portrayed in the Documents of the Cairo Genizah*, 6 vols. (Berkeley, 1967–93); id., *A Mediterranean Society, An Abridgement in One Volume*, rev. and ed., Jacob Lassner (Berkeley, 1999); N. de Lange, *Greek Jewish Texts from the Cairo Genizah* (Tübingen, 1996).
22 Michael the Syrian, ed. Chabot, III.130; see G. Dagron, 'Minorités ethniques et religieuses dans l'orient byzantin à la fin du Xe et au XIe

siècle: l'immigration syrienne', *Travaux et Mémoires* 6 (1972): pp. 177–216.

23 V. Grumel, *Les Regestes des actes du patriarcat de Constantinople*, rev. J. Darrouzès, I.2–3 (Paris, 1989), nos. 838–40, 846.

24 For a review see Giles Constable, 'The historiography of the Crusades', in Angeliki E. Laiou and Roy P. Mottahedeh, *The Crusades from the Perspective of Byzantium and the Muslim World* (Washington, DC, 2001), pp. 1–22.

25 Alongside Steven Runciman's *A History of the Crusades*, 3 vols. (Cambridge, 1951–4) one can put R. J. Lilie, *Byzantium and the Crusader States, 1096–1204*, Eng. trans. (Oxford, 1993), as well as Angeliki E. Laiou and Roy P. Mottahedeh, *The Crusades from the Perspective of Byzantium and the Muslim World* and Jonathan Harris, *Byzantium and the Crusades* (London, 2003), with Mary Whitby, ed., *Byzantium and the Crusades: The Non-Greek Sources* (Oxford, 2006); see also the relevant sections in Magdalino, *The Empire of Manuel I Komnenos* and chapters in *The New Cambridge Medieval History*, Vols. 4 and 5.

26 Lilie, *Byzantium and the Crusader States*, p. 247.

27 Magdalino, *The Empire of Manuel I Komnenos*, pp. 95–9; M. Hendy, *Studies in the Byzantine Monetary Economy c.300–1450* (Cambridge, 1985), pp. 146–54.

28 Donald Nicol, *Byzantium and Venice: A Study in Diplomatic and Cultural Relations* (Cambridge, 1988), p. 96.

29 A. Piganiol, *L'Empire chrétien (325–395)* (Paris, 1947, 2nd edn 1972).

30 Some examples from the debate: Maria Grigoropoulou, 'The artistic world of the crusaders and oriental Christians in the twelfth and thirteenth centuries', *Gesta* 43.2 (2004): 115–28; Sharon E. J. Gerstel, 'Art and identity in the medieval Morea', in Laiou and Mottahedeh, eds, *The Crusades from the Perspective of Byzantium and the Muslim World*, pp. 263–80; Lucy Anne Hunt, *Byzantium, Eastern Christendom and Islam: Art at the Crossroads of the Medieval Mediterranean*, 2 vols. (London, 1998, 2000), for example, 'Art and colonialism: the mosaics of the Church of the Nativity in Bethlehem (1169) and the problem of "Crusader art" ', ibid., vol. 2, no. 18, pp. 224–60 and 'Artistic and cultural inter-relations between the Christian communities at the Holy Sepulchre in the twelfth century', ibid., no. 19, pp. 261–300.

31 M. Balard, 'A Christian Mediterranean, 1000–1500', in Abulafia, ed., *The Mediterranean in History*, pp. 183–218, at pp. 192f.

32 Eustathius of Thessalonike: see Alexander Kazhdan, 'Latins and Franks in Byzantine perception and reality from the eleventh to the twelfth century', in Laiou and Mottahedeh, eds, *The Crusades from the Perspective of Byzantium and the Muslim World*, pp. 84–100, at p. 99.

33 See R. Ousterhout and D. Fairchild Ruggles, 'Encounters with Islam. The medieval Mediterranean experience: art, material culture and cultural exchange', *Gesta* 43.2 (2004): 83–5.

34 Jonathan Riley-Smith, 'Government and the indigenous in the Latin king-
    dom of Jerusalem', in David Abulafia and Nora Berend, eds, *Medieval
    Frontiers: Concepts and Practices* (Aldershot, 2002), pp. 121–32.
35 For inter-cultural relations see Peter W. Edbury, 'Latins and Greeks on
    Crusader Cyprus', ibid., pp. 133–42.
36 See the essays in Benjamin Arbel, Bernard Hamilton and David Jacoby, eds,
    Latins and Greeks in the Eastern Mediterranean after 1204 (London, 1989),
    with Bernard Hamilton, *The Latin Church in the Crusader States: The Secu-
    lar Church* (London, 1980).
37 Psellus, *Chronographia*, VII.65, p. 315 Sewter.
38 Michael Angold, *Church and Society in Byzantium under the Comnneni,
    1081–1261* (Cambridge, 1995), pp. 22–7.
39 J. Richard, 'The establishment of the Latin church in the empire of Con-
    stantinople (1204–1227)', in Arbel, Hamilton and Jacoby, *Latins and Greeks
    in the Mediterranean*, pp. 45–62.
40 See Tia M. Kolbaba, 'Byzantine perceptions of Latin religious "errors"', in
    Laiou and Mottahadeh, eds, *The Crusades from the Perspective of Byzan-
    tium and the Muslim World*, pp. 117–43; on the Armenians, pp. 122–3.
41 Michael Angold, 'Greeks and Latins after 1204: the perspective of exile',
    in Arbel, Hamilton and Jacoby, *Latins and Greeks in the Mediterranean*,
    pp. 63–86.
42 Elizabeth Zachariadou, 'Holy war in the Aegean in the fourteenth century',
    ibid., pp. 212–25, at pp. 217–18.
43 Vividly described using the Ottoman records by Anthony Bryer, 'Byzantium:
    the Roman Orthodox world, 1393–1492', in Christopher Allmand, ed., *The
    New Cambridge Medieval History*, Vol. 6, c.1415–c.1500 (Cambridge,
    1998), pp. 771–95.

CONCLUSION

 1 See N. G. Wilson, *From Byzantium to Italy: Greek Studies in the Italian
    Renaissance* (London, 1992).
 2 Donald Nicol, *The Byzantine Lady: Ten Portraits 1250–1500* (Cambridge,
    1994), pp. 96–7, 105–6.

Index

Page numbers in *italic* refer to illustrations.